# RETURN VIA RANGOON

M.E.W; M.E.Williams. Captain-Retd. 2KoRR

# RETURN VIA RANGOON

A Young Chindit Survives the Jungle
and Japanese Captivity

by

P. G. STIBBE

LEO COOPER
LONDON

First published in Great Britain in 1994.
This paperback edition published in 1995 by
LEO COOPER
190 Shaftesbury Avenue, London WC2H 8JL
an imprint of
Pen & Sword Books Ltd,
47 Church Street,
Barnsley, South Yorkshire S70 2AS

© Philip Stibbe, 1994, 1995

A CIP record for this book is available from the British Library

ISBN 0 85052 476 8

Co Published in Thailand, Burma, Laos and
Cambodia by White Lotus Co Ltd,
GPO Box 1141, Bangkok 10501, Thailand.

ISBN 974-8496-47-3

White Lotus: Sole Distributor for Thailand, Burma, Laos and Cambodia.

Printed at Redwood Books, Trowbridge, Wiltshire.

# Contents

To

Rifleman Maung Tun
The Burma Rifles
Hintha, March 1943

# Author's Note

This book was first written in the summer of 1945 and published two years later. After forty-five years I have revised this account of my experiences. I hope the result is a more objective and a more readable piece of writing.

Basically the tale is the same. I have left the Epilogue as I wrote it in 1945 because what I said then still seems to me to ring true, and because I feel indebted to those who shared my experiences, and, especially, to the man who deliberately gave his life for me.

In the words of T. P. Cameron Wilson:

> ". . . still through chaos
> Works on the ancient plan,
> And two things have altered not
> Since first the world began –
> The beauty of the wild green earth
> And the bravery of man."

P.G.S
1993

# Foreword

by
JAMES LEASOR

When Christopher Columbus set out in 1492 to discover the New World, he found it difficult to sustain the courage and confidence of his crew.

The prospect of sailing into totally unknown seas terrified and distressed them. Many believed that, beyond sight of shore, the earth ended suddenly and they would plunge down into a measureless and fearful deep. Some threatened Columbus. All begged him to turn back while they could. Why should they attempt what no-one else had ever attempted before them? Columbus resolutely ignored such faintheartedness. After each day of discord and danger he made the simple entry in his log: 'This day I sailed on.'

Reading Philip Stibbe's account of his experiences in Burma as one of Brigadier Orde Wingate's Chindits during the Second World War, I was reminded of Columbus's stoicism and his determination not to give in. Like Columbus, Stibbe never lost confidence in himself, in his comrades, or what they set out to achieve. His book is a remarkable testimony to human resilience and the strength of human spirit.

Stibbe was· at Oxford when war broke out. He joined the army, was commissioned, and in 1942, exactly 450 years after Columbus sailed West, Stibbe was marching East in Wingate's first column of British and Gurkha troops, plus a contingent of the Burma Rifles. They took the name Chindits from the mythical stone creature, *chinthes*, that guard Burmese temples.

Until they set off British and Indian armies in Malaya and Burma had been in constant retreat. Humiliated, and defeatist, confidence in themselves and their leaders had eroded.

Wingate was determined to prove that, under his leadership, they could achieve what no other army in history had ever attempted: to fight through the monsoon. He was convinced that they could not only beat the Japanese, but also the climate and the jungle itself. Supplied by air, they would attack bridges, railways and other targets in the heart of Burma, then melt away to appear elsewhere unexpectedly, days or even only hours later. Such strategy may be commonplace now, but then it was revolutionary.

They could only be given rudimentary equipment, because that was all there was. In addition to the enemy, they would also face malaria, dysentery and unknown fevers so strange and malignant that medical officers would simply declare them 'NYD' – Not Yet Diagnosed. Wounds would rarely heal in monsoon conditions; even minor cuts could suppurate, often becoming open sores as big as saucers.

Before they set out, Wingate, an unorthodox leader with a close knowledge of the Old Testament, addressed them in Biblical terms: "The River Chindwin is Jordan. Once across, there is no turning back. The only way out of Burma is via Rangoon." That is how Philip Stibbe returned – three years after he went in.

During the campaign he was so badly wounded that he had to be left behind. A Burmese rifleman loyally volunteered to stay with him. Foraging for food, this brave companion was captured by the Japs who believed that a wounded British officer was hiding nearby. They tortured him to reveal Stibbe's whereabouts. He died rather than do so.

Despite this, the Japanese eventually found Stibbe. Almost as a matter of course, they tortured him. Then, starving, ill, suffering from his fearful wound, he was taken south to Rangoon jail. Here he stayed a prisoner until the end of the war.

Philip Stibbe wrote and published the first edition of this book shortly afterwards. At that time, we were both undergraduates, reading English at neighbouring Oxford colleges, Merton and Oriel, and both back after years with the Army in Burma.

I was impressed then, and now, by the amazing way in which he seemed able to rise above all hardships.

"Whether I am wiser than I was when I joined the Army as an undergraduate, I cannot tell," he writes, "But certainly I am happier."

In the Bible, the psalmist praised as blessed a man who, passing through the valley to Bacca, a fearful, arid area on the way to Zion, was able to regard this waterless desert as a well.

Philip Stibbe's Bacca was Burma. He did not simply pass through. He stayed there for years, towards the end under daily fear of execution by the Japanese. Living on bamboo shoots, scrapings of bad rice, roots and leaves, his credit at the bank of health became seriously overdrawn. Now that debt is being called in.

Yet despite ill health, Philip Stibbe's experiences have given him the rare ability never to worry about anything beyond his control: "There is nothing to be gained from anxiety, and in any situation one can only do one's best – and then leave the outcome to Providence."

What the reader gains from this modest and inspiring book is the wonderful sense of comradeship and brotherhood, even unto death, which in that campaign, long ago and far away, flourished between Indians, Gurkhas, Burmese and British. Philip Stibbe's account provides an example all the world could follow with great advantage today.

# Acknowledgements

I have been overwhelmed by the generosity, kindness and help given me for this project by apparently innumerable friends, family and supporters, such as vital tasks like painstaking typing by Pat Mather, Elisabeth Macquire, Karen Alfrey and Sue Wright. The Imperial War Museum photographic library, my ever tolerant publisher Leo Cooper, and my brother-in-law Andrew Thornton have all supplied evocative wartime and recent photographs. I am also particularly grateful to Geordie, Bernard Fergusson's son, for allowing me to use the photograph from *Beyond the Chindwin* of his father's officers at Christmas 1942. Other kind advice and superb material was provided by The Royal Sussex and The King's Regimental Headquarters, and Michael Moore of Norwich. Mrs Elsie Bertram MBE suggested this revised version would be an ideal retirement project; my family took her seriously, especially my son Giles who has done most of the "legwork"! My wife Joy, brother Paul, brother-in-law Bob, daughter Claire, son Mark, and daughter-in-law Alison have been constantly reassuring.

The encouragement from the institutions that have played such significant roles in my life have been phenomenal; I have been really touched by the care and support of firstly the educational establishments that have tolerated me all my life, except wartime, Nevill Holt, Mill Hill, Merton, Bradfield, and Norwich; secondly the wonderful armed forces welfare agencies who do so much marvellous work through their global networks on behalf of veterans like me: The Chindits' Old Comrades', and The Far East Prisoners of War Associations. Tribute must also be paid to individuals like Mr P. S. Cairns

*Acknowledgements*

MBE of Manchester for his tireless voluntary work on behalf of those veterans like me who suffer from diseases such as Parkinson's that are most probably the result of the diet and regime we suffered as Japanese prisoners of war.

Throughout my life colleagues and friends have been tremendously encouraging: Hugh Murray Wells and Clive Gimson, Denis Thomas, Willie Wilding, and, perhaps the definitive "Rat of Rangoon", Lionel Hudson! I could not have wished for kinder supporters than Murray Argyle, Basil Johnson, Tim Potts, Francis Templer, Charles Lepper, Michael Ricketts, Pat Huish, Pauline Ingan-Jones and the late Tony Chenevix-Trench.

I must also thank the fellow authors including one "distinguished former pupil" who have endorsed this book. James Leasor reviewed the first edition when we worked on "Isis" at Oxford together after the war. His own tales have won him deserved international acclaim. Ewen Southby-Tailyour's knowledge of the Falkland Islands' coastline was crucial to winning the war "Down South"; his *Reasons in Writing* is surely the fairest account of what happened there. Civilian mariners acknowledged his feat by making him "Yachtsman of the Year". Alan Clark needs no introduction as a robust military historian and politician of conviction. David Owen had to put up with me as his housemaster; I'm not sure to what extent I inspired his politics! Clive Gimson and I started a discussion group at Bradfield called the 1952 Society and David was a most enthusiastic member. He knows how much I admire his patient work in Bosnia, and I am immensely grateful to him for finding the time to endorse this book. Finally and above all I thank my publisher Leo Cooper, his wife Jilly, partner Tom Hartman, and assistant Georgina Harris for their boundless enthusiasm and hospitality!

# *Prologue*

According to my watch it was 10 a.m. I guess the day was 31 March, 1943. I suddenly realized that I had been alone for 48 hours, alone in the Burmese jungle somewhere east of the Irrawaddy River and probably further east at that moment than any British soldier on active service. I had practically nothing to eat or drink and I was wounded in the chest. The Japanese, our enemies who had conquered Burma, were certainly occupying the nearest village. The Chindit column of which I was a member, and which had been operating behind the Japanese lines for about six weeks, had been ordered to return to India. Due to my wound I could not accompany them. Altogether the outlook was extremely gloomy.

Yet as I lay there I did not despair. I was not particularly cheerful, but at no point during those 48 hours do I remember feeling despondent. I certainly spent some time praying to be given courage to face whatever lay ahead, and this was an immense source of help. I also remember asking myself whether, if the possibility ever arose, I would be able to write an account of my comrades and the events which had led up to my present predicament. This made me recall in detail all that had happened since the day in May, 1942, when I first left my native land. Now that I have come to write my story this is the point where I will begin.

# PART I

# Preparation

"Not all the modern, easy ways of life have been able to eradicate the hard core of native toughness in the British race ... The modern British soldier, once trained, is capable of feats of endurance as great as any of the past."

*The Good Soldier* by Viscount Wavell

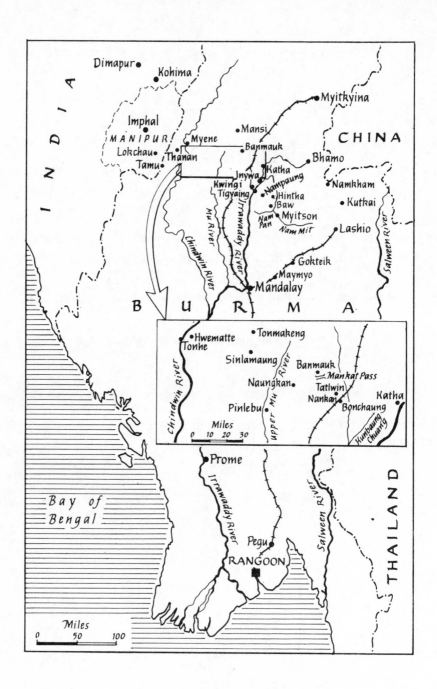

# CHAPTER 1

## *Travelling*

The damp blanket of sea mist that enveloped us, the strident calls of seagulls, fog horns, and ships' sirens, all melancholy, formed a fitting background to my mood as I leant over the rails watching the water slide by the ship's side. For a few moments the mist lifted to reveal a glimpse of Scottish coastline, steep grey cliffs below and brown bracken slopes above, with patches of vivid green pasture where some very bedraggled sheep grazed. Lucky sheep, I thought; at least you can stay in your own land with your own flock instead of being herded on to a boat with a crowd of strangers, and not only sent abroad, but sent to India, the last place on earth anyone in their senses would want to visit. The mist closed in again and the ship slid on, carrying me and my alternating sorrow and resentment out into the Atlantic.

It is more than forty-five years, since that day but it remains as clear as yesterday in my memory. At that period of my life I was utterly insular. My passion for the English countryside is part of me still, but then it was so intense that I could not imagine why anyone ever wanted to leave this island. I am a different person now, so different that sometimes I think it cannot have been me that sailed so reluctantly from England at the beginning of May, 1942.

We were a mixed convoy. There were ships from nearly all the allied nations. Ships of every size, shape and age, but all wearing the same grey war paint. We were escorted by a cruiser and several destroyers, some British and some Lend-Lease American. Over the horizon, we were told, lurked one of our battleships and an aircraft carrier.

Our own ship was the *Athlone Castle*, one of the newest vessels of the Union Castle line. She had been converted into a troop carrier and now carried about five times her peacetime complement of passengers. Forty-eight of our draft of officers were given bunks in a room rather less than half the size of a Nissen hut. The bunks were arranged in tiers so that we were no more able to sit up in our bunks than a corpse can sit up in its coffin. The rest of the officers slept four to a cabin. We felt far too crowded for comfort, but we were waited on by peacetime stewards and served with peacetime food in the dining saloons. Those of us who visited the men on the lower deck, where the rations were meagre and the atmosphere stifling, realized that no officer had any cause for complaint. Down there the overcrowding was indescribable; nobody suffering from claustrophobia could have survived. Black-out regulations were very strict and all portholes had to be kept shut at night; portholes on the lower decks were never opened.

The draft of officers in which I found myself was not my idea of a fine body of men. Most of them did nothing but sleep, eat, drink and amuse themselves in unimaginative ways, not even bothering to appear for the daily physical training parade. The officers' lounge in the evening soon became a place to be avoided. I have enjoyed having too much to drink on occasions as much as anybody, but to get drunk every evening in the same place with the same people singing the same bawdy songs seemed to me depressingly monotonous. It certainly did nothing to endear the officers to the troops, whose drink ration was severely limited. Sometimes I could not help wondering how many of the officers on board had been sent to India because their commanding officers wanted to be rid of them. My own C.O. had said he was sorry to lose me. He had been ordered to send some of his junior officers. Why, I wondered, did he choose me? Did he think I was 'bolshie'? I wished now I had not been so critical of and frustrated by the slowness and inadequacy of our training. How delightful those months of muddle in Lincolnshire and Suffolk now seemed.

In George Borrow, another officer of my battalion of the

Royal Sussex Regiment, I found a kindred spirit. An East Anglian, like his famous forebear, George was slightly built, quiet and studious, with a face like a baby owl. At first sight definitely not the kind of person one would expect to feel at home in the army; an academic, I decided, and not a man of action. I soon discovered my mistake. There was about George a remarkable integrity and sincerity and a wonderful gift of being able to devote himself entirely to what he was doing. This, combined with a phenomenal amount of determination, enabled him to endure far more than most of those who appeared to be better equipped for warfare. He was also one of the gentlest and least selfish men I have met. Everyone who met him came to like and admire him. Before joining the Army he had spent a year at Cambridge and, as I had spent the same period at Oxford, we had much in common. There was ample time for reading and talking, and I remember that, among other books, Lord Elton's *St George or the Dragon* and C.S. Lewis's *The Problem of Pain* stimulated much discussion.

We also managed to enjoy some music. One of the officers had managed to bring with him a fine collection of gramophone records which he played to us in the evenings. Perhaps because it provoked such home-sickness for the English countryside, it is his record of Delius's *On Hearing the First Cuckoo in Spring* that I remember best. Some very good programmes were broadcast over the ship's loudspeaker system and, on the lighter side, we found among the troops much talent for staging amusing variety shows.

Among those on board were a draft of Somersets and Gloucesters who were going out to reinforce a battalion which had suffered heavy casualties in the recent withdrawal from Burma. I met several of their officers and offered to give them a hand as they seemed very overtaxed, while we unattached officers had no duties. This involved me in the censoring of letters. Many of the men wrote at least one long letter a day throughout the voyage, although they knew that there was no chance of posting them until we reached port. It was a sickening chore to have to read the pathetic outpourings of so many sorrowful souls, but for security reasons it had to be done. Sometimes I was overwhelmed by a feeling of utter disgust with a world in which there could be so much misery, and at these times the war seemed nothing but a wretched mixture of evil and suffering, with no gleams of hope. Fortunately my sense of proportion usually reasserted itself quite quickly. I soon realized that I was not expected to try to bear the burden of the whole world's sorrows.

We had frequent boat drills, the alarm bells usually sounding when I was enjoying the luxury of a bath, so that I arrived dripping and breathless on the boat deck to be greeted by much mirth and the information that it was only a practice alarm.

Freetown was quite as sweltering as everybody always says it is. Because of the risk of infection no one went ashore, but we spent several uncomfortable days lying in the harbour. Much to the disgust of the natives, we were not allowed to throw coins to them when they rowed out in their bumboats as there was a shortage of small change on board. Mercifully the appalling heat was relieved every night we were there by a violent tropical thunderstorm; as soon as it began everyone stripped and rushed on deck; it was like watching some tribal dance to see hundreds of naked bodies leaping about in the blessed cool of the rain, the whole scene vividly lit by flashes of sheet lightning with the hills of Africa forming a spectacular backdrop. Describing our stay in Freetown, I burst into verse:

> . . . You must realize
> The ship was crowded, grossly overcrowded;
> It carried many times its complement
> Of bodies; I say bodies purposely,
> For in that climate you become aware
> With emphasis that you are physical;
> Your bodily being overrides all else
> And every part clamours for recognition . . .
> . . . During the day
> We lay becalmed in silence, till the sun
> Relieved us of its pressure. Then we stood

*Travelling*

Talking beside the rail of this and that,
Of what the future held and what the past,
Of things we loved and things we wanted changed
(Of those we'd left we spoke not, only thought).
Others would sing sweet songs whose very notes
Bring flooding back a thousand memories
Of times in England. Thus the cooler air
Of evening blotted out the consciousness
Of what and where we were. There was no room
For most to sleep on deck. We spent the night
Tossing in sodden heat and airlessness
Until we heard the wind, which always came
Before the morning. Then like souls in hell
That leap up at a glimpse of Paradise,
We scrambled to the deck with shouts of joy
And laughter, revelling in the God-sent rain.
The lightning tore the startled air and showed
A thousand naked bodies bounding up
To drink delight. We had not been forgotten.

The ship was so crowded that we were spared the ceremonial of crossing the line. Just before we reached the Cape the convoy divided, our half putting into Cape Town and the other going on to Durban. I was watching this manoeuvre with an officer, who knew everything about every ship in the convoy, and we began discussing the progress of the war at sea. He was full of interesting information.

"The crew say they have never been on a trip where there have been so many submarine alarms," he told me.

"Really?"

"The Jerries are going all out now with their U-boats. You know they have sunk the *Queen Mary*?"

"No! When?"

"A few months ago."

"I didn't hear about it."

"Well, of course, they will never announce it until the end of the year but it's a fact."

For a few minutes we watched our cruiser pass closer than usual and make several runs at top speed through the middle of the convoy. The coast sparkled in the sun and we could see Table Mountain in the distance. Suddenly everyone on deck began to move to the other side of the ship. We followed. It was impossible to reach the rail, but we could easily see what was attracting all the attention. Rapidly overtaking us was the largest and one of the loveliest ships I have ever seen. As she passed us she came so close that anyone who was still in doubt could read her name – *Queen Mary*!

Before landing at Cape Town we were warned about the notorious District Six, the potency of Cape Bandy, and the colour bar. Before we left, several men from the convoy had been stabbed in District Six and a couple of men from the *Athlone Castle* who had decided to test the strength of the brandy were carried back to the ship where they remained unconscious for about twenty-four hours. The colour bar was the only thing I did not like about Cape Town. I was not persuaded by the argument that if I were to live there for any length of time I would soon realize how necessary it was, and I objected to being reproved by a white woman for speaking to an elderly black woman in the street, especially as I was only asking the way to the Post Office.

The hospitality was tremendous; every man in the convoy was royally entertained. The South Africans invited us into their homes, took us to see the sights, and to shows, and did everything to make us remember our four days with them as one of the most pleasant times of our lives. After the years of black-out in England, it was a joy to see the lights at night; this meant more to us than the unrationed food and the luscious fruits. Everywhere we met the same genuine friendliness. One day George Borrow and I escaped from the organized hospitality and went for lunch to the Mount Nelson Hotel. The head waiter proved to be an old Sussex man, which was a good start. Before long he had brought us a bottle of wine, a present from a gentleman lunching nearby. We went over to thank him and he at once asked us to dine and go to the theatre with him. We had hardly been talking to him for five minutes when he offered us jobs on his farms if we returned to South Africa after the war. It seemed that the British in South Africa were particularly anxious to lure as many Britons as possible into the country.

Later that day George and I received further evidence of South African friendliness. We emerged from a cinema about midnight to find that it was pouring with rain. We had no raincoat with us and we had to return to the boat, so, seeing what we took to be a taxi standing at the side of the road, we leapt in and ordered the driver to take us to the docks. It was only when we were nearly there that the driver good-humouredly revealed to us that he was a very senior officer in the South African Air Force and that the "taxi" was his private car.

The rest of the voyage was uneventful. We had some rough weather rounding the Cape before we collected the other half of the convoy from Durban. There was a distant view of Madagascar and another magnificent close-up view of the *Queen Mary* at full speed. Later a number of ships left the convoy to go on to the Middle East. We heard afterwards that the Armoured Division they had on board went straight into action in the Desert.

I was sorry when the trip was over. As we steamed into Bombay on 4 July I tried to feel some of Kipling's enthusiasm for the place. Many officers did not know what regiment they were to join in India. Soon after we had docked a list was sent on board giving the number of officers required by various units in different parts of the country. We spent a merry half-hour posting ourselves to the ones we thought the most attractive. I chose the unit furthest away from Burma and the Japanese. Our plotting ceased with the arrival of definite posting orders for us all. There were four Royal Sussex Officers on board besides George Borrow and myself. We were all to report at once to the 13th Battalion of The King's Regiment at Patharia in the Central Provinces. We had heard of the King's and knew they were a Liverpool regiment, but nobody knew anything about Patharia. Enlightenment was not long delayed.

# CHAPTER 2

# *Training*

We did not have time to see much of Bombay as our train left at midday, but we took a short stroll through the streets around the docks, which I afterwards discovered gave a very false impression of the place. The first thing we noticed was that peculiar smell that is found in every village of India: it can best be described as the Oriental version of the English farmyard smell.

We were soon surrounded by beggars, and a host of small children with outstretched hands wailing the inevitable "Baksheesh, sahib". After you have been in India a while, you manage to ignore all this and stroll along sublimely indifferent to the swarms surging around you. This is a technique which takes time to develop; some of the beggars are so hideously deformed, and all are so pitifully thin, that a new arrival soon succumbs. Later I was told that in certain Indian families children are deliberately deformed in infancy in order to excite more pity, but we were new to India and it was not long before one of us had parted with a couple of annas to get rid of a particularly persistent child. This was fatal. The news seemed to spread in a moment and before long we were surrounded by a clamorous crowd. It took us some time to struggle back to the dock gate.

Meanwhile George Borrow had appointed himself our Cook's agent. When we arrived at Victoria Station we found him there with all our tickets, baggage and reservations complete. This was typical of George. Without any fuss or bother he would slip quietly away, and when we slower and lazier members of party eventually began to stir ourselves into action, we would find that George had already taken all the action necessary, not only for himself but for us all.

George and I had already become firm friends on the boat, so we shared a compartment on the train. In India there are not many corridor trains, so usually you walk along to the restaurant car for your meal at one halt and return to your compartment at the next. We remembered to lock the doors of our compartment while we dined that evening, but forgot to do so before settling down for the night; the results of this omission became apparent in the early hours of the morning when I awoke from an easy sleep and noticed that the compartment felt rather stuffy. I was in the top berth, so I bent down and switched on the light. There, on the floor, blinking and grinning up at me, were five or six very dirty Indians, all quite happily chewing nuts. For a moment or two I was completely nonplussed; then I reached out and grabbed my revolver which was hanging on a peg. At this they all murmured, "Sahib, Sahib" in deprecating tones and then continued to chew. Happily, while I was meditating on the next move, George woke up. He grasped the situation in a moment, there was some quick crosstalk in Urdu and then George ushered them firmly into the lavatory and bolted the door on the outside. At the next halt he unlocked them and propelled them into the night with a few special terms of Urdu abuse. I began to wish I had learned the language; George had taught himself on the voyage out.

The country we passed through was sufficiently interesting to prevent us from doing much reading. For the most part it was jungle or scrub-covered plains, but there were frequent ranges of hills which I found intriguing. Compared with the outline of their more conventional British counterparts, the Indian hills often seem to have been twisted and worn into fantastic and sometimes almost hideous shapes. The railway crossed innumerable rivers or river beds which the monsoon would shortly fill with raging waters and many of the bridges were fine examples of British engineering.

Every station provided entertainment in the shape of small boys who sang or danced for a few coins, dozens of men selling sickly looking food or drink and the usual host of "char-wallahs" offering their noxious brew of tea, not to mention the chocolate, cigarettes and the newspaper sellers. There were three refreshment rooms on most of the stations, for Europeans, Hindus and Muslims, the standard of the European ones being far higher than in England. We had no idea what sort of a place we were going to but we all imagined that the King's would be in barracks and, as we had heard of the tremendous smartness which was expected on and off the parade ground in India, we all donned our most immaculate suits of khaki drill, polished our buttons and Sam Browne belts, and prepared to make a good first impression. As we approached Patharia we scanned the countryside for the sight of a town, but we only saw hills and jungle intermingled with scrub and cultivated land on the plain. Eventually the train stopped at a desolate little station with a small village straggling behind it. We alighted gingerly, while some Indian porters unloaded our baggage. It made an immense pile on the platform, for we had each brought a large tin trunk and several other bulky pieces, as well as useful accoutrements such as tennis rackets; one of the party even had a large bag of golf clubs! Suddenly a British officer appeared. He has since become famous both for his exploits and for his appearance, which better pens than mine have described. So I will only say that he had no apparent teeth, that he was dressed in a motley array of English, Indian and Scottish garments, and that he looked a complete thug. He packed us on to a truck driven by a smart little Gurkha, promising that our luggage would follow. There was no time to gather much information from him but he said something about jungle warfare and mentioned a Brigadier.

The truck bumped along for several miles until we reached a river where a large quantity of stores had been dumped under a tree. This was our road-head, and from here, after crossing the river on stepping-stones, we were directed up a jungle track. We must have looked comical; six officers, dressed in immaculate uniform, stumbling along a rough track through the jungle, watching the trees on either side apprehensively and starting at every rustle in the undergrowth. There was a distinct lack of enthusiasm among all present to take the lead. After about a mile and a half we came to a stone hut and some tents beside a stream. This was the Quartermaster's Stores; from here there was another half mile before we reached the Battalion Head-quarters. By the time we arrived there we were not in the best of spirits, but the welcome we had from the Commanding Officer, Colonel Robinson, and from his Adjutant, David Hastings (a son of the famous lawyer) was reassuring. They were dressed informally, as for jungle warfare, and displayed kindly amusement at our parade-ground rig. They soon put us in the proverbial picture.

The 13th Battalion of The King's Regiment was made up almost entirely of Lancashire men, mostly from Liverpool and Manchester. It had been formed in Scotland, trained in England, and, after some time on coastal defence it was sent out to India for garrison duty at Secunderabad. Most of the men were married and in their late twenties, and it was generally believed that they were to remain at Secunderabad. Life there was enjoyable. Most people were satisfied that this should be so, and there, no doubt, the battalion would have remained, doing an occasional exercise just to show that there was a war on somewhere. For the officers the morning ride, the afternoon siesta, a swim or a game of tennis, dinner in the Mess and then perhaps a dance or a game of bridge at the Club; and for the men, plenty to eat and drink, plenty of sport and dancing, and, if they had to do an occasional parade or guard duty, that was very little trouble because the Indian bearers always kept their kit spotlessly clean. All this would probably have gone on indefintely had it not been for Brigadier Wingate.

Much has now been written about Wingate and his career[*] but in 1942 when we found ourselves members of his 77th Indian Infantry Brigade, most of us had not even heard of him.

---

[*] The best account is *Orde Wingate* by Christopher Sykes published by Collins in 1959.

His brilliant achievements in Ethiopia received practically no publicity, but doubtless it was the knowledge of these that inspired General Wavell, the Commander-in-Chief in India, to give Wingate a chance in Burma. He had appeared in Delhi after the fall of Burma with a scheme for beating the Japanese which seemed little short of crazy to everyone but Wavell. Many people thought Wingate was slightly mad, but if he was suffering from any form of insanity, it was of a kind the modern world badly needs. Wavell could not spare any highly trained fighting troops for an experimental scheme like Wingate's, so he gave him a Brigade made up of a Battalion of freshly-recruited young Gurkhas and a Battalion of British troops (the 13th King's) who had really been intended for garrison duties. To these were added a contingent of the Burma Rifles, the 142 Company (a mixture of Commandos and Sappers), some signallers and some RAF personnel. It was not by any stretch of imagination a body of first-class fighting troops, but Wingate was determined to make it into a force that would carry out his plans. So the 77th Infantry Brigade was assembled in the jungle of the Central Provinces, near Patharia, at the beginning of July, 1942. The King's were short of officers, so we six officers of the Royal Sussex Regiment were attached to them.

Training was due to start the day after we arrived. George and I were to be in 5 Column, which was commanded by Captain Waugh, or Ted, as he was invariably called. He was a Manchester man, Lancashire to the core, with a wonderful knack of mixing with people. He greeted us warmly, telling us there was a special treat on the menu that night – a hare he had shot himself. This proved to be the toughest animal I have ever set teeth in, but Ted ate it with relish while George and I did our best to appear to be enjoying ourselves, though secretly we were thinking that if this was considered a special treat it boded ill for future meals. The other officers in the Column were extremely friendly, especially Alec Macdonald, the Administrative Officer. Alec was a Liverpool medical student, tall, freckled, with a pleasant lazy smile and an amazing capacity for doing things without any apparent effort. The Column sergeant-major was Jock Cairns of the King's Own Scottish Borderers; a less dour Scot it would be hard to find. He had a grand sense of humour and was the personification of the Scots word 'leal'.

There were eight Columns in the Brigade: 1, 2, 3 and 4 Columns were mainly Gurkhas, and 5, 6, 7 and 8 Columns were mainly King's men. Each Column had three ordinary rifle platoons, a support platoon with 3 inch mortars and Vickers machine guns, a platoon of Burma Riflemen or "Burrifs" as we called them), a mixed platoon of Sappers and Commandos from 142 Company (usually known as the Commando Platoon) who were to carry out demolitions, some signallers and medical orderlies, and quantities of mules and muleteers. Not all these component parts of the Column had arrived at the beginning of the training but they drifted in gradually as we proceeded, and anyway there were quite enough on the spot to start. I was put in command of No. 7 Platoon, which was one of the three rifle platoons in 5 Column.

I cannot honestly say that I took to my platoon at first or they to me. To begin with, I was about eight years younger than most of them and I often suspected in the early days that they, as married men with families, rather resented being ordered about by someone who appeared to them little older than a schoolboy. Again, I was not used to dealing with Lancashire men or that particular type of Lancastrian, the Liverpudlian. After my old platoon of Cockneys and Sussex men, I found them difficult to understand and, at times, exasperating. Later, when I had become accustomed to their rather sardonic attitude to life, and stopped taking everything they said too seriously, we got along much better. In this I was helped by Sergeant Bob Marchbank who was my platoon sergeant until he was whisked away to Brigade Headquarters. Always immaculate and cheerful, this highly intelligent Liverpudlian quickly summed me up and, with immense kindliness and good humour, smoothed over my early blunders and initiated me into the Liverpool way of doing things. He and George's Sergeant Rothwell were a splendid pair, always calm and efficient and always able to see the funny side of things.

The memories of my first night in the jungle are not rosy. I had seen the usual jungle films and always thought that the sound-track version of jungle noises at night must be an exaggeration. It is not. The noise of the crickets and bull-frogs alone is tremendous and continues all night. Added to this there is the doleful howling of jackals. Sometimes a whole pack of them will come shrieking through the middle of camp until someone makes a loud noise. Then they slink silently away. The jungle is never completely quiet; it probably comes nearest to silence in the heat of the day, but during the night the racket sometimes seems deafening. I was thankful that Ted had offered me a tent near his own, but even so, stories I had heard that evening of a panther and a cobra having been seen nearby quite recently were not conducive to sleep. I also found it very hot under my mosquito net.

The following morning all the English-speaking personnel of the Brigade were assembled for an address by Brigadier Wingate. When the Brigadier appeared, we were called to attention by Colonel Robinson, who then saluted him and reported that we were present and correct in the best parade ground manner. It was clear that the Brigadier had little use for these time-wasting formalities. We were stood at ease and he launched straight into his address.

It was impossible not to be impressed by Wingate; in appearance, in speech and in manner he was dynamic. Thick-set and not very tall, he seemed endowed with immense physical energy, but it was his face which was so striking, particularly the deep-set eyes glaring out from beneath his now famous sun-helmet. He was inclined to stoop as he walked and, with his head and jaw thrust forward and his eyes half closed as though in concentration, he looked what he was, a genius and a fanatical man of action. Some have likened him to one of the fiercer Old Testament Prophets and the comparison is apt. He lectured us at length and at speed without notes, but everything he said was worth hearing, and every point was driven home in a memorable way.

He began by telling us that we were going to play a decisive part in the coming recapture of Burma; we were going to prove to the world that the British soldier was a better fighter than the Japanese. We were to enter Burma ahead of the main force and penetrate far behind the Japanese front line. Then, while the main attack was put in against the front-line troops, we were going to create havoc behind them, cutting their lines of communication, destroying their supplies and generally making a thorough nuisance of ourselves. Sometimes our columns would operate individually and sometimes in a group. We would have no supply lines of our own on the ground but we would be supplied from the air by parachute and our only means of communication would be by wireless. We were to avoid large concentrations of Japs, and if we were heavily attacked we were to disperse in small groups and reassemble at a pre-arranged rendezvous some distance away. Similarly, after blowing up a bridge, ambushing a convoy, destroying a dump or carrying out some such project, we were to disappear into the jungle, reassemble, have another dropping of ammunition, explosives and supplies from the air and then strike again. All this sounds quite commonplace today because Wingate's ideas have been so widely adopted, but in 1942 they were brand new and, as such, extremely suspect to many people. Nevertheless, when Wingate was talking it was difficult not to be persuaded of the essential soundness of his plans, so convincing were his arguments and so hypnotic his manner. Churchill and Roosevelt were later to be persuaded by the same arguments and the same manner to support his ideas on a large scale. By the time he had finished talking, although he had not concealed from us that an extremely hard task lay ahead, even those who were not prepared to admit it were inspired with at least some of his enthusiasm.

The date for our entrance into Burma was not yet fixed, he told us, but there was no time to waste. We were to start training at once and ignore the monsoon which was just breaking. First we were to get used to living in and moving through the jungle. "Ridiculous," he said, "to be afraid of snakes or animals. Man, equipped with human intelligence and armed with a modern weapon, can cope with any animal." Then we were to learn and practise the special tactics which Wingate himself had devised for our particular kind of warfare, working first as sections and platoons and then by columns, until at the end of the training we could have a few exercises operating as a Brigade. Simultaneously, we must keep up to scratch with our weapon training, non-swimmers must be taught to swim, muleteers must be trained to look after mules, signallers must learn to use the various types of wireless sets we were to take with us, and all the other specialist personnel must be brought up to a high pitch of efficiency in their respective jobs. Above all, we must make ourselves fit to march unheard-of distances, carrying unheard-of loads on our backs. It was quite a full programme!

After the parade had been dismissed, the Colonel took his six new officers to be introduced to the Brigadier. We stood uneasily outside the tent which was Brigade Headquarters. After a few minutes Wingate stalked out, glared at us and then shook hands in silence. As he turned on his heel to withdraw, he growled, "I hope you will all enjoy yourselves."

"We hope so too," one of us murmured as he disappeared.

For the first week or so, although we had some rain, the weather was quite good and we began to be less afraid of the jungle. When we had got used to moving through the undergrowth by day, we started doing night work. Soon we realized that any snakes or wild animals there might be were really far more frightened of us than we of them. In fact, during the whole of my time in India and Burma I saw remarkably little wild life. Most of the men did not dare to go through the jungle alone at night for the first few weeks, but in the end they would walk anywhere alone as unconcernedly as they would stroll down their own street at home, and, considering that they were nearly all townsmen, they got used to the jungle remarkably quickly.

Wingate was not one of those Brigadiers who only put in an occasional appearance. He was liable to turn up anywhere at any time, and thus he became well known to all ranks in the

Brigade. It was extremely dangerous to relax even for a few moments in his Brigade; he expected everyone to be ready for everything every minute of the day. On one occasion I had to take my platoon to a certain spot in the jungle where an officer was to give a demonstration of something or other. When we arrived at the spot, the officer was not there, so I told the men to sit down and have a smoke while I went to look for him. I returned with the officer two minutes later, to find my platoon fallen in, with a fuming Brigadier pacing up and down in front of them. What was the meaning of this? Why was my platoon sitting here doing nothing? I explained the circumstances. Then why hadn't I given them something to do while they were waiting? Let them practise taking bearings with a compass, or climbing trees or doing anything so long as they were not wasting time. This must not happen again. It didn't.

A constant stream of orders, pamphlets, information, encouragement and invective showered down on us from Brigade Headquarters, all written in Wingate's striking style and all worth reading. Some of the orders were, or seemed, unorthodox in the extreme, but in the end we usually found that they were right. Saluting was to be cut down to a minimum. Everything was to be done at the double. Everyone must eat at least one raw onion per day. Only shorts would be worn when it was raining. Swearing must stop. Thursday was to be Sunday. When marching in mass formation through the jungle we were to ignore thorn-bushes and only look upon thick plantations of bamboo as obstacles. (This order was subsequently modified. Wingate did not mind admitting the occasional mistake.) Every officer must learn 800 words of Urdu and 800 words of Gurkhali. (Fortunately no steps were taken to see whether this order had been carried out.) No officer was to go sick and a man must either be sick or fit; if he was sick he was to do nothing; if he was fit he was to do everything. Orders were to be obeyed at once.

There were many stories current about Wingate in those early days. I repeat a few, but I cannot vouch for their complete accuracy, although they are all in keeping with the character of the man. He was very keen on sand table exercises and had a huge sand table constructed on such a large scale that men could be represented by matchsticks. On one occasion some officers were ordered to meet the Brigadier at the sand table to be put through their paces. They stood waiting for him in the rain and wondering how long he was going to keep them. Suddenly, Wingate burst from the bushes behind them, dancing like a dervish, firing his revolver jut over their heads and shouting, "Hands up, the lot of you, hands up. You are all quite helpless; not one of you is armed." After that no officer was ever seen without his revolver.

Whether he was dealing with men, mules or motors, Wingate always drove hard. A party of officers arrived back at Brigade Headquarters after a hair-raising drive with Wingate at the wheel of the truck, but instead of stopping and letting them get out, the Brigadier drove round and round in circles at high speed. The officers looked at one another uneasily, wondering what to do, and after they had been going round in circles for a few minutes, Wingate suddenly looked into the back of the truck and exclaimed, "What, are you still there? Jump off. Do you expect me to stop and let you get off?"

Another time, when a party of officers was summoned to a conference at Brigade Headquarters, they found their way barred by what was usually a small stream but had now become a raging torrent, swollen by the monsoon rains. Even the strongest swimmers did not like the look of it, so the Colonel sent off two officers to look for a more suitable crossing place; they returned unsuccessful. Eventually Wingate appeared on the opposite bank and shouted to the party to swim across. There were signs of hesitation in obeying this order, so Wingate, who was a powerful swimmer, dived in and swam across himself, much to the relief of the officers. However, no sooner had he set foot on the bank than he turned and, shouting "Follow me", dived in and swam back again. I think it is true to say that he never ordered anyone to do anything he could not do himself.

Another of his characteristics was his dislike of clothes. There were many stories of his issuing orders or receiving senior officers while naked. One officer, attached to his Brigade Headquarters, tells how, on joining the Brigade, he was extremely worried because he had no clean clothes to change into for dinner on the first night. While he presented himself at the mess tent very diffidently at dinner time, he found nobody there, so he felt sure that the Brigadier and his staff must all be changing. After a few moments there was a sound outside of someone shouting to the orderly for his dinner, and in rushed Wingate without a stitch of clothing.

The most unpleasant part of the training as far as I was concerned was the daily swimming parade in the nearby River Suner. We always had a man with a rifle on the watch for crocodiles but they seemed to give us a wide berth. Teaching grown men to swim is not easy, and most of the non-swimmers only achieved a few strokes even after several months of real effort. Inability to swim later proved fatal to several soldiers in Burma.

Thursday, being Sunday, by order, was supposed to be a day of rest. In a burst of enthusiasm on our first Thursday at Patharia, Sergeant Marchbank and I took out a small shooting party from our platoon; it was not a success. We had several shots at deer, but our stalking was not good enough. The only member of the party to hit anything was a man who got lost and, while wandering about on his own, found a cobra standing in his way, obviously about to strike. He put a shot right through its head and when the rest of us arrived back at the camp hot, tired and rather ashamed of ourselves, we found him displaying his trophy to an admiring crowd. After that, Thursday *was* Sunday as far as I was concerned.

After a week or two the monsoon broke in real earnest, and Ted Waugh decided that, as our column area was rapidly deteriorating into a quagmire, we should move to another area. There was a muddle over the move and the mules to carry the tents did not turn up until very late. I went ahead to look for a suitable area for my platoon. It rained all day as usual and we sank up to our ankles in mud at every step. I chose the least boggy area I could find and waited angrily for the tents to arrive. There had been several hitches, including a halt at the canteen en route, so it was nearly dark when the team finally arrived. It was still raining at 10.30 that night and we were still struggling to put up the tents in the dark. The Brigadier's order about bad language was not, I fear, obeyed to the letter. It was fortunate that we had moved, for two days later the river rose to such an extent that, in the area we had just left, only the tops of the trees were visible above water. Several men from other columns were drowned. The complete Gurkha battalion disappeared for a whole day and we all feared the worst, as the area of their camp was completely submerged. We found them all in the evening, damp but cheerful, perched in the tree-tops where they had been living for nearly twenty-four hours.

On August Bank Holiday Monday it stopped raining and our column marched to an airstrip which had been cut in the jungle about fifteen miles away. We did an exercise here under the eye of the Brigadier and started to march back to camp about three o'clock in the afternoon. We had not gone far before it started to rain again. Soon it was raining harder than ever. When we reached a small river which we had forded with ease that morning, we found it impassable. We moved along the bank for about half a mile and found a spot where it looked a bit easier to cross. The water was in full spate and it was extremely difficult to remain upright once you had left the bank; as soon as you put your foot down, the ground was washed away from under it. About a dozen of us succeeded in crossing somehow after narrowly escaping being swept away by the current, but it was obviously not worth risking the lives of the whole column in this way, especially as so many men could not swim. Eventually Ted shouted across to us to make our own way home while he took the rest of the column back to a nearby village for the night.

Our little party squelched its way forward but, whichever direction we went, after about half a mile we found ourselves faced with raging flood waters. It was rapidly getting dark and we began to think we must be on an island with the floods

rising all around us. One of the officers was swept away trying
out a possible crossing place, but he managed to seize an
overhanging branch and drag himself to the bank. When night
fell we found that our torches would not work as they were
damp, and we decided that the only thing to do was to stay
where we were and hope that the water would not rise to our
level before morning. As usual we had taken off all our clothes
except for shorts when it started to rain but it had been
impossible to keep them dry. We had nothing to eat, we were
soaked to the marrow and it was now extremely cold. We could
not make a fire, so we huddled together under the scanty leaves
of a tree and prepared for a sleepless night. Somebody remarked
that at any rate we were not suffering from thirst. I spent the
night clinging to another officer for warmth under a sopping
blanket. We derived a certain amount of amusement from
recalling how, as children at home, we used to be popped into a
hot mustard bath if we came home with wet feet.

At first light we moved off, stiff and tired and hungry. It had
stopped raining, and the floods were beginning to subside as
rapidly as they had risen, so that we did not have much
difficulty in reaching the camp. We found a party just starting
out to look for us under Bill Edge. We had not met Bill as he
was on a weapon training course when we joined the Brigade
and had only returned to the battalion the previous evening. As
we moved wearily along the track, he bounced brightly out of
the camp to meet us.

"I say" he boomed heartily, "You *do* look as if you've had a
night out."

There was no reply.

He tried again: "By the way, I'm Bill Edge; are you Borrow
or Stibbe?"

"Stibbe," I snapped, ignoring his outstretched hand.

In spite of this unpromising first encounter and my appalling
display of bad manners, Bill and I struck up a lasting friendship
and, with George, we soon formed a very happy triumvirate of
platoon commanders. Bill was a Balliol man, so the ancient
universities were well represented in our column. As he had

been with the King's since the battalion was formed, every man knew him and, because of his genial, good-natured attitude to life, he was universally popular. Yet George was easily the most energetic of the three of us. Some days he would not be still from dawn to dusk; he was incredibly conscientious and never spared himself. He rarely walked anywhere but usually rushed about at a miraculous speed. Sometimes late at night I would hear him crashing through the jungle long after I had settled down under my mosquito net. From my tent I would call out to him, "For goodness sake relax, George; you make me feel so lazy."

"It's just that you're better organized than I am," was his invariable but untrue reply.

Our August Bank Holiday jaunt was the first piece of training for a draft who had joined us, fresh from England, a few days before. We were amazed at the way these newcomers stood up to the strain and they proved a very valuable addition to our strength. Among the new arrivals sent to my platoon were the Dennett twins. They were short and thick-set, with very fair hair, pink faces and blue eyes and they were absolutely identical; there was literally no way of telling which was which and, as they were devoted to one another, nobody suggested that they should be parted. Their home town was Warrington. They were a perpetual source of amusement and I was delighted to have them in my platoon.

Our last weeks at Patharia were not particularly happy. It rained almost incessantly so that one became resigned to being wet from morning till night. It was foolish to wear anything except shorts, and the dry boots and socks we used to put on optimistically in the morning were soon full of mud and water. Even in our tents everything was covered with mildew. I remember with shame how sorry I felt for myself at having to spend my 21st birthday under these conditions; it rained especially heavily on that day and, to crown my festive feelings, one of my men accidentally shot off two of his fingers while cleaning his rifle. Rations were bad as it was difficult to obtain them owing to the floods, and the sick list began to grow at an alarming rate. There was a certain amount of dysentery, but the most prevalent ailment was a most unpleasant type of ulcer; we called them jungle sores. The medical staff did some fine work but it soon became apparent that there was too much for them to cope with. I found that men in my platoon with quite small sores were having to wait for hours in a queue for dressing, so I took to holding my own unofficial sick parade. The worst cases I sent to the medical officers, but I dressed many minor sores myself and the results of my amateur efforts were usually satisfactory.

Eventually over half the battalion were on the sick list and at last Wingate was forced to call a temporary halt. We marched away down the road to the little station where we had arrived; a train was waiting to take us to Saugor where we were to go into barracks for at least a week. There were rumours that the Wingate show had been cancelled and that we were going to do internal security work at Delhi, but nobody really knew what the future held.

The first few days at Saugor were delicious. To be under a roof, to be dry, to eat civlized meals and wear civilized clothes, to be able to have a hot bath and to feel clean, this was happiness enough for a few days. Then we began to look around for further amusement, only to find that Saugor was not such a wonderful place after all. When we heard definitely that the Wingate show was to go on we calmed down and began to take stock of ourselves.

The time we had spent at Patharia had not been wasted, even if it had ended rather lamentably. We all knew how to live and move in the jungle; we all had a pretty good idea of the special tactics we were going to employ and every man in the column had some idea about how to use a map and compass, a skill which was later to save many lives. The sickness rate in the batallion was depressing, but at least it enabled us to sort out those who were obviously not going to be able to stand up to the strain. For the most part they did not seem sorry to go, and this was hardly surprising; to serve under Wingate was no joke even for the fittest, and for the ailing it must have been unbearable. There was some concern because many of the men openly expressed their envy of those who were being sent away. Colonel Robinson, who regarded the chance of going into Burma with Wingate as the most wonderful luck, was horrified and genuinely mystified by this attitude. The battalion was paraded and I can still remember how he stood before us with gleaming eyes and said, with deep emotion, "As you know, some unfortunate members of the battalion have been found unfit to carry on with us. I understand that some of you have been calling them 'lucky blighters'. They are *not* lucky blighters. They are poor devils, to be pitied because they will not be with us in this great enterprise."

Alas, this stout-hearted eager spirit was not with us when we entered Burma. A few weeks before we finally set out Wingate told him that he had decided it would be wrong to take anyone of his age, despite his efforts to prove that he was perfectly fit. He was, in fact, by far the oldest man in the Brigade, but it was a shattering blow to "Robbie" and he always spoke of it with bitterness in later years.

Secretly I shared the men's feeling of envy. Those who were being sent away were going to miss "blood, tears, toil and sweat" and probable death. As they were genuinely sick they had no need to feel ashamed of themselves. To me they seemed very fortunate, and all the envious talk and grumbling among the men seemed perfectly natural. On the other hand, if the Colonel had asked those of us who were fit whether any of us wanted to be sent away with the unfit, I doubt whether one of us would have stepped forward.

We had soon exhausted the possibilities of Saugor, which consisted of one cinema and a typical club, but while we were there Gandhi was arrested for his anti-British activities and his Congress Party supporters went wild. We all walked about armed for a few days, but, although there was trouble in the town, it never spread to the Cantonment where the British lived, much to the disappointment of some of us who were beginning to be bored. After about a fortnight of riding about in lorries and on bicycles, we got back on our feet again and marched twenty miles by night on a dusty road. By morning we had reached the village of Abchand and close by, in the jungle, we found our new camp site.

I remember Patharia as a place dominated by rain, mud and gloom, but the jungle at Abchand was much more pleasant and the sun shone every day. Wild flowers abounded on the short turf and there was an almost park-like atmosphere. A clear stream babbled through our column's area but the greatest attraction was our perfect natural swimming pool, half a mile away, where a river ran through a gorge. In the mornings we were awakened by the cry of "Garrum dood" from an Indian selling hot milk. Then, instead of early morning physical jerks which I abominate, we would double down to the river for a swim and double back for breakfast. Our rations arrived here regularly and the food was good. Corporal Jones, a cheery soul from Ellesmere Port, presided over the camp fire cooking with remarkable skill, although he had had no culinary training. The results seemed far better than the food produced in barracks from well-equipped kitchens.

During the day we made good progress with our training, and we had several short column exercises. Now that the monsoon was over, the heat became more intense and during these exercises we began to experience real thirst; sometimes as we moved through the jungle under the midday sun we would come across a herd of Indian cattle; the sound of cow-bells tantalizingly recalled the sound of ice tinkling against the side of a long cool glass.

Some of our best men went to be trained to handle mules, and we all began to become acquainted with these animals for whom I have never managed to feel anything warmer than admiration. At this stage we saw little of the other columns but we had one or two camp-fire concerts and once, when the King had appointed a National Day of Prayer, we had a Church parade attended by all the English-speaking members of the Brigade. This followed conventional lines, and the Chaplain told us in his sermon that the war was a crusade and a struggle between the forces of good and evil. After the final hymn, Wingate announced that everyone was to stand firm. Then, having escorted the Chaplain from the scene, he returned to the parade and addressed us in the most memorable way.

He began by saying, "I entirely disagree with what the padre has just said about the war being a crusade. It may be so for some people, but for all of us it is a fight for survival." Having elaborated on this, he went on to review the course of the war and told us that in some places our military reputation had sunk as low as that of the Italians. It was being said that the British would fight till the last Russian soldier in Europe and the last Indian soldier in Burma. He finished by saying that he intended to prove to the world that British troops could fight anywhere under any conditions as well as anyone *and win*. It was a most stirring speech, revealing his religious convictions and his intense admiration for Churchill. When he finished even the King's men joined in the spontaneous applause.

Before we left Abchand a platoon of Burma Riflemen joined our column. They had two British officers, Captain John Fraser and Lieutenant P. A. M. Heald, invariably known as Pam. John was a Scot and had been in Steel Brothers, a large civilian firm in Burma. He had joined the Burma Rifles and been captured by the Japs during the withdrawal from Burma; he escaped and, after incredible hardships, reached India with a small party, having crossed over the Chaukkan Pass, a route which had only been used three times before and never in the monsoon period. Pam had been in the Burma Oil Company, so they both knew Burma and its inhabitants well.

I believe that, strictly speaking, the term "Burmese" should only be applied to one of the many races which inhabit Burma. The inhabitants of Burma as a whole should be called "Burmans", a term which covers all the various races, the Burmese, the Karens, the Kachins, the Chins and the Shans. The Burma Rifles attached to our column were all Karens and mostly Christians. The American Baptist Mission has done fine work in Burma; the Karens' sincerity and spontaneous goodness and happiness are unique in my experience and make them a wonderful advertisement for their religion. To see the gaiety and serenity of their lives is an inspiration not easily forgotten. Dr Gordon Seagrave's book, *Burma Surgeon*, gives a fine account of the American Baptist Mission and of the Karens. It certainly changed my ideas about missionaries.

Some of the Karens spoke English, but in any case language difficulty is negligible with people like the Karens. They had magnificent physiques, loved living in the jungle and, as they were crack shots, brought many a welcome addition to our diet, including monkey, python and peacock. Subedar Ba Than, Jemadar Aung Pe, Po Po Tou, the Quartermaster and Havildar-Major Billy ran the Burma Rifle Platoon in a calm and efficient manner which set an example to us all. Many of the Karens have English or American names; among ours were Jameson, Nelson, Washington and Robert. Robert was so striking in physique and appearance that we all felt he could have made a fortune in the film world. They were a cheerful crowd; in fact, they seemed to like us as much as we liked them. We little realized then how much we were all to owe to them later.

CHAPTER 3

# And More Training

About 20 September we struck camp and started on our first Brigade exercise. I cannot remember much about it except that some mules were with us and I was infuriated by one poor frightened mule which kept on sinking into the mud up to its belly and that Ted, in an exasperating burst of energy, marched half the column off their feet one night and I finished the march hanging on to the tail of a mule for support. Before the exercise began I had told my platoon that there could be no question of anyone deliberately falling out on the line of march. "If the pain from the blisters on your feet becomes more than you can stand," I said, "you will faint, and if you become completely exhausted you will lose consciousness; until this happens you must carry on." How I wished I could lose consciousness that night.

Tactically, as far as our column was concerned, the exercise was a fiasco owing to the non-arrival of certain messages, but it made us much tougher and more aware of our powers of endurance. General Wavell, who had flown down from Delhi, seemed quite impressed with us.

We went back to Saugor for a short rest and on 4 October we marched north to a new area near Malthone. By this time we were really getting used to the life and had discarded our tents. An extract from a letter I wrote home from Malthone gives some idea of the kind of existence we led: "We are now in a rather more remote part of the jungle than before. Life is very pleasant at the moment as we are having a breather and I am just eating or lying under a shady tree either sleeping or reading Shakespeare . . . I think that you would agree that this is rather enjoyable if you were here. This is a strange life; our diet is plentiful but plain, chiefly biscuits, raisins and tea, with a stew sometimes, and sometimes bacon. Our sleeping quarters are under trees and bushes; our bathroom is a river, and yet, in the middle of this wild and uncivilized existence, I have managed to procure a bottle of sherry. We sit round on the ground in our bush shirts and shorts and hats and sip it out of enamel mugs just as if we expected to be told any minute that dinner is served. I wish you could see us ... It is much more pleasant now that the monsoon is quite finished. We don't expect to see any more rain until next July but we have had more than enough to last us till then. The weather is much hotter but we don't do much work in the heat of the day."

It was at Malthone that Dunn became my batman. Since leaving England I had been looked after by a series of batmen and, though they had all done their best to please me, it looked as though I would never find one in the same class as the trusty Atkin who had looked after me so well in the Royal Sussex. Then one day I suddenly decided to try Dunn. He had been a leather worker in Warrington but had been in the Army since the start of the war. He was dark and well-built, a good swimmer and, although he had always lived in a town, he had liked country pursuits. He also had a mind of his own and did not hesitate to say what he thought; but what appealed to me was his tremendous keenness and his dry sense of humour. When I asked him if he would like to take on the job of being my batman, he at once said he would not. However, I urged him to try it for a while and, rather reluctantly, he consented. As far as I was concerned the experiment was a success; he looked after me admirably and kept me amused with his witty and sometimes caustic comments on life. Often he gave me very sound advice when asked, and occasionally, very respectfully, when not asked. I was relieved when he said that he would carry on at the end of the trial period. Nevertheless, although he never showed it, I sometimes suspected that he felt that he could have taken on a more responsible job.

There were a number of departures and arrivals at Malthone.

Colonel Cooke of the Lincolnshire Regiment took Colonel Robinson's place. He seemed very calm, good-humoured and efficient, a typical example of the best type of regular officer, but our contact with him was to be limited. A change which affected us much more closely was the departure of Ted, which all ranks much regretted. George and I were particularly sorry, as he had been extremely good to us ever since our arrival, but he had been struggling all the time against ill-health and it was clear that he could not go on.

Ted's successor as our column commander was Major Bernard Fergusson, a regular officer of the Black Watch. I don't mind admitting now that I was not looking forward to having a new column commander and, when I saw this tall military figure, moustached and monocled, coming through the jungle, I felt sure that he and I were not going to mix at all well, and I deliberately avoided him until we inevitably met at supper. By the end of that meal I had completely reversed my first opinion of him and I think we all felt extremely happy about our new commander from then on. His invariable title in the column was "The Major" and I shall henceforth refer to him thus. His own account of our exploits, *Beyond the Chindwin*, although written with becoming modesty, gives the reader a far clearer impression of his character than I can hope to give. He was an intellectual and a man of action, an unusual combination, and he had joined us because of his genuine thirst for adventure. He brought with him his servant, the redoubtable Peter Dorans.

Shortly after the Major's arrival, the post of Intelligence Officer at Battalion Headquarters fell vacant. We all urged George Borrow to take it. It meant that we no longer had his company in our mess, which was a particular loss to me, but he was the ideal man for the job and although, of course, he worked as hard as ever, I think the work was more congenial to him. In any event he seemed to settle down very quickly and happily and there was no doubt about his efficiency. About the same time I lost Sergeant Marchbank; we did our best to keep him in the column, but his reputation had spread to Battalion Headquarters and they took him away to be their C.Q.M.S. I was most put out but before long I was given Sergeant Thornburrow to console me.

Thornburrow was a good-natured giant of a man from Kendal. He used to work as a bottler in a brewery and he was certainly a good advertisement for beer. We liked one another from the start and I could not have wished for a more pleasant platoon sergeant. I sometimes thought that he was rather too good-natured and that some of the men took advantage of this, but it was not a bad fault and, when it came to the test, the men had just as much respect for him as they would have had for a martinet of a sergeant. Certainly he was held in genuine affection. I am perfectly ready to admit that in theory it was a bad thing for an officer like myself to have a sergeant like Thornburrow; I was far too easy-going, as the Major told me several times, and therefore I suppose I should have had the kind of sergeant who would compensate for this. In practice the combination was quite a success. The Major was a great admirer of Edmund Blunden's book, *Undertones of War*, and it gave me immense pleasure to hear him compare my Sergeant Thornburrow with Blunden's Sergeant Worley, as Blunden had been my tutor at Oxford. As far as I was concerned, Thornburrow was the best of sergeants. I could always rely on his being at hand, patient and unperturbed, whatever happened and I shall always remember with pride and gratitude his unswerving loyalty to me.

At the beginning of November we started to go on leave in relays and I had four days in Bombay, which I now discovered to be a far better place than I had at first supposed. As this looked like being my last bit of civilization for some time, I made the most of it and lived in luxury at the Taj Mahal Hotel; I doubt whether I could have enjoyed its comforts more even if I had realized that two and a half years were to elapse before I slept on a bed again. While I was in Bombay, I thought my parents might like to have a photo of me in my bush hat so I steeled myself and entered a photographer's shop on Hornby Road. Here I should explain that, with one exception, my features are remarkably nondescript, but nobody who has seen me can fail to have been impressed by the size of my nose; it is, as a friend once remarked, outstanding.

"Do you want full face or profile, Sahib?" asked the Indian photographer.

"Full face," I said.

"But, Sahib, I think the profile would be better. Did you particularly want full face?"

"Yes," I replied, and then, thinking some explanation was necessary, I added, "You may have noticed that I have a very large nose and it won't be quite so obvious in a full-face photo."

"But, Sahib," he protested, "It is a *beautiful* nose."

Not wishing to prolong the discussion, I eventually allowed him his way and, strangely enough, the profile turned out to be less hideous than the full-face photograph. I still suspect that the photographer tampered with the plate in order to modify the outline of my snout.

On my return I found that the column had moved about twenty miles to a site on the Narain Nullah, near Bahron. On 15 November I wrote home: "Here I am, back in the jungle, after being in Bombay for four days. I can't say that I was looking forward to coming back but we are in a new camp and life is so pleasant that now I am back I don't mind a bit. This is the best camp we have been in – plenty of shady trees and a lovely river which we usually swim in twice a day. I have managed to do a bit of fishing but have not been very successful. The trouble is, there are too many fish and they all jostle each other round the hook and never give each other a chance to take a really good bite. I am, as usual, feeling horribly healthy.

"I am very thrilled because at long last I am to have a horse of my own, complete with groom. I shall soon have quite a retinue of servants if I go on at the present rate. I am quite lazy enough as it is. My new platoon sergeant is a great success; he is only 22 so I don't feel so terribly young.

"We are feeding awfully well at present; we have an excellent native cook for the mess, which now consists of a log table with log benches on either side, constructed by Karens. After dinner at night we usually sit round the fire talking; we have the most interesting and deep discussions. The Major puts up with my rather left wing views very good humouredly."

We certainly did have some very enjoyable evenings round the fire. The Major had been in Palestine and Syria and been A.D.C. to General Wavell; he had been with Anthony Eden to Turkey and he had fought in the Western Desert besides being at G.H.Q. in Cairo and Delhi, so that he had a wonderful fund of experiences from which he could draw. He also had a remarkable gift for bringing each one of us into a discussion so that none of us ever felt out of it, whatever the subject under debate. He was as voracious a reader as I was, and books were an inexhaustible topic of conversation between us. Under his good-humoured influence even the most incompatible of us mixed well together, and I shall always look back on those days at Bahron as some of the happiest of my life.

Three new arrivals enlivened our circle at Bahron. Flight Lieutenant Denny Sharp, our Column RAF Officer, was a New Zealander. Like many worthwhile people, he took a bit of getting to know but the effort was well rewarded. He would throw some perfectly outrageous remark into the discussion, scowling fiercely as if challenging anyone not to take it seriously, and then he would lose control of his face and a most infectious grin would spread over his features. Denny brought with him several RAF signallers to work our largest wireless set.

John Kerr, who took over George Borrow's old platoon, was a land agent from South Wales. I think we disliked each other at first. I thought he was far too self-opinionated and full of bounce, and he obviously did not think much of me. The Major had told him that I would show him the ropes but I gained the impression that John thought I needed showing the ropes myself. When we knew each other much better I realized that once again my first impressions were wrong. On one occasion we really let fly at each other and after that we were the best of friends.

John was never short of words. I remember the first occasion when we went out together just after he had arrived with a party of men whom we were to instruct in compass reading. Every time we stopped we divided the party into two halves to explain to them what was happening. I would finish my explanation and stroll over to where John was explaining to his half of the party, hoping that he would be ready to move on. John would be just finishing the preamble to his talk so I would go back to my group and say, "Now, we'll just run over that again." By the time I had done this three or four times John would be about ready to move on. We were late back for lunch that day.

The third new arrival brought all our mules with him; he was our Animal Transport Officer, Bill Smyly. He was a wonderful horseman and although, being only nineteen, he was the youngest man in the column, woe betide anyone, officer or other rank, who did not show due respect for his mules. He brought with him some Gurkha muleteers, who were all devoted to him, although he ruled them with a rod of iron. The King's men called all the Gurkhas "Johnny" and relations between British and Gurkhas were always friendly. I never ceased to admire the calm efficiency with which Bill carried out his most exacting job.

Most of the time at Bahron was occupied with river crossing. We knew that crossing rivers like the Chindwin with mules and equipment was going to be one of the most difficult tasks in front of us, and we tried several methods with various types of equipment before we finally decided which was the best. The Burrifs, as we called the Karens, were as much at home in the water as they were in the jungle, and with their strong overarm stroke they would swim backwards and forwards for hours without tiring. By this time a good many of the non-swimmers in my platoon had gained confidence and even some I had regarded as hopeless cases could swim a few strokes.

Now the pace of our training began to quicken as we approached the date of our entry into Burma. As well as practising river crossings, we practised striking camp in the dark without noise or confusion and dispersing to a pre-arranged rendezvous; in fact, we practised everything we were likely to need to do behind the Japanese lines. In all this training it was the mules who caused the most difficulty. First they objected to having their loads put on their backs. Then, when the load was safely hooked on to the saddle, they would appear to become resigned to their burden and the muleteer would begin to think his troubles were over. Not so; with a wicked gleam in its eye and a shrill grunt of indignation, the mule would throw its hind legs into the air and its load would land several yards away. This was so frequent an occurrence in the early days with mules that the column never moved more than a few yards before the cry "Mule out" brought it to a halt. In the end we had to detach a man to help the muleteer and hope they would eventually catch us up. At the end of one exercise, so many of my men had been detached to help the muleteers deal with "barbary" mules that my total platoon strength was four men. Gradually mules and men grew accustomed to one another, and by the time we went into Burma a satisfactory relationship had been established.

The mule I remember best was looked after by Private Baxter. Private Baxter and his mule marched with my platoon and carried a Bren gun and its ammunition. During the course of one exercise we passed through a village where Private Baxter espied a small pond. Being a good-hearted fellow, he thought he would let his mule have a drink. The mule stepped gaily forward into the water and then disappeared! To Private Baxter, standing on the edge, anxiously watching the surface of the pond, it seemed hours before the mule reappeared. In the end up it came, but minus the Bren gun and ammunition. The apparent pond really concealed the head of a disused well, and at the bottom of this well lay one of His Majesty's Bren guns and several hundred rounds of ammunition.

"Well, Philip," said the Major when I told him what had happened, "I'm afraid you'll have to stay behind until you've recovered it."

"Yes, sir," I said, swallowing hard and resisting the temptation to ask him how on earth he thought we were going to do it.

I arranged for the platoon to go on under Corporal Drummond while I kept Sergeant Thornburrow, Dunn, Baxter, and
the mule with me. When I got back to the well, I found that
Bill Smyly already had his clothes off and was diving down to
see how things lay. After a bit I half-heartedly followed his
example, but it seemed hopeless; we could not get down far
enough and, besides being a local rubbish dump, the well
seemed choked up with thorn bushes. By this time the whole
village had turned out to watch the fun and, by flapping a few
rupee notes under their chins, I managed to persuade some of
them to assist us. They would take a deep breath, hold their
noses, leap off the side and disappear for an incredible length of
time, but they never brought anything up. At last, when
improvised grappling hooks had failed, I bribed them to bale
the well dry. Bill Smyly had to act as interpreter and, once they
had made up their minds, they emptied that well remarkably
quickly. We soaked the gun with shark oil before setting off
after the column.

Shark oil was plentiful at this time. Wingate thought that, if
necessary, we ought to be able to survive on a diet of biscuits,
raisins, and shark oil which was issued to us in two gallon tins
at the beginning of the exercise. As it is far more objectionable
than cod-liver oil it was not easy to persuade the men to take
their ration. Nobody seemed to know what the correct ration
was, but I discovered eventually that I had been giving my men
a quadruple dose. We soon found that the least revolting way
of taking it was to fry our biscuits in it. Later we found it very
good for cleaning rifles and leather harness.

Much of our training took place at night, and, as we were
going to avoid roads in Burma, we usually moved across
country in single file, platoons taking it in turn to march at the
head of the column where one set the pace. At the rear of the
column, for some inexplicable reason, the pace was always
much faster than at the head.

I remember so well some of those night marches along dusty
tracks, especially on the nights when there was a moon and
one's imagination began to play tricks. Did we really march for

miles along a flat terrace one night, with the moonlit waters of a lake below us on our left, and on our right a long line of grotesque ruins of palaces and temples? Bill Edge was convinced, on one occasion, that we had passed a line of London buses parked at the side of a jungle track. Another night when we were at the head of the column, the Major and I became so engrossed in our philosophic discussion that C.S.M. Cairns had to bring us gently down to earth by informing us that the column behind were wondering what had happened to their hourly halt.

It is tradition in the army to march for fifty minutes and halt for ten minutes. We adjusted this tradition to suit our own particular needs; we marched for an hour and stopped for a quarter of an hour. A cunning man like Dunn could light a fire and brew tea in fifteen minutes, still leaving time to drink it!

By this time we had been issued with our Everest packs. They had a steel frame and were designed to keep the weight off a man's back. When properly fitted they enabled us to carry far heavier loads than we would have been able to carry with ordinary equipment and we were soon able to average at least twenty miles a day fully loaded.

"Basically," Wingate had once said to a group of officers, "there is no difference between officers and men. We all have the alimentary canal but, because they have had less education, the men have little to occupy their minds. Officers should have well-stocked minds." The truth of this came home to me on our long marches. At school I had been made to learn by heart at least twelve lines of verse each day; "repetition" we called it, and we thought it an archaic custom. Now, tramping through the Central Provinces of India, I passed the time recalling these lines, and the miles seemed so much shorter. The Major would always tell us how far we had to go, and I would calculate the distance we had covered by imagining that we were on the well-remembered road between my home in Leicester and my prep school at Nevill Holt. The first hour's march brought us to Great Glen, the second hour to Kibworth and the final hour always involved the laborious climb up Medbourne Hill. Oddly enough, this proved a fairly accurate way of gauging how far we still had to go.

My memories of this period of our training are vivid but disorganized. Once we bivouacked near a huge cantilever railway bridge and, as we sat round our camp fire, we looked up to watch the mail trains, rumbling across the bridge, their lighted restaurant cars and sleepers giving us a glimpse of a luxurious way of life none of us were to know again for many months, and some of us never.

On another occasion, as part of an exercise, we were to attack and "destroy" another railway bridge. We aimed to put in a surprise night attack on the troops guarding the bridge, so we removed our ammunition boots to deaden the sound of our approach. It was almost pitch dark when we made the final charge and I ran headlong into a barbed-wire entanglement with such velocity that I hung upside down, helpless as a joint in a butcher's shop, until Dunn came back to rescue me. It was not until some time later that I discovered that my boots had parted company with me in the barbed wire, so that I had to finish the exercise in a very tight pair of the Major's brogues.

A figure that pops up in almost all my memories of 5 Column is the imperturbable stocky form of Brookes, the bugler. Always with Column Headquarters, it was he who transmitted the Major's orders to the rest of the column, by bugle or by whistle. At a signal from him we loaded the mules; at another signal we moved off; at another we halted. Sometimes he summoned the officers to conference with the Major, and at other times he blew the call which told us to disperse into the jungle and meet again at a prearranged rendezvous. We all knew what each of his signals meant, and we all took it for granted that he would be at hand to blow his bugle with impeccable clarity.

Gradually we became aware of the kind of life the Indian peasant lives: the squalor, resignation and dignity. We became familiar with the shrill hoarse cries of the villagers standing in the river to bash the water out of their clothes on the gleaming rocks; the smell of burning cow-dung in the villages, the bullock carts creaking along the tracks in the dark, the sleeping drivers huddled in a blanket between their slow, patient animals; the cheerful bartering for a plate of rice and tomatoes or a pile of chapatties; the hills trembling with heat and the whole plain panting for the evening. We felt that we were getting to know the real India that would continue thus regardless of what might be decided in London or New Delhi.

I remember so well the evenings in bivouac spent talking round the fire, our discussions punctuated by the popping of bamboo sticks. I remember John Kerr shocking the Major by saying that he felt no personal allegiance to the King.

"I never thought," spluttered the Major, "to hear an officer holding the King's commission say anything so disgraceful."

"But why should I have any *personal* feelings for someone I've never seen or talked to?" asked John. "Have you ever talked to the King?"

"Well, actually I have . . ."

On another evening, the Major shocked John. John had been telling us about a course he had been on in Scotland to learn what was called "unarmed combat". It seemed to consist mainly of hurting your opponent in the most vulnerable parts of his anatomy. John was very keen to train our men in this kind of warfare.

"I absolutely forbid it," said the Major. "It's utterly barbarous and if we can't win the war without going in for that sort of thing, I think I would rather we didn't win it."

The Major never lost sight of the romantic, one might even say the poetic, side of the war. I remember him saying one night by the fire that he thought that having served under Wingate would be counted as great an honour as having been with Lawrence in Arabia. Even the most sceptical among us caught some of his enthusiasm, but only a few of us (and I was not one of the few) managed to be so invariably high spirited.

Our final Brigade exercise took the form of an attack on Jhansi, which was an important railway centre from where we were to set out for Burma. After various adventures and having covered 180 miles in nine days, we were not as fresh as we might have been when we at last reached our objective. Nevertheless, Jhansi station, which was heavily guarded by "the enemy" soon fell. The men immediately started to invade the refreshment room in relays, always leaving a sufficient number to guard against counter-attacks, while our Commando Platoon, under David Whitehead and Sergeant Pester, had the time of their lives "blowing up" the various installations on the station and causing great alarm and bewilderment to peaceful passengers. The Major established himself in the station lamp-room and soon his servant, the invaluable Peter Dorans, had procured numerous tins of sausages from the refreshment room which we ate cold. Having temporarily satisfied my hunger, I noticed a large pile of blankets on the platform and suddenly realized how tired I was. I lowered myself heavily on them, much to the dismay of an Indian who was curled up asleep at the bottom of the pile. Finally the signal box "blew up" with a shattering explosion and the umpires decided to call it a day.

Morale was very high and the march from the station to our new camp nearby was soon accomplished to the strains of:

> "We joined the Navy to see the world,
> And what did we see? We saw the sea."

For some reason or other it seemed peculiarly appropriate. The indefatigable George Borrow was there before us, although he had marched as far as we had. He had already discovered which tents were for whom and he handed us each a batch of letters which were awaiting our arrival.

There was a large Anglican Church at Jhansi and the Major quickly organized a choir to lead the singing of carols on Christmas morning. In those surroundings the words of the carols were strangely moving and I shall not forget Bill Edge, with his exceptionally fine voice, reading aloud in our tent Milton's poem *On the Morning of Christ's Nativity*. Having served the men with their Christmas dinner, the officers consumed a vast meal in their mess. As I had been persuaded to be

Mess Secretary, I was responsible for this meal and did not enjoy it as much as the second Christmas dinner we had at the Club that evening. We walked back to the camp about midnight, happily singing carols and found a stray goat wandering among our tents. We caught it and tucked it up in Alec Macdonald's bed.

The officers' chargers arrived whilst we were at Jhansi. Mine was a beautiful black animal but, as it bit anyone who tried to go near it, we never saddled it and I did not ride much until I was given a good-looking chestnut to replace it. Another arrival was Judy, our column dog. Two of our men had been trained with her and they acted as her masters. If the column was divided, one master went with each part of the column and Judy would faithfully carry messages from one master to the other over incredible distances. Apart from her masters, nobody was allowed to feed or make a fuss of her and she did excellent work in Burma.

When we had recovered from Christmas and Hogmanay, which the Major celebrated in style with Athol brose, our column went out on a final river crossing exercise. Without doubt this was the most delightful exercise I have ever experienced. The marches were easy and we bivouacked in most pleasant surroundings. The crossing itself was quite a success but the mules needed much persuading to swim across. I found the best way was to swim part of the way with them and then hold on to their heads when they showed signs of wanting to turn back. We had quite a struggle in mid-stream with some of them and had to turn on our backs and cling around their necks with our legs while we tried to keep their heads in the right direction with out hands. One officer got a snapshot of me in this position which, I am glad to say, did not come out. I must have looked like a centaur doing contortions!

The last few days at Jhansi were a frantic series of kit inspections and last-minute purchases from the bazaar, but Bill Edge and I managed to give a small party to our respective platoon headquarters. C.S.M. Cairns came and needless to say a thoroughly good time was had by all. My recollections of the end of the party are conveniently hazy, except that I do remember finding Sergeant Thornburrow lying across the entrance of my tent and declaring that he would not move until he knew that I was safely back. My platoon headquarters now consisted of Sergeant Thornburrow, Bill Dunn, my batman, Paddy Feeney, my runner, and one of the Dennett twins as my groom. They worked well together and gave me totally loyal support, but it was not until long after the war that Paddy Feeney told me how he and Bill Dunn spent a good deal of their time rallying the less enthusiastic member of the platoon.

My Section Commanders were Corporal Litherland and Corporal Berry, and a lance-corporal whom I later replaced. I am afraid my Section Commanders found me very hard to please and it must sometimes have seemed as if I expended all my surplus spleen on them. However, in spite of several stormy periods in India, they never let me down in Burma. Their conduct in action exceeded my wildest hopes and the same may be said of all my platoon.

I cannot tell of all my men, much as I would like to, but this book would not be complete without some mention of Private Byrne, who was with me right from the start. Red-haired and very thick-set (he had been a champion wrestler in Liverpool). He was probably the strongest personality among the men and I could usually gauge the mood of the rest of the platoon by his. Apart from a very occasional burst of temper, for which he always subsequently apologized, he was cheerful and a tremendous worker. I often thanked my lucky stars for him.

Now for the first time the column was complete. At the last minute the Major had managed to arrange for Duncan Menzies, also of the Black Watch, to join us as Column Adjutant. Duncan was an Australian of Highland descent and one of the finest men I have ever met. He had been a Rhodes scholar at Oxford and I often thought that he was a perfect example of the type of man Rhodes intended to encourage. He was a splendid addition to our number. By this time there had been several other new arrivals. David Whitehead, who joined us before the Jhansi

Exercise, was a typical Yorkshireman. He had already had more than his share of excitement in the war, having been with the Royal Engineers in France and Holland and on several Commando raids. Jim Harman of the Gloucesters, experienced, cool and efficient, took over the Commando Platoon and Gerry Roberts, ex-Welsh Guardsman, took over the third rifle platoon, No. 9. Bill Williamson, who had been in the King's since before the war, came to us from another column and became Second-in-Command of the Support Platoon, and Tommy Blow, another genial giant, joined as a spare platoon commander in case of casualties. To everyone's delight, Bill Aird came to 5 Column as medical officer just before we left. Everyone had liked Bill ever since he came to the Brigade in Patharia days. It was a triumph to have "bagged" him for our column. Scotland was well represented in Column Headquarters with the Major, Duncan Menzies, Alec Macdonald, Bill Aird, C.S.M. Cairns and the Major's servant, Peter Dorans, all coming from north of the border. I sometimes wondered if Bill Edge, who had joined Column Headquarters as cipher officer, ever needed an interpreter. By now the reader must be thoroughly confused about the organization of the column, so I will refer him to the end of the book where I have laid it out more clearly.

Two things worried us: how to write home and what to do with our wounded? The mail problem was solved by arranging for a printed airgraph to be sent home on each man's behalf once a month during the campaign. This airgraph explained that due to the nature of the operation in which he was involved, the man was unable to write himself, although mail could be delivered to him. It also informed his next-of-kin that he was well and would write as soon as he could. This was a most satisfactory arrangement and, of course, the names of any casualties would be wirelessed back to India. The other problem was not so easy. Obviously, as we were operating behind enemy lines, it was impossible to evacuate the badly wounded, but they could perhaps be left in friendly villages. Each officer carried several copies of a letter in Burmese which was to be given to the villagers to whom the wounded were entrusted. In fact, many villages did prove most friendly and co-operative and, as Wingate himself said, a wounded man would probably have a much better time in a Burmese village than he would in a military hospital. All officers were issued with morphia, taught how to use it to relieve pain and how to give a lethal dose if necessary.

At a final talk with his officers before leaving Jhansi, the Major gave us all a last chance to withdraw from the undertaking if we so wished. Nobody took advantage of this offer and I am sure that, to this day, none of us regrets his decision.

At last, on 10 January, 1943, we were ready. Horses, mules and muleteers were loaded on to one train, the rest of us on to another, and, for better or worse, we were off. In his final written instructions before we left, the Brigadier had said: "The Chindwin is Jordan. Once across there is no turning back. The only way out of Burma is via Rangoon."

# PART II

# Action

"My God, I thank thee that my course is set,
with others of Thy choosing, at this hour;
to see the right discerned, the challenge met,
and battle given to the evil power;
to share the upward thrusting to the light,
and all the grandeur of the stony ways."

Richard Elwes, *Sonnets in War.*

# CHAPTER 4

# *Jhansi to the Chindwin*

I cannot remember how long the train journey lasted, but after a few days we changed trains and proceeded on a metre-gauge railway. On this part of the line officers and NCOs took turns to ride on the footplate and take driving lessons, so if we captured any locomotives in Burma we could use them. Our passengers did not have a very smooth ride but it was very interesting, and what impressed me most was the way the driver made his tea. He suddenly pulled the train to a standstill and disappeared under the engine with his teapot. Then the fireman pressed a button and a few minutes later the driver emerged with a pot of tea straight from the boiler.

We left the train at a place called Dhubri on the banks of the Brahmaputra and spent the night in a transit camp. Here I had my last hot bath for more than two years. The following day we loaded everything on to a river steamer. I remember the Major coming up to me while we were loading and repeating to me the very apt quotation, "All was bustle and confusion aboard the little vessel".

The twenty-four hour trip up the river was delightful; John Kerr, who was a keen photographer, took numerous snaps of the really impressive scenery, including a group of my platoon, which unfortunately has been lost. At Gauhati we unloaded our kit from the boat up a steep bank to another train. It was a very hot day but we managed to procure some coolies to help. That evening the local WVS gave us our last civilized meal and we entrained at about 10.00 p.m. It was here that John Kerr had one of his laughing bouts. They used to come upon him periodically but this was the most spectacular I had experienced.

Anyone who has read Martin Armstrong's description of Mrs
Rees laughing will have some idea what the laughter of John
Kerr was like:

> "It germinates, it spreads, dimple by dimple,
> From small beginnings, things of easy girth,
> To formidable redundancies of mirth."

Some quite innocent remark of mine set him off and he rolled
helplessly about the floor of the compartment, bellowing with
laughter, for at least five minutes. Of course it was quite
impossible not to join in, so for some time the air was full of
mirth. What the Indian railway staff made of it all I cannot
imagine.

The next day we reached Manipur Road, the station at
Dimapur which was our railhead. We spent a night in a camp
about six miles outside the town. From this camp we could see
the Manipur Road winding into the mountains, a sight which
made many of us discard certain superfluous items of kit we
had intended to carry.

When fully equipped, each man carried a load of about 70
lbs, about half his own weight for an average sized man. In his
Everest pack he carried:

> seven days' rations
> spare shirt
> spare slacks
> spare socks
> rubber-soled hockey boots
> "Housewife" (Needles, cotton and other repair kit)
> water sterilizing tablets
> mess tins
> eating utensils.

In addition to this he carried:

rifle
bayonet
ammunition
a dah or kukri (Burmese or Gurkha knives)
three grenades
water bottle
canvas water container
water wings
toggle rope
jack knife.

All these articles had to be carried; anything else was optional.

Officers also had revolvers, Verey pistols, binoculars, torches, compasses and maps. At first each officer had been issued with half-inch maps for the whole of Burma, parts of Assam, China, Thailand, French Indo-China and Malaya. After strong protests the more superfluous of these were withdrawn but we still carried about fifty maps each. Most of mine went on a mule and I only carried those immediately relevant. My binoculars, rifle and Verey pistol went on my horse but some officers insisted on carrying theirs. My horse also carried a sausage-shaped bag, which the ingenious Dunn had made out of an old trouser leg. We filled this with spare clothes, a few books, medical kit and emergency rations; it rode very comfortably behind the saddle, while in the rifle bucket with my rifle was a very fine shot gun which had been issued to help us supplement our rations and which Dunn was determined to add to his collection when he got back. We also kept a wary eye on a water bottle full of Martell brandy which I had managed to procure in Jhansi. Finally, although Bill Edge read it more than I did, I carried in my map case Everyman's edition of Milton.

All ranks also carried a supply of Attabrin tablets. The country in which we were to operate is one of the most malarial in the world, and as a precaution we were all to start taking Attabrin regularly from April 1st, which is the beginning of the worst season for malaria. I believe Attabrin was the latest thing for malaria in 1943. It did not cure it but suppressed it, and anyone with malaria was all right as long as he took the tablets regularly. The idea was that we should take the tablets and suppress the malaria until we returned to India.

We moved by night as the road had to be left free for convoys by day. The marches were not long compared with some we had already done, but we climbed to a height of over 5,000 feet and we were always happy to see the morning which meant that our rest camp was near. On the first night I was detailed to bring up the rear of the column and stop any lorries passing us and frightening our animals with their head lamps. I stood with my horse and watched the column wind away up the road. The Major, as always, was in front with Column HQ and the Burrifs; then came the reserve rifle platoon, then some outsize mules carrying our wireless sets, followed by Tommy Roberts and his Support Platoon with the mules carrying their mortars and machine guns. Behind him were Jim Harman and his Commandos, with their mule loads of explosives, and David Whitehead stumping along at the back; then a long string of second-line mules carrying spares of all kinds. These were led by Bill Smyly's Gurkhas and escorted by another rifle platoon. Then followed Alec Macdonald and Doc Aird, with rear headquarters or hindquarters, as we used to call them, and at the back of them the third rifle platoon, known as the perimeter platoon, because in bivouac this platoon furnished sentries round the perimeter. The three rifle platoons took it in turn to act as Reserve, Escort to the second-line mules, or Perimeter Platoon, changing every twenty-four hours. Reserve was the most popular job as it meant marching near the head of the column. Escort was less pleasant because it meant helping the Gurkhas load and unload their mules at every halt, and the Perimeter job, which seemed to come round to us with amazing rapidity, was distinctly distasteful as it meant sentry duty round the bivouac instead of sleep, followed by a gruelling march at the rear of the column.

Stretched out in single file the column was over half a mile long and Bill Smyly had an endless and difficult task riding up and down keeping an eye on his ninety-odd mules. It was a fine sight and the men were in good heart that night. I waited until the Perimeter Platoon had gone by and then prepared to follow a few hundred yards behind. Just at that moment I heard a musical Welsh voice indulging in a delightful flow of bad language and round the corner came Private Akerman and his bullocks. These bullocks were a last-minute addition of Wingate's and, with specially constructed bullock carts, they proved extremely useful for carrying extra loads and eventually for eating purposes. That evening Akerman and his band of "bullocketeers" were finding them troublesome. They never liked going up hill and later on one of them lay down and refused to budge an inch until a fire was lit under its tail. We then had difficulty in preventing it from overtaking the Major!

Our first rest camp was a good one with bamboo huts and we all slept well after the stiff climb. It was here that Bill Edge, on rousing his men in the morning, heard one of them remark, "I bet bloody old Stibbe isn't getting his bloody platoon up yet." Bill repeated this with relish at breakfast and thenceforward I was always "bloody old Stibbe" to him.

The marches were all much the same. The road was cut out of the mountainside so that there was always a drop of several hundred feet just over the edge and we counted the wreckage of scores of lorries far below. The nights were cold, which made the marching easier. We had a fifteen-minute halt after every hour's marching and one long halt during the night when we could brew up tea, although sometimes Dunn miraculously used to conjure up a cup of tea during a fifteen-minute halt.

Sunrise on the Manipur Road was magnificent. The vast mountain ranges flaunting themselves against the vivid morning sky, the silver sheen of the rivers gleaming below through the gaps in the mist, the long line of men and animals, each standing out in bold relief as the column topped a rise in the road, all made an unforgettable impression. It was perfect material for a film.

At Kohima we were sped on our way by a piper, and indeed the bagpipes seemed very much at home in that ultra-Scottish scenery. Sometimes at the end of the march we would find our camp perched high above the road and the last climb up several hundred feet of rough-hewn stairs tried even the best-tempered among us. Usually there was a clear, cool mountain stream nearby and here we would bathe, often with a crowd of native road-menders looking on.

After nine nights of marching we reached the Imphal plain. Our camp was well off the road by a river about five miles from Imphal. We were to stay here until everything was ready for our advance. We had a certain amount of rain, but there was an abundance of bamboo and banana leaves for building huts, and we were soon all under cover. Nearly every day the officers went into Imphal by truck. Here the Brigadier had established himself in what used to be the golf clubhouse and his Intelligence Officer, Graham Hosegood, had a remarkable room full of information about Burma, with maps spread all over the floor; Wingate insisted on everyone removing their shoes before entering. Here, squatting on his haunches in the middle of a map, his heels showing through enormous holes in his socks, he delivered his final instructions to us, firing his usual devastating questions and filling his audience with admiration and a surprising amount of enthusiasm. After the lectures we were bumped back to camp in our lorry singing our favourite "Green grow the rushes O" at the top of our voices.

Although the Major always said that riding was an unnatural pastime, and insisted that the first man to ride a horse must have done it as a joke, he was very keen that the officers should have a race and one morning we all lined up, some of us extremely apprehensive, and the column turned out to watch the fun. Once we had started, my horse needed no urging on; in fact he took the matter entirely out of my hands and we were soon galloping along in fine style about third or fourth from the front. Then suddenly he noticed that we were passing the spot where the fodder was kept and, without warning, he swerved to the left and headed for food. I was too busy holding on to do anything about it and poor Duncan, who was close behind me, was forced to swerve off course to avoid a collision.

We reached the winning post just as the crowd was beginning to disperse.

On 5 February I was sent ahead with a small party to guard a ration dump which had been formed for the Brigade at Lokchau. I left Dunn behind with most of my kit and travelled light. The road beyond Imphal was even more tortuous and steep than the Manipur Road, but we reached Lokchau that night after a hair-raising drive and found that our dump was situated by a river about a hundred feet below the road level. My instructions were to prepare suitable camp sites for the various columns of the brigade who would be spending twenty-four hours there as they marched through, but as the hillsides fell almost sheer down to the river and were thickly covered with bamboo, this was not going to be easy. However, the following day I found a battalion of Gurkhas stationed nearby and the Colonel very kindly lent me a party of men to clear the bamboo away from the few pieces of level ground available. In the officers' mess they showed me a list they had stuck up on the wall of about twenty different ways of serving bully beef, their staple diet for months past.

I learnt that the mules of this Gurkha battalion lived almost entirely on bamboo leaves and seemed to thrive on them. This was a new idea to us and I passed the information on to Wingate when I saw him a few days later. He at once ordered that all the mules in the Brigade should be introduced to this new diet, and later in the campaign mules and horses had nothing else for weeks at a stretch. This discovery meant that we did not have to depend so much on fodder being dropped for our animals.

A welcome arrival on my first day at Lokchau was a sanitary corporal who had been sent to help me with his squad. He seemed to find working with us more pleasant than his usual gruesome job which was burying the bodies of the hundreds of refugees who had died near the road in the trek out of Burma in 1942.

I enjoyed my stay at Lokchau. It was glorious country, we had a perfect pool in the river for swimming and there was plenty to eat. There was a Divisional Headquarters a little way down the road with the usual bevy of signallers and a splendid Indian Major who rejoiced in the name of Huknawuz. The colour sergeant belonging to this HQ was extremely helpful and gave me various items of kit which I had been unable to obtain elsewhere. I asked him down one evening to try out tinned meat-and-vegetable stew which was a treat for him after bully beef. The road above us was being widened by a gang of Nagas, fine looking men and quite friendly in spite of their reputation as head-hunters. Later a bulldozer appeared and for some hours huge boulders came crashing down all round us, several nearly missing our precious pile of rations.

On 10 February, the first of the columns arrived, drew their rations and rested. They told me that General Wavell had been up to see the Brigade at Imphal and, after addressing them, had saluted them as they marched off. Even he had been made to remove his shoes before entering the sacred map room. Later I heard that for several hours during his visit there were grave doubts as to whether we should be allowed to go on. It had been decided to postpone the big attack on Burma, at any rate until after the monsoon, and if the big attack was off it meant that our task of aiding the big attack by creating havoc behind the Jap lines was off too. However, Wingate urged that we could still make ourselves a nuisance to the Japs and, in addition, it would be a very good plan to see, before the real thing, whether our particular type of warfare was going to prove a success. After all, Wingate's ideas still had to be tested. We were all keyed up to go in and, although at the time some may have doubted the wisdom of General Wavell's decision to let us go ahead, subsequent events proved him right. Wingate's feelings at the time were summed up in a statement he made to Alaric Jacob of the *Daily Express*:

"If this operation succeeds, it will save thousands of lives. Should we fail, most of us will never be heard of again.

"If we succeed, we shall have demonstrated a new style of warfare to the world, bested the Jap at his own game and brought nearer the day when the Japanese will be thrown, bag and baggage, out of Burma. Most of my Chindits are not in their first youth, but married men between 28 and 35, who have previously done coastal defence and internal security work and never dreamt that they would serve as shock troops, doing one of the toughest jobs any soldiers have undertaken in this war.

"If ordinary family men from Liverpool and Manchester can be trained for this specialized jungle war behind the enemy's lines then any fit man in the British Army can be trained to do the same, and we show ourselves to the world as fighting men second to none, which I believe we are."

We did not know that we were being called Chindits. This name, however, which was later used for everyone under Wingate's command, arose from the mispronunciation of the word *Chinthé*, which was the Burmese name for the griffin-like beasts whose statues are found guarding pagodas all over Burma. These griffins were eventually adopted as the Divisional sign of the Chindits.

Five Column arrived at Lokchau on 12 February and I gave them all the rations I had left, but as they nearly all had stomach trouble they were not able to appreciate them. They brought with them some mail for me including a parcel from home which I had no room to carry in my pack and a ten shilling postal order with a verse by Patience Strong, a Christmas present from the village at home. As we moved off, my friend the Colour Sergeant from Divisional Headquarters rushed up with a very acceptable present of a dozen boxes of Bryant and May's matches.

The night's march from Lokchau was made pleasant by the singing of several of the Burriffs who decided to march with their friends in my platoon. Their favourite song was, "When It's Springtime in the Rockies". Morning found us near Tamu, where Bill Williamson had a ration dump similar to mine. Here we lay up for the day. I always find sleeping by day difficult even after a long march. John Kerr and I spent a long time in the river scrubbing one another's backs.

From here I went on again by lorry to our last ration dump. Bill Smyly, who had a bad fever, came with me and we drew rations from the dump ready for the arrival of the column. An officer from 7 Column called Tom Stock was in charge of this dump and I remember making myself very unpleasant to him when he would not give me what I wanted, little knowing that we were soon to meet again. We drew from this dump our first instalment of the kind of rations which were thenceforth to be dropped on us from the air. A day's ration consisted of:

> twelve Shakapura biscuits (for bulk)
> two ounces of cheese
> one ounce of milk powder (often damp and unusable)
> nine ounces of raisins or dates
> three-quarters of an ounce of tea
> one packet of salt
> four ounces of sugar
> one ounce of chocolate (or acid drops if you were unlucky)
> twenty cigarettes
> one box of matches.

Before we left Jhansi 6 Column had been disbanded and its men dispersed among the other Columns to bring them up to strength. Now the Brigade was split into three groups. Brigade Headquarters with 3, 4, 5, 7 and 8 Columns were to cross the Chindwin at a place called Tonhe; 1 and 2 Columns, under Colonel Alexander, were to cross further south to draw attention away from the Tonhe crossing; and Major Jeffries, dressed as a Brigadier, was to provide an additional feint further south still.

After another night's march we reached the end of the road at Thanan. We were now in Burma and before we set out again the Major read us the Brigadier's Order of the Day. It is so typical of the man and made such a fine prologue to our enterprise that I shall quote it in full:

"Today we stand on the threshold of battle. The time of preparation is over and we are moving on the enemy to prove ourselves and our methods. At this moment we stand beside the soldiers of the United Nations in the front-line trenches throughout the world.

"It is always a minority that occupies the front line. It is a still smaller minority that accepts with good heart tasks like this that we have chosen to carry out. We need not, therefore, as we go forward into conflict, suspect ourselves of selfish or interested motives. We have all had the opportunity of withdrawing and we are here because we have chosen to be here; that is, we have chosen to bear the burden and heat of the day. Men who make this choice are above the average in courage. We need, therefore, have no fear for the staunchness and guts of our comrades.

"The motive which has led each and all of us to devote ourselves to what lies ahead cannot conceivably have been a bad motive. Comfort and security are not sacrificed voluntarily for the sake of others by ill-disposed people. Our motive, therefore, may be taken to be the desire to serve our day and generation in the way that seems nearest to our hand. The battle is not always to the strong, nor the race to the swift. Victory in war cannot be counted on, but what can be counted on is that we shall go forward determined to do what we can to bring this war to an end which we believe best for our friends and comrades in arms; without boastfulness or forgetting our duty, resolved to do the right so far as we can see the right.

"Our aim is to make possible a government of this world in which all men can live at peace and with equal opportunities of sacrifice. Finally, knowing the vanity of man's effort and the confusion of his purpose, let us pray that God may accept our services and direct our endeavours, so that, when we shall have done all, we may see the fruit of our labours and be satisfied.

O. C. Wingate, Commander."

I found and still find this a moving and inspiring statement, but, not surprisingly, it did not go down so well with the men. I can still hear, as I was intended to hear, some of the comments of the men in my platoon:

"What did he mean – 'We're here because we've chosen to be here'? I never chose to be here."

"He may be fighting for the United Nations and all that but

I'm fighting for my missus and children, and if I don't get back to them in one piece it won't make much difference to them if we win the war or not."

"Him and his war aims. My aim is to get back to Birkenhead as quick as may be."

I sometimes wonder whether Wingate realized that his eloquence was wasted on many of the troops serving under him. It is difficult to believe that he was so ignorant of their mentality. Perhaps he was aiming his remarks at his officers and relying on them to "jolly" the troops along. Not many ordinary soldiers have ever had the time or the inclination to think about ideals and war aims. It is difficult not to suspect that Wingate may have been addressing himself in part to posterity. Perhaps I am completely wrong about this. Certainly Wingate's biographer, Christopher Sykes, had no doubt about his powers of leadership. He says:

"Most commanders who can compel the devotion of their men do so by being able to convey a sense of close sympathy, by appearing in some sort as a big father or brother, by appearing essentially the same, in larger version, as the men they lead. Wingate belonged to a different and older fashion. When he addressed his men he seemed to speak from a different world. If he entered into small humdrum details of administration, discipline or equipment, he would as often as not relate them to principles of war, to the virtues of the cause for which his men were fighting, to the historical implications of the hour. A more dangerous method can hardly be imagined of exhorting British soldiers, always prone to Philistine cynicism and a laugh at authority. Wingate never failed in seizing and dominating the attention of his audience. He never indulged in comfortable assurances. He was capable of telling men outright before an operation that not a few of them were likely to meet their deaths soon, and when he did this it did not lower their morale but strengthened it. He could always convey all his own self-confidence. One man, remembering a particularly grim address of the 1943 days, added that after hearing it he would 'have followed Wingate to Hell and back.' This was not an exceptional reaction. His sincerity always struck home with the same telling response."

I certainly have no doubts about Wingate's sincerity nor do I doubt that if he had been able to deliver personally this final Order of the Day before crossing the Chindwin, it would have carried far more weight with the troops.

The track from Thanan to the Chindwin was the worst we had experienced. Before long we bumped into the tail of the column ahead of us. They were having trouble with their mules and they sent word back that the track was not wide enough for our bullock carts, so we abandoned them and henceforth used the bullocks as pack animals. When it grew dark the track seemed to become worse. In places it was difficult to stop the mules slipping over the edge and at least one animal was lost in this way. It is only fair to the mules to say that in our column they really did seem to try to behave themselves from Imphal onwards. Eventually we halted and slept as we were on the track. The next morning I was told that during the night's march my sausage-shaped bag of kit had fallen off my horse and my groom had not been able to find it again in the dark. Dunn volunteered to go back but he only found the bag empty. It was extremely annoying to lose so much even before we had crossed the Chindwin.

About midday we pushed on, my platoon bringing up the rear. The path was steeper than ever, but less fearsome by daylight. We passed several skeletons and skulls by the side of the track, grim relics of 1942, and then at the top of the range we halted and there below us lay the Chindwin, just as we had seen it on the aerial photographs back at Imphal. The crossing at Tonhe was not proceeding very well, so the Major obtained permission to attempt to get his column across at a place called Hwematte, a few miles upstream. At about seven-thirty we arrived on the banks of the river. A brief rest was decreed before we attempted the crossing and we cooked our evening meal under cover, very much aware of the four hundred yards of water between us and the far bank.

It was a moonlight night and the river looked strangely

beautiful as it flowed between its high wooded banks but we did not have much time to appreciate this. We were all more than ready for a good night's sleep and I was feeling particularly disgruntled; one of the mules had kicked me on the thigh without the least provocation and walking was painful for several days as a result. I couldn't help feeling that if it had to kick me it ought to have kicked me hard enough to break my leg so that I need go no further.

For several hours it seemed as though we were never going to start. We had several R.A.F. rubber dinghies and the Major decided to make a large raft by putting a wooden platform on two of them; we began to construct the platform from planks of wood taken from derelict houses in the village. Meanwhile David Whitehead and the Commandos had got a rope across, but it fouled the bottom in several places and it was only after many hours' work by Sergeant Pester and others that it could be used to haul the raft and dinghies backwards and forwards. Nevertheless we ferried a platoon across to form a bridgehead, using a rubber dinghy and a native boat, which held about six men with their packs. The Major put me in charge of the boat, remarking optimistically that as I was an Oxford man I should be able to manage it. I spent quite a pleasant night paddling to and fro.

We snatched two hours' sleep before dawn and then set to work again. The mules were not too difficult once we had a few of them across to encourage the others; those who were unwilling to swim were pulled across behind the boats and raft. On one trip two of them got their legs caught in a rope and it was terrible to see them threshing wildly about in the water and getting themselves more and more entangled. Eventually we dragged them ashore, but artificial respiration failed to revive them. Apart from this, the crossing proceeded smoothly. By nightfall we were all across and the Major decided that we would sleep where we were. Except for the watchful sentries of the Perimeter Platoon we slept soundly, thankful that we had crossed our first major obstacle with no interference from the Japs. So far, so good.

# CHAPTER 5

# The Chindwin to Tonmakeng

It was so dark the following morning when we attempted to start that we gave up and went to sleep again until it was light. Then we made good progress moving parallel with the river; soon, striking inland we came to a village. Some of the Burrifs had gone ahead of us to gather information. One of them, Robert, whom I have already mentioned, did not seem as if he could do enough for me since an occasion when I had let him ride my horse and he appeared in this village with a present of eggs. By midday we had joined the other columns in the neighbourhood of a place called Myene, where supplies had already been dropped for us, and the remainder of the day was devoted to discussing plans, issuing orders, preparation and rest.

Myene was the first Burmese village we had seen properly and we at once noticed how superior it was to the average Indian village with its mud huts and general atmosphere of squalor and poverty. Most villages in Burma are dominated by their golden pagodas, cared for by the Buddhist priests in their orange robes. The houses are well built of teak and bamboo and usually they are raised several feet from the ground on posts. There is always at least one well, often sunk by the Government, and the general air of the place is clean and prosperous, although there was not much prosperity under the Japs. Many of the men wear the traditional "lungi", a length of brightly-coloured material which they wrap round themselves and tuck in at the waist. It is like a kilt but longer and with no pleating. The average Burman looks far better fed than the average Indian.

Our first supply drop had been a complete success, except

that our mail was dropped in the wrong place and fell into enemy hands. The following morning we collected our rations from the dropping area and set off. This time our column was in front. Three Column, under Major Mike Calvert, were off on their own and a party of Burrifs had gone on ahead to reconnoitre the next dropping area at a place called Tonmakeng, but we were at the head of the main body. It was an easy march along a good track through a teak forest, which meant that we were shielded from the sun. At the midday halt a message arrived telling of Japs in a village to the south of our route and the Major, eager for our first brush, obtained permission to investigate.

We struck off south from the track in the afternoon, but we had not gone far when we realized that our maps were not complete in all respects, for we ran into a shallow marsh which promised to hold us up indefinitely. It might have been possible to get the men across, but our animals would quickly have sunk under their loads. When night fell we were still looking for a way round and the following morning we at length decided that the only solution was to fell some small trees and build a causeway. This took some time and when it was finished the mules did not like it much, but at last we were all across and ready to set off again. We had hardly gone fifty yards when we came to another similar marsh and this was followed by seemingly countless others. I don't know how many causeways we built that day, but I do know that even the usual Army expressions of disgust seemed quite inadequate before we had finished. As always, the Major had just the right remark to make and even the most "browned-off" could not help grinning at his quips. At length, as night began to fall, we emerged into the valley where the village lay, but the Japs had left several hours before.

We spent that night on a steep hillside about a mile and a half from the village. My platoon was acting as Perimeter Platoon and we carried out the normal routine on reaching bivouac. The Major considered that three posts would give us sufficient protection, so, having established my platoon headquarters near the centre of the bivouac area, I placed my three sections at suitable points on the perimeter. I then reported to the Major to see whether he approved of the sites I had chosen for my posts. These posts always had one sentry standing on guard throughout the night. It was necessary to check that everyone knew the password and recognition signal and the position of platoon headquarters, of column headquarters and of the other posts. Also I had to make arrangements for Sergeant Thornburrow and myself to be woken at intervals during the night. When all was done I returned to my platoon headquarters where Dennett had groomed and watered my horse which, incidentally, he had christened Billy, and where Dunn had one of his wonderful concoctions ready for me. Meanwhile Feeney had been running messages for me with his usual quiet efficiency.

After the meal we did not waste much time preparing for the night. I always slept in my boots, as, in an emergency, it takes so long to put them on again, but some of the men used to wear their hockey boots at night. When we were Perimeter Platoon I insisted that everyone should sleep with something on their feet so as to be ready for instant action. Normally we had no time for shaving and beards were encouraged. We usually arrived in bivouac at dusk and left at dawn, so that even if there was a suitable river for washing, we did not have time for more than a cursory rinse. At times I must have gone for a week or more without a proper wash and without removing my boots or clothes, but at the time I did not notice it. At night I never bothered with a ground sheet but just rolled up in a blanket as I was.

Sergeant Thornburrow, who slept close at hand, took turns with me at going round the posts at intervals during the night. On this particular night I was woken at a pre-arranged time by one of the sentries who had just stood down. It was a moonlit night and I sat for a few minutes listening to the jungle noises. The only sound from the column was from my horse, grazing a few yards away. At the first two posts I visited all was well; the sentries were alert and had nothing to report. I approached the third post quietly but there was no challenge, not a sound. For a moment I wondered if I had mistaken the position of the post in the dark, but I found the section and their Bren-gun mule asleep in the bushes nearby, so that I knew that I was at the right spot. I woke up the section commander and asked him who was supposed to be on sentry duty. He told me. "Isn't he there, sir?" he gasped. We soon found the man sound asleep. He explained, quite casually, that he had not been feeling very well. So he had decided, without a word to anyone, to leave his post and lie down again. I cannot recall what I said to him, but I returned to my blanket sick at heart.

The next day the Major had a tricky case to handle when the man was brought before him. He had put the whole column at risk. Obviously a very severe and speedy punishment was called for, but, cut off as we were from the rest of the world, the normal procedures – a court martial, penal servitude, detention, loss of pay and so on – were out of the question. The Major decided that the man must choose between making his own way back to India alone or being flogged. He chose to be flogged. C.S.M. Cairns made a cat-o'-nine tails from parachute cord and administered the flogging. I think we all felt that this was a fair way of dealing with the matter and I still feel this more than forty years later. The man took his punishment well and subsequently bore no ill will. The whole incident left me suspecting that as a platoon commander I was far from adequate.

The next few days were easier. Our route lay over a series of low hill ranges, heavily wooded with bamboo, replacing the teak forests through which we had marched at first. In each valley we found a village by the river surrounded by paddy fields. The villagers seemed pleased to see us, but they were frightened of the Japs. We followed the track of the other column again and kept on bumping into one another, which was very annoying, but it gave me a chance to see George Borrow once more. He was looking ghastly with yellow jaundice and must have been feeling terrible, but he was as cheerful as ever and determined to ignore his illness.

It was during these few days that we finally solved the

problem of fires. The Major quite rightly foresaw that if every man had his own little fire to cook on at halts, the smoke from scores of fires would soon give the column away to enemy aircraft. He therefore ordered that, except in special circumstances, only one fire was to be lit in each platoon. But thirty men cannot cook on one fire, however large it may be, without a certain amount of difficulty as we very soon found out, so, instead of the whole platoon jostling round one big fire, each man built a fire of his own on the circumference of a small circle laid down by me. The smoke from these fires all went up together as if from one big fire and it was easy to put them all out if enemy aircraft were heard.

The paddy fields at Tonmakeng were an ideal dropping area, surrounded by low wooded hills with a river running down one side and the village and pagoda at one end. The Brigadier decided to have a mammoth three days' dropping and, much to the Major's disgust, our column was chosen to organize the dropping while the other columns were sent off to attack a Japanese garrison that had been reported by the Burma Rifles at Sinlamaung.

Various platoons of the column were put out round the Tonmakeng valley to prevent any Jap interference with the dropping, but although several patrols were reported nearby and it must have seemed strange that British planes were hovering over the same valley for three days, we were left in peace. Denny Sharp, as our RAF officer, was put in charge of the technical side of the dropping, and my platoon were to have the job of collecting supplies as they dropped and stacking them ready for distribution to the columns.

Early on 24 February we lit a series of fires in the shape of a large letter "T" on the dropping area, and at the appointed time we heard the hum of planes. Greenstuff was piled on the fires to make them give off smoke and in a few moments two Dakotas and a Hudson were circling round with their fighter escort. The leading plane signalled to Denny that the dropping was about to begin and the men at the fires took cover under the trees at the edge of the field while the first plane swooped low over the area. We could see the men in the open doorway of the plane push the bundles out, three parachutes opened and in a few moments our first instalment of rations had landed gently in the middle of the field. The second and third planes followed behind, and then the first one came round again, and so on until they signalled that the dropping was over and headed back to India to be reloaded. They came over twice a day regularly while we were at Tonmakeng and dropped all that we had asked for and more.

Each parachute had a container with four petrol tins of rations in it, each tin containing ten packets of one day's rations. Unfortunately the Hudson did not seem able to fly as slowly as the Dakotas while it was dropping and, as a result, some of the parachutes did not open. Thus the tins were badly buckled when they landed, but we wirelessed this information back to the airbase and they sent us replacements. We soon removed the parachutes and stacked the things for each column under cover of the woods, while we made a dummy stack of bags of mule fodder in the open to draw enemy fire if we were attacked. The bags of mule fodder were dropped without parachutes and it was as well to stand clear of the dropping area as they landed. One column later lost a man who was hit by a bag in a night dropping.

By the third day we had enough rations and mule fodder for all the columns; the planes then started dropping clothing and equipment. Boots, shirts, socks, shorts, torches, batteries, rifles, ammunition; a quartermaster's stores started to rain on us from the sky. By this time the other columns were returning from Sinlamaung. They had found that the Japs had heard of their approach and fled, so they had to content themselves with destroying the Jap huts and stores. The distribution of supplies ran as smoothly as could be expected though there were one or two amusing incidents.

Eight Column collected some of their rations on an elephant they had added to their number, much to the alarm of our horses and mules. We began to feel that with mules, horses, dogs, bullocks and elephants our nickname "Wingate's Circus" was well deserved. Tom Stock, to whom I had been so rude at his ration dump before the Chindwin, came to draw his column's quota and, in the course of the ensuing argument, the Major came up and happened to catch one of his remarks.

"I won't have you speaking to one of my officers like that," he said. "What rank are you?"

"Lieutenant, sir."

"Oh, that's all right; I thought you must be a private soldier from the way you were swearing at him."

My third meeting with Tom Stock took place in less happy but more friendly circumstances.

During the dropping an officer from Brigade Headquarters came up and asked me, confidentially, if any packages with a white streamer attached had been dropped. Apparently he had arranged for some whisky to be delivered with a streamer to distinguish it. He was somewhat dismayed when I told him that all the bags of mule fodder had white streamers on them, but he found his precious package in the end.

The Major had spare monocles dropped to him and later the press made much of this. It was not generally realized that his monocle was not worn for show purposes; it was a very vital part of his equipment and he could not manage without it.

On the third day, while the planes were still dropping sacks, Wingate appeared. He was very anxious to move Brigade Headquarters. They had already loaded up their mules with as much as they could carry and they were all lined up ready to leave, but he thought it would be a good idea if the mules, before they started, had a good feed from the sacks which were still being dropped. I sent some of my men to collect a dozen sacks from the dropping area and we lined them up in front of the mules who were getting quite excited about the prospect. I have never seen animals look·so crestfallen as they did when I cut open the tops of the sacks and revealed that they were full of boots and socks!

When all the columns had taken away all they could carry, there was still a lot left, so 5 Column were issued with an extra two days' rations each. My platoon had already been allowed to take some of the rations which had been broken because the parachutes attached to them did not open, so that most of them could not carry any more. We gave everything that was left to the villagers. They were particularly delighted with the material from the parachutes, as, since the Japs had arrived, cloth had been unobtainable. Shortly after we had left, the Japs reported that they had wiped out a force of paratroops that had landed at Tonmakeng. The Japs who had fled from Sinlamaung spread exaggerated rumours about us. Already we were causing considerable alarm and confusion among our enemies.

By the evening of 26 February we had finished our work and at last I managed to go down to the river for a bathe. It had been a busy period and this was my first chance to relax. During the three days of the dropping Dunn had produced some extra special meals with things bought from the village but I had only had time to snatch at them. All the same, I had enjoyed myself and taken the opportunity of riding my horse as I went from one part of the dropping area to another. We went to sleep in good time that night to be ready for an early start.

# CHAPTER 6

## *Tonmakeng to Bonchaung*

The valley in which Tonmakeng lies runs more or less north and south and so do the tracks running along it. To the east lies a mass of hills separating it from the Upper Mu Valley. It was no longer possible to try and conceal our presence from the Japs, but our plan was to appear in the Upper Mu Valley several days before we could possibly be expected there. We were to achieve this by taking a secret track which the Japs did not know about, through instead of round the hills to the south which was the normal route. Mike Calvert, with 3 Column, was off on his own as usual, but 4, 5, 7 and 8 Columns were to take the secret track. We had heard by now that 1 and 2 Columns, operating far to the south, with Colonel Alexander, had already drawn blood.

The two days' march along the secret track was one of the most trying of the campaign. Our way ran along the top of a ridge and our packs were especially heavy after the dropping. Marching along a watershed is a good idea if you want to avoid being ambushed, and no doubt it has many other advantages, but all I know about that track was that it never remained on the level for more than a few yards. Every time we had struggled to the top of a rise we saw a dip and another rise in front of us. Many of these rises were so steep that the only way the mules could climb them was at a run. The muleteers did wonderful work throughout the campaign, but I never admired them more than I did during these two days. Most of us found that it was difficult enough to march along the track ourselves without the additional effort required to bring a mule along too. Certainly those muleteers deserved a medal and, for that matter, so did the mules.

We came across no water on the first day but we bivouacked near a good river for the night. The following morning we followed this river for several miles, alternating between wading and marching along the bank. After removing and replacing our boots several times, we gave it up and kept them on to wade. By this time our feet were so hard that it was unlikely that they would blister through marching with boots full of water, but I decided to mount my horse and ride along the river dry-shod. It would have been a good idea if Billy had not decided to have a roll in the water while I was still on his back, with the result that I finished up wetter than anyone else. I hope the poor animal could not understand some of the names I called him. By the end of the march we were utterly exhausted and I don't mind admitting now that several times that day I told myself that if I had not been an officer I would have fallen out at the side of the track and told everyone to go to hell. Yet nobody gave in and I well remember that Dennett, worn out and exasperated with the effort of leading Billy, still fed and watered him with the same affectionate care when we stopped that night.

The Brigadier sent for all the officers that night to tell us his plans. We were nearly at the end of the secret track and, as soon as we reached the end of it, 5 Column was to go off on its own and head for the Mandalay-Myitkyina railway line at Bonchaung. Here we were to blow up a bridge and blow down a cutting where the line runs through a gorge. Three Column were also heading for the railway, while the other Columns were to draw the attention of the Japs elsewhere. The Brigadier, not for the first time, reprimanded us with memorable scorn for leaving a trail of litter wherever we went. He also emphasized that Columns were making far too much noise. There was no need to talk in whispers but equally there was no need for any shouting. Mules and horses could be heard whinnying miles away and they must be taught not to do so by being struck sharply on the nose very time they gave tongue. Strangely enough, after a while the whinnying in our Column almost ceased, though whether this was the result of disciplinary action or whether the poor animals were too tired to whinny we could never tell. Billy, my horse, never learnt his lesson and used to look at me most reproachfully every time I beat him on the nose. He whinnied cheerfully to the end.

I think it was here that Wingate issued one of his most unpopular orders, that nobody was ever to brew tea before starting off in the morning. Needless to say this was a blow to most of us, but there is no doubt that it did waste time and there was always a risk that we might give away our presence by lighting fires before dawn. Rumour had it that Wingate did not like tea and that on the rare occasions when he did take it he always strained it through a sock!

From now on we developed a regular daily routine. We would move at first light, each stage of an hour's marching being following by fifteen minutes' halt. The second halt of the day would be our tea halt and, if we had any, our breakfast halt. At midday we always stopped for three hours. This gave us a chance to have a meal, clean and inspect weapons and feet, do any first aid necessary and various other jobs. Then we marched on until we reached the night's bivouac.

We started early the following morning in an effort to move well clear of the secret track and the rest of the Brigade, but before we had gone far the Brigadier caught us up with last-minute instructions. The descent into the Upper Mu Valley was steep and one of my muleteers lost his pack in the dark. So he had to be fed by the rest of the platoon until the next dropping.

The main road from Mansi to Banmauk runs through this part of the valley and there is a road, motorable in dry weather, running south from this road to Pinlebu. Our intention was to go south in the direction of Pinlebu for about twenty miles and then to strike eastward through the hills to the Meza Valley and the railway line. We knew of Jap garrisons at Mansi and Pinlebu and one or two smaller places nearer to us in the valley, so that it looked as if the valley was pretty strongly held. This was confirmed by some Burmans who gave us information of Japs in several nearby villages, and also by a Burma Rifles officer who had been fired on by the Japs while making a propaganda speech in one village.

As we wanted to reach the railway unobserved if possible, we kept clear of tracks that day, but the jungle was pretty thick and my platoon who were up in front as Reserve Platoon often had to cut a way through the bamboo with their dahs and kukris. Duncan assisted us and hacked carefully and tirelessly all day. We halted that night near a place where a lot of trees had recently been felled, so, as my platoon were guarding the perimeter, I took extra special precautions that night.

We had not gone far next morning when we reached a motorable road which had not appeared as anything more than a track on our maps. There were Jap footmarks in the dust of the road made by the black rubber-soled boots they so often wore. My platoon blocked the road while the Column crossed and the Burrifs skilfully concealed all traces of our crossing. While this was happening a party of coolies came down the road and informed us that they were carrying baggage for some Japs nearby. The Major was eager to attack these Japs but decided against it as we were in a hurry to reach the railway. In addition, one of the coolies had made off into the jungle as if to warn the Japs, so we bribed the others not to tell in which direction we were moving and pushed on towards the Pinlebu road.

My platoon, as Perimeter Platoon, was at the back of the column and it was not long before I heard someone approaching from behind. To my astonishment, instead of Japs, I saw the Brigadier coming up at high speed on foot surrounded by his Gurkha bodyguard. He wanted to know why we were moving so slowly and I explained to him that at the front of the Column they were having to carve a way through the jungle. He fumed at the back for a few moments while I told him of the incident with the coolies and then he fought his way up to the front to demonstrate the best way of hacking a path for the Column. Thereafter speed increased somewhat until we stopped to brew up just short of the road. Several explosions to our left had puzzled us but we discovered, on reaching the road, that it was 7 and 8 Column who, impatient of the jungle, were marching down the road and blowing up the wooden bridges behind them as they went.

Progress since we left the secret track had been infuriatingly slow and we had not moved away from Brigade Headquarters and the other Columns. We now, under Wingate's orders, found ourselves marching briskly and brazenly down the road to Pinlebu with 7 and 8 Columns and Brigade Headquarters behind us. By this time 4 Column had left the others and was on its way to attack a Jap garrison at a place called Pinbon. During the course of the day the Major sent me back down the road with an urgent message. I mounted my horse and galloped off. As usual when Billy moved faster than walking pace, items of equipment, such as map cases, binoculars, and revolvers flew off him and me in all directions. As I passed a startled group from 7 Column I heard one of them shout, "Look out, here comes John Gilpin."

There was a violent storm that afternoon and we were soon ankle deep in mud even on the road and at places we had to wade over our knees. The Brigadier caught us up again during the storm and I had my first and last long conversation with him. It is sad that I cannot remember what we talked about but I do recall feeling that the conversation was proceeding surprisingly well and I know that I tried to impress him with my enthusiasm and intelligence as we trudged through the rain. At length the weather began to clear and he said, "Well now, shall we stop and have a meal and light fires or shall we march on until our clothes have dried on us? What do you think?"

"I think we should march on until we have dried out," I said heartily, anxious to enhance my reputation for enthusiasm and intelligence.

"Hm," he said as he stepped to the side of the road to await the arrival of the Headquarters who were following behind. A few minutes later we received from him an order to bivouac off the road. The rain had soaked everything, even the remains of our rations in our packs, but we lit fires after some considerable difficulty and tried to dry ourselves and some of our belongings. We cheered up a bit when we were warmer.

Our column moved off again after dark and this time we really did leave the other columns. It was unpleasant marching through the blackness down the muddy road which was now full of potholes. At one of the hourly halts an officer discovered that he had left his map-case behind at the previous halt and, not being a keen horseman, he asked me to ride back and look for it. For once I was glad of an excuse to get on my horse. I rode back along the road, half-expecting to run into some Japs following us up but too tired to be really worried. I could not find the map-case and nearly fell asleep before I had caught up the column again, but Billy seemed anxious to return to them so that if I dozed in the saddle it did not matter.

In the early hours of the morning we left the road just before Naungkan. The other columns were going to march straight on down the road and we were to try to march through the hills by going up the valley of the Nam Maw. We fully expected this valley to be blocked by the Japs, so we made very careful arrangements to collect at a rendezvous near an alternative route should we be attacked and forced to disperse. Yet for the moment all that we wanted was sleep. We had covered thirty-two miles since our last bivouac, which was no mean achievement with the weight we were carrying. It was nearly light when we halted and settled down for a few hours' rest on a wooded hill, except for the poor Perimeter Platoon which, thank goodness, was not mine.

We were woken at noon and after a hurried meal we moved on. Soon we found ourselves entering a long narrow valley. It had several villages in it and looked extremely attractive. Later we christened it the Happy Valley, but at first we were not at all certain what it held for us. Some of the Burrifs put on their "lungis" and went ahead to the first village to gather what news they could. We were delighted when they came back to say that, although the villagers had been ordered to store food and build air raid shelters for them, the Japs had not yet set foot in the valley. Also they were willing to sell us rice for ourselves and paddy for our animals. This was especially good news as our rations were practically exhausted and the Major did not want to have another supply drop until we had done our job on the railway. We filled everything we could, including water-wings and socks, with rice and paddy. Then we followed the path which ran up the valley beside the river. We were soon brought to a halt at a place where the river ran through a rocky glen and the path crossed the river just below a waterfall on a series of extremely dangerous stepping-stones. It was obvius the mules could go no further this way. The villagers told us of another way round, which meant retracing our steps and climbing up one side of the valley, but we were stiff after the previous day's soaking and, to our delight, the Major decided to spend the night in the glen, trusting the report of the villagers that there were no Japs about. The glen would have been a death trap had we been attacked during the night but it was by far the loveliest of all the places in which we had bivouacked. The rocks rose up on either side and the river poured down into a series of pools lined with grassy banks. We stuffed ourselves with rice and settled down for the night, except for Dennett, my groom, who insisted on having a swim. I felt very tempted to follow but decided I needed sleep more than a wash.

Some of the villages we passed through as we continued up the valley the next day had brine wells, which supplied the whole area with salt. They looked pleasant and prosperous. We had our usual halt at midday and Dunn made a fine dish of rice and cheese. As always at the long halt, Duncan Menzies pinned up on a tree a map showing our route and the distance covered, and also the latest radio news bulletin, so that everyone could follow the course of our campaign and the course of the war. On this day the news had been broadcast that the guerrillas, operating behind the Japanese lines in Burma, had blown up a ralway line at several points. Like the British forces in the Falklands 39 years later, we did not know whether to be amused or annoyed that this announcement of our intentions had been made two days too soon. We only hoped the Japanese would not pay too much attention to it.

The Major always tried to keep everyone in the picture as far as possible. We suspected what the Japs might do to extract information from prisoners. So anything really vital was known only by those who had to know. Nevertheless, the policy of telling everyone as much as possible obviously made all ranks far keener than they would have been if they had been kept in complete ignorance.

At the head of the valley we left the river behind and, after a stiffish climb, reached the top of the Mankat Pass. Ahead of us we could see the country through which the railway ran. We could hardly believe that the Japs had let us come through this pass unmolested. It was perhaps the most obvious of the few ways to approach the railway and they could easily have blocked it with a small force. The suspense as we neared the top of the pass had been tremendous; we felt like dancing down the other side. We were in a cheerful mood when we bivouacked that night, despite our long march. My own happiness was increased by a quite undeserved but very welcome verbal bouquet from the Major, perhaps intended to compensate for an equally undeserved verbal rocket which had been delivered the day before.

The next day's march was a comparatively easy affair. As usual the Burrifs had gone ahead to gather information and we kept to a track as there were no reports of any Japs in the immediate neighbourhood. During the heat of the day our way lay through another teak forest so we avoided the worst of the sun. In the evening we passed through the village of Tatlwin and marched several miles down a newly constructed motor road which led to a village on the railway called Nankan. We made our night's bivouac in the jungle well away from this road. As a rule we bivouacked at least five hundred yards from any road or track and we developed a special technique for leaving no sign of the place where we had turned off the track. On this night, of all nights, we wanted to be absolutely sure of being undisturbed. We had now arrived within a few miles of our objective at Bonchaung without seeing a Jap, although it was eighteen days since we had crossed the Chindwin. Tomorrow was to be our day and it was impossible not to notice the air of anticipation about the column as we ate our evening meal.

Our orders from the Brigadier were to blow up the railway and then cross the Irrawaddy and make for an area on the far side where he intended to collect the Brigade before further operations. The method of carrying out these orders was left to Major Fergusson. Most of us imagined that we would blow up the railway by night and then try to reach the Irrawaddy unobserved and cross it in some secluded spot, hoping the Japs would imagine that we had turned back to India. Yet the Major's final plan was far bolder and more inspiring. As there were so few Japs about, we would blow the railway by day and then, instead of trying to make a long-drawn-out crossing of the Irrawaddy with our rubber dinghies, we would make for a large place where there would be plenty of boats and, having taken it by storm if necessary, cross the river there in style. The place chosen was Tigyaing. The map indicated that it had a steamer station and ferry. It was too much to hope that the ferry was still running but we thought there would be no difficulty in finding plenty of boats. The plan appealed to us as we were rather tired of slinking about and trying to avoid being noticed.

The Major issued his orders on the evening of 5 March. The following morning the column was to be divided into four parties. Party 1 was John Fraser and some Burrifs who were to reconnoitre Tigyaing, which was nearly thirty-five miles away, and if possible make arrangements for us to cross there on or about 10 March. Party 2 was Tommy Roberts with the mortar section of his Support Platoon, John Kerr with his rifle platoon (Number 8), Pam Heald with some Burrifs, Doc Aird and Bill Edge who, although he was acting as cipher officer, wanted to see the fun. This party was to attack the Japs who were reported to be at Nankan, the village on the railway about six miles down the road from our bivouac and the next station on the line south of Bonchaung. Some of the Gurkha muleteers, who were always itching for a fight, were allowed to go with this party. Party 3 was Jim Harman, Sergeant Pester and half the Commando Platoon, escorted by my platoon, with two Burrifs. We were to move across country to the gorge, about two miles south of Bonchaung station, and blow it. Party 4, led by the Major, was the rest of the column. They intended to proceed along the track to Bonchaung station. There David Whitehead and the other half of the Commando Platoon were to blow up the steel girder bridge over a stream which runs into the river just south of the station, while the Major and Duncan, with 9 Platoon under Gerry Roberts and the Support Platoon's machine-gun section, made sure that their work was not interrupted. Meanwhile the rest of the party, under Alec Macdonald, would go on, crossing the line and the river which ran almost beside it, and prepare a bivouac for the bridge-blowing section of their party. All parties, except Number 1 (John Fraser's), were to meet at a rendezvous about twenty miles beyond the railway on the banks of the Kunbaung Chaung* by midday on 8 March. The rendezvous with John Fraser's party was near Kwingi, a village about five miles short of Tigyaing.

The Major gave us these orders at dusk that evening and when we were all quite sure we understood them, we dispersed to our various platoons and passed them on to our men. Then, having made some last-minute arrangements for the morning with Jim Harman, I rolled up in my blanket and, in spite of the feeling of excitement in my stomach, I was soon asleep.

On 6 March each party, before it left the bivouac, took its share of one of our bullocks which had been slaughtered that morning by the Burrifs. Parties 1 and 2 were off punctually and Jim Harman and I followed down the road about ten minutes behind Party 2. We intended to keep to the road for a bit and then strike off eastward across country towards the gorge. We

---

* The words Nam and Chaung both mean river or stream.

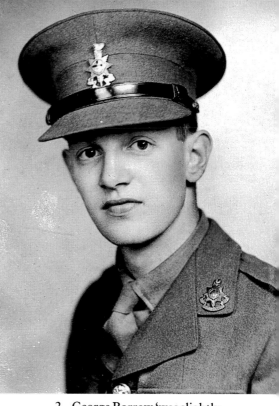

1. The author in 1942.

2. George Borrow 'was slightly built, quiet and studious, with a face like a baby owl.' (p.5)

3. 'Bill Edge and I struck up a lasting friendship.' (p.23)

4. 'Sergeant John Thornburrow was a good-natured giant of a man from Kendal.' (p.33)

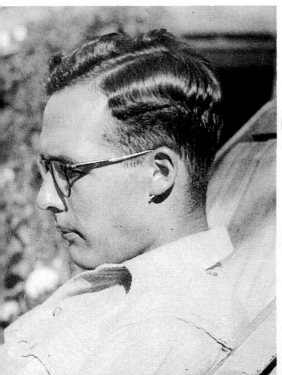

5. 'It was impossible not to be impressed by Wingate.' (p.16)

6. Bernard Fergusson, 'an intellectual and a man of action' (p.32)

7. John Kerr 'was a land agent from South Wales' (p.35)

8. *Left to right:* Lieutenant 'Pam' Heald, General Wavell, Captain John Fraser, Major Fergusson, Brigadier Wingate. (*Imperial War Museum*)

9. Officers of no 5 column, Jhansi, Christmas Day, 1942.

10. Chindits marching up a river bed in Burma.

11. Preparing mules for a river crossing.

had gone about three-quarters of a mile and were just approaching the village of Kyaik-in when we heard the sound of firing and grenades going off some distance ahead of us. After a hasty consultation, Jim and I decided to conceal our party in the jungle at the side of the road while we went forward with Dunn to see what was happening. Fitzpatrick, Tommy Roberts' groom, came galloping back along the road with a message from Tommy to the Major, but he could only tell us that there was a lot of firing, which we already knew. He galloped on towards the bivouac we had just left and the three of us went on up the road for about three hundred yards to where a track led off to the left towards Bonchaung. Just as we reached this point about eight Japs burst out of the jungle on the right of the road, dashed straight across and disappeared in the jungle on the other side. They were only about fifty yards ahead of us but obviously they had not noticed our presence and they were gone so quickly that we had only just time to recognize what they were. The firing ahead of us now seemed to be coming from several directions but we could not see what was happening, and it was difficult to know what to do. The obvious course was to go in and help Tommy Roberts and John Kerr and their party, although it was impossible to see how the land lay; then we reflected that our task was to blow the gorge and that, by joining in the fight and revealing our presence to the Japs, we would not achieve that task. We therefore decided to make straight for the gorge across country. It was a hard decision and Dunn was thoroughly disgusted at not being allowed to have a crack at the Japs. We comforted ourselves with the thought that, if Tommy and John had bumped into a much stronger force, they would be able to employ Wingate's dispersal tactics which were designed to meet such an eventuality; in fact we had no reason for thinking that they had met a larger force than they could cope with. All the same I did not feel entirely happy about our decision until I heard the full story later on, and the Major had told us that we had acted quite rightly.

Having joined our party, we set off through the jungle in the direction of the gorge. At the top of a ridge we paused to take our bearings. Behind us we could still hear firing and, for a few minutes, there was a series of blood-curdling screams. I heard later that these screams came from the Japs as they worked themselves up to put in a bayonet charge, but, at the time, not knowing what it was, we felt most uneasy. Ahead of us we could see some thickly covered hills between ourselves and the railway and, as we looked, three planes swooped down and fired their machine guns at some invisible target in the direction of the line. It was impossible to make out whether or not they were our planes, and this added to a growing feeling of bewilderment, but we knew our objective so we pushed on.

The next few miles lay through the worst country we had experienced. The jungle was incredibly thick and we had tremendous difficulty in hacking a way through for our mules. In addition to this, the hills were fiendishly steep and rocky. The mules were laden with explosives and, at some points, the way was so narrow that we had to unload them to get them through and then manhandle the loads. I remember Pester, the Sergeant of the Commando Platoon and, incidentally, the only Leicester man in the column beside myself, the sweat pouring down his face after his own exertions with a particularly heavy box, quietly supervising the passage of the next obstruction. After about three hours of a struggle, during which we made little progress, we stopped for a short while at the foot of a rocky slope. We had a small wireless set so we took the opportunity to see if there was any message for us. The signallers could pick up nothing so we pressed on again. I shall never forget that day. Nature seemed to have contrived to put every available obstacle in our path. As we overcame one we were confronted by another. Nevertheless, everyone, even the hard-pressed muleteers, kept their temper, and some hours later, to our immense relief, we came upon a track which we rightly presumed would lead us to Bonchaung station.

It was late afternoon when we reached the railway line. At the station we found Duncan was in charge and David White-head and his Commandos were already preparing the bridge to be blown. Duncan told us what he could about the events of the morning. When Fitzpatrick had arrived with the message from Tommy Roberts, the Major had immediately rushed down the road with Gerry Roberts and 9 Platoon to the scene of the fighting, ordering Duncan to make straight for Bonchaung with the rest of the party and carry on according to plan. So far no more had been heard of the Major or of any of the others. Duncan and his party had found the station deserted. A derelict train in a siding gave evidence of good work by allied planes and there was no sign of the station buildings having been inhabited for some time, though the line was obviously still in use. Alec Macdonald had gone on with his party to prepare a bivouac as arranged. Clearly we were to go on with our part of the plan as before, except that we would not be able to blow the gorge until some hours after David had blown the bridge. As we moved off down the line we could see him and his men working happily astride a girder, obviously in their element.

Between the station and the gorge, a distance of about two miles, the line ran for the most part along an embankment beside the river. We had hoped that it would be easier going along the railway over streams running into the river. The rails were supported on girders but there was nothing under the sleepers and it was too much to expect the mules to walk across on the sleepers as we could. At each bridge the mules had to be taken down the steep embankment, across the stream at the bottom and then up again onto the line at the otherside.

On our way we met a solitary Burman. Our Burrifs spoke to him and he seemed a pleasant enough fellow but we kept him with us till our work was done just in case he should be questioned by some Japs. I think he quite enjoyed our company for the evening. Our two Burrifs took the opportunity of finding out about conditions in Burma under the Japs and also pumped a bit of propaganda into him.

It seemed hours before we reached the gorge, but when we did arrive we found that it might have been made to be blown down. From our maps we had been able to tell that at this point the hills ran up to the water's edge and it looked as though the line ran round the end of the range between the last hill and the river, so that we expected to find the hillside falling steeply to the line on the right and on the left a steep drop down from the line to the river. In fact we found that the line curved away from the river at this point and ran through the hills for about two hundred yards in a cutting. The sides of this cutting were almost perpendicular and, for the most part, solid rock. Jim and Pester chortled with glee at the sight of it.

As we walked along, Jim and I had been discussing plans for making a quick getaway as soon as the gorge was blown. Somehow or other we had to cross the river, but the only possible crossing place we had seen was near the bridge which David was blowing. Although we felt certain that the sound of the explosion would draw every Jap within miles towards Bonchaung, there was no alternative but to make our way back along the line when we had done the job and cross the river there. So that we would not be delayed by the mules on the line, we took off all the explosives as soon as we reached the gorge and I sent Sergeant Thornburrow back to the ford at Bonchaung with one section and all the mules, instructing him to wait there under cover until we arrived. This was a hard blow for Thornburrow and his section. They were dog-tired after the day's exertions and, just when they hoped to have a bit of a rest and see some fireworks, I sent them back again along that confounded railway.

It was dark by this time and I posted men at both ends of the cutting and arranged a system of signals in case a train or a party of Japs approached. Jim's men were soon at work picking holes in the side of the cutting for their charges and the rest of my men lit fires in a disused hut and prepared a meal of tea and bullock meat for the whole party. We found a box of Jap ammunition in this hut. It was almost identical to our own but did not quite fit our rifles so we threw it in the river. Once we thought we heard a train in the distance. Naturally we would have been delighted to blow down the gorge on top of a train but, as the charges were not yet ready, we were quite relieved when it did not materialize. Actually there was no chance of a train coming from the south as, although we did not know it,

Mike Calvert and his column had blown the line at Nankan that day.

It was a calm evening with no wind and a clear sky full of stars. Everything suddenly seemed to be perfect. The hills stood out against the sky and the river chuckled below us. We might have been on the West Highland line in Scotland. How lucky I had been to be sent on this glorious adventure in this delightful country when I might so easily have been "sweating it out" in the Libyan desert. It was nearly nine o'clock when we heard the bridge go up with a roar which echoed round the hills; we knew then that no trains would be running from the north for some considerable time. What fun it all was.

At about a quarter to twelve everything was ready and Jim let his men have a mug of tea and a bite of food. Then, while he and Pester stayed behind to press the button, the rest of us stumbled off along the line, looking eagerly back over our shoulders. The explosion, when it came, was bigger and better than any of us had expected and it brought hundreds of tons of rock and earth crashing down on to the line. In a few minutes Jim and Pester had caught us up, both trying not to look too pleased with themselves.

"Good show," I said.

"Not bad," replied Jim.

It seemed almost too much to hope that the Japs had not been attracted by the noise of David's explosion, so we moved rapidly but cautiously towards the bridge, parting company with our Burman guest who was by this time goggle-eyed with amazement at what he had seen and heard. At Bonchaung Thornburrow and his party were waiting for us and we could not resist going to have a look at what remained of the bridge. David and his men had excelled themselves. One complete span lay in the bed of the stream and the rest of the bridge looked as if a giant had been trying to play cat's cradle with it. Having gloated, we crossed the river and, after covering about four miles, settled down for the night, tired but triumphant.

# CHAPTER 7

# Bonchaung to Tigyaing

Our feeling of elation had not left us the following day as we
marched towards the column rendezvous stopping at each
village for refreshment in the shape of tea, bananas, coconuts
and eggs. We also filled up again with rice. The villagers were
friendly and lent us guides but our two Burrifs were wary at
our entering so many villages and, looking back, we do seem to
have been incredibly reckless on that day and the next. However, our luck held and the only thing that went wrong was our
wireless. We had two first class signallers with our set, but,
although we had arranged to contact the Major on the air every
day at a certain time, we never managed to pick up a message. I
had always professed to disbelieve in wireless and I used to tell
the signallers that they just pretended to use their apparatus and
then made up the messages they had allegedly received. On this
occasion I began to wonder if there were not a grain of truth in
my chaff.

We waded across the Meza River about noon and arrived at
the rendezvous on the Kunbaung Chaung late that evening. To
our amazement we found nobody there. We knew that the
bridge-blowing party had at least three hours' start on us from
Bonchaung so we were certain that we would find them waiting
for us. There was still no sign of the rest of the column the
following morning, so I made a thorough reconnaissance of the
whole area on horseback. Dunn and Dennett were very concerned at my going alone but I did not want to waste any time.
I came across some Burmans building a road for the Japs and
they dropped their tools in amazement at the sight of a solitary
Englishman riding down the road. Of the column I could find

no trace. The rendezvous was supposed to stay open until noon but Jim and I felt certain that the others must have joined John Fraser, who was to wait for us at Kwingi. We knew they left Bonchaung ahead of us and it seemed most unlikely that they were still on their way to the Kunbaung Chaung. This was an unwarranted assumption on our part, as we discovered later, but we decided to move to Kwingi at once.

Again the villagers were very friendly. They told us the Japs had ordered them to make various tracks motorable before the monsoon. Our two Burrifs were very suspicious of a man with a bicycle whom we met en route. The food shortage seemed acute in these parts and nearly all our requests were met by the pathetic answer, "Mashibu" – "There is none."

As we approached Kwingi that afternoon one of John Fraser's Burrifs emerged from the bushes and led us to the spot in the jungle where John had his headquarters. We were delighted to see him but surprised to find that only his party was there. He was in contact with the Major and able to tell us that the Major had now arrived at the Kunbaung rendezvous with the whole of his party and that Tommy Roberts was also there. Being more sensible than us, they had tried to avoid tracks and villages on their way from Bonchaung and they had been delayed by very bad country. However, their advance party, under Duncan, had pushed ahead and reached the Kunbaung Chaung at ten o'clock that morning, just half an hour after Jim and I had left. Naturally the Major was worried at not finding us there, and, not knowing that we had gone on to Kwingi, he had decided to wait for us for twenty-four hours. Unfortunately, as he would not be on the radio again until noon next day, John could not tell him until then that we had joined him at Kwingi. Jim and I felt very bad about all this. It meant that because we had not waited at the original rendezvous the whole programme was put back twenty-four hours. The only comfort was that it meant a welcome twenty-four hours' rest for everyone.

John's men had been into Tigyaing in plain clothes and there were plenty of boats and no Japs. The nearest enemy garrison seemed to be at Katha, about twenty miles away, but John had received unfavourable reports of the headman of a nearby village so after dark we moved our bivouac several miles in case he had sent the Japs information of our whereabouts. Later one of our Burrifs intercepted a message from this headman to the Japs at Katha informing them of our presence. We regretted that we did not have time to pay him a visit. The following day, 9 March we rested. At midday John reported by wireless to the Major that we were with him and the Major said he hoped to join us that night, so we moved to a fresh bivouac in the evening to await the arrival of the rest of the column.

They came in just after dark and Jim and I at once reported to the Major and told him our story. Apart from our having left the rendezvous too soon, about which he was less angry than I had feared, he seemed well satisfied with what we had done. He then told us the story of the battle at Kyaik-in on 6 March.

Tommy Roberts and John Kerr, with their party, had run into a truckload of Japs in the village. They killed two of them before they could get out of the truck and the driver drove off neatly with the corpses. In the fight that ensued two of our men were killed and several wounded, including Bill Edge, but it looked as though all the Japs were killed, so Tommy Roberts pushed on with his men. John was just collecting his platoon and preparing to move on when another Jap machine gun opened up, hitting John, Sergeant Drummond and two section commanders. Some of the Japs then came in with the bayonet (this was the screaming we had heard from the top of the ridge), but John's men shot every one of them before they got near the wounded. Shortly after this, the Major and Gerry Roberts arrived on the scene with 9 Platoon and finished off one or two small parties of Japs who were still firing. Altogether sixteen Jap bodies were found and two had been driven away on the truck. One of Bill Smyly's Gurkhas had shot three with his rifle and decapitated two with his kukri. When it was all over, one of the Jap "corpses" on the road came to life and pointed his rifle at the Major, who was talking to John Kerr nearby. Peter Dorans, always the perfect servant, shot him before he could fire.

Our own losses were comparatively light, but none the less grievous. Besides the two men who had been killed, there was no hope for two of the wounded and three more obviously could not march. John had a burst of machine-gun fire in the calf of his leg and the Major told me he doubted if he would be able to use that leg again. Poor John. I thought of how he had always been bursting with energy and enthusiasm and how he had told me, in a typical burst of exuberance a few days back, that his body was running like a Rolls Royce. There was nothing for it but to leave these wounded behind. Mercifully we had plenty of morphia, though John refused to use any until he had given the Major a full account of what had happened. They were left in the deserted village with their packs and a supply of water, and, as their heavy-hearted comrades moved off towards Bonchaung, they shouted cheerily after them to "make a good job of the bridge". As far as is known, John Kerr was the only one of the five to survive, but at least they had the satisfaction of hearing our explosions and knowing that their courage and self-sacrifice had not been in vain.

Bill Edge's wound was not very serious and he was in good spirits when they rejoined us, but nine of Tommy Robert's men, one Burrif and one Gurkha had become separated in the fighting and did not rejoin the column. They had good N.C.O.s with them and eventually most of them got back to India. Tommy Blow now took over John Kerr's platoon. The men in my platoon were especially saddened by the news of Sergeant Drummond who had been a corporal with us for so long.

A message had come through from Wingate saying that, as no news had been received from 1,2 and 4 Columns for some time, it might be rather hazardous to cross the Irrawaddy. He left it to the Major's discretion whether to carry on as arranged or stay on this side and harass the reconstruction of the railway. The prospects of crossing at Tigyaing seemed very good, so, after careful thought, the Major sent a message back saying that he intended to cross the Irrawaddy and then make for the suspension bridge over the Shweli River near Namkham (not to be confused with Nankan). The road which runs over this bridge branches off from the famous Burma Road and runs up through Bhamo to Myitkyina. Thus by blowing the bridge we would have cut both road and rail communications between Myitkyina and the rest of Burma. To us it sounded a splendid idea.

Tigyaing proved to be a pleasant spot. It lies on the west bank of the Irrawaddy at the southern tip of a range of hills and is overlooked by a glorious pagoda. To the south stretch miles of flat paddy fields and marshes. In the Irrawddy just opposite the town there is a large sandbank which can be reached by wading. The distance from this sandbank to the opposite side of the river is more than half a mile and the current is strong.

The advance party for Tigyaing left our bivouac at a reasonable hour on 10 March. It consisted of John Fraser, Pam Heald and the entire Burrif Platoon, Jim Harman, David Whitehead and the Commando Platoon, and my own platoon. The rest of the column followed an hour later. Though we knew there were no Japs in Tigyaing itself, John did not like the look of a number of columns of smoke we could see forming a kind of semicircle round us in the distance. He had seen these signal fires used to indicate the presence of British troops to the Japs during the withdrawal of 1942. A little later in the day reports started coming in of a considerable body of Japs about eight miles to the south.

As we approched the town a Jap aircraft circled over it dropping pamphlets. These propaganda efforts caused much mirth among our men and the local inhabitants. There were two kinds of pamphlet, one for us, the other for the Burmans in Tigyaing. Ours, addressed to the "pitiable Anglo-Indian soldiery", informed us in English, Burmese and Urdu that we were beaten and surrounded, but that if we went to the nearest Japs with one of these pamphlets in our hand we would be well treated. Later in the day the Major read it out in resonant tones before an assembly of troops and local inhabitants in the centre of the town, to the delight and amusement of all present. The other pamphlet, addressed to the Burmans, informed them that we were stragglers and that they were to take us to the nearest Jap garrison. To demonstrate that we were not stragglers, we made ourselves look as smart as we could, beards or no beards, and we marched into the town with rifles at the slope. To heighten the impression, I mounted my horse and rode down the main street at the head of my platoon. The effect was somewhat marred when we arrived at the waterfront as Billy suddenly decided to have a roll in the sand. This was the second time the idea had occurred to him while I was still on his back and this time it was even more embarrassing.

There was no time to waste. John told the Burman authorities to issue orders that nobody was to leave the town until we were all across the river. The authorities proved most co-operative and did all they could to help us. Meanwhile, Pam and some of the Burrifs started buying up rice, eggs, vegetables, fruit and Jagri (a kind of brown sugar rather like fudge), and gathering these supplies on the waterfront, while the Commando Platoon started collecting boats at the point on the sandbank nearest the other side. The boatmen were very willing to assist us and some of their boats were large enough to take about a dozen men and their equipment so there was no need for us to use our own rubber boats. I posted my men on the various tracks leading out of the town. They served the double purpose of guarding against the arrival of Japs from outside and the departure of Burmans from inside.

While I was visiting one of my posts, a Burman driving a bullock cart approached from the direction of the town. Whether he had not heard the order to stay put or whether he was trying to take information to the Japs I don't know, but, as he approached my sentry, he whipped up his bullocks to a gallop and the sentry, not unnaturally, stepped aside to avoid being trampled to death. By the time he had recovered himself the cart was almost out of sight round a corner in the track. I told him to fire a shot just over the man's head, but, of course, that only made the bullocks go faster. There was only one thing to do; I leapt on to Billy's back and, for once, he rose to the occasion and we were soon nearly level with the cart. By this time the bullocks were quite out of control and the wretched man was nearly being flung off the cart as it careered madly along the rough track. Glancing back over his shoulder, he saw me galloping up behind him, brandishing my revolver threateningly with one hand while I hung on to Billy's reins with the other. This sight completely unnerved him and, abandoning all efforts to control his animals, he turned round and knelt facing me with the most imploring expression on his face. Obviously the matter was no longer in his hands and I was beginning to be rather tired of brandishing when the bullocks brought the whole affair to a sudden end by running the cart into the ditch. I did not think it likely that the man would try to escape from the town again that day.

By now the rest of the column had arrived and the crossing was proceeding smoothly. The mules seemed to know what was expected of them and we had very little trouble this time. After their first doubts had worn off, the people of Tigyaing turned out to welcome us in force. The shops opened up and Pam managed to buy the last few tins of food they had left. The atmosphere was extremely friendly. One Burman proudly introduced me to his wife, a most beautiful and charming girl. They both spoke good English and from them we heard the same tale we heard everywhere we went of Jap cruelties and of the terrible shortage of every kind of supply. It was most touching to find that, in spite of everything, they had not lost faith in the British. "We knew you would come back one day," the girl said. It was hard to have to explain to them that this time we were not stopping. They understood when we told them that we were preparing the way for the real thing. As I made my way back to my platoon headquarters, Robert appeared with smiles all over his face and presented me with a huge parcel of cakes. Dunn had been very busy all morning and produced boiled chicken for lunch.

Everything was going according to plan. As boats became available, platoons were marched to the waterfront where they drew their share of the supplies which Pam Heald had bought; then they waded across to the sandbank and so on to the boats.

By the early evening nearly everyone was across and I brought my men in from their posts to collect their rations from Pam. We then made our way to the sandbank and the Major told me to put out two Bren guns for protection while the last boats were being loaded up. The last men of Tommy Roberts' platoon and the first men of mine were just climbing into a boat when there was a sudden change in the atmosphere. The waterfront had suddenly emptied and the other boats were not returning from the far side but seemed to be heading downstream. We thought we knew what that meant and our fears were confirmed when the only boatman we had left on our side of the river said that he could not make another trip because two hundred Japs were approaching from the south. However, the persuasive powers of a gun are almost unlimited and the boat was just going to set off when we heard the sound of aircraft engines and a Jap plane appeared flying low up the river. There must have been nearly thirty of us left on the sandbank and several animals. We all stood stock still, fighting the urge to look up. It was a helpless feeling, standing there as the plane flew directly over our heads. We waited for it to turn and come back but, to our surprise, it went straight on as though it had not noticed us. We loaded a few more men on to the boat and pushed it off, the men on board holding the bridles of the mules which swam alongside. At that moment another boat appeared, returning from the other side. One of the Burrifs had seen what was happening and had just been in time to prevent the boatman making off down the river with the others. All the animals had gone now, so we loaded as many men as possible onto the boat, C.S.M. Cairns and Peter Dorans being the last. As it disappeared into the gathering dusk we looked at our watches and realized that the whole crossing had been accomplished in just over three hours.

There were six of us left on the sandbank: the Major, John Fraser, Duncan, Po Po Tou (the Burrif Quartermaster Sergeant), Nelson (John's Burrif groom) and myself. We were just looking round to see if we had left anything behind when we heard machine-gun fire from the direction of the town. It was impossible to tell for certain what they were firing at, but, exposed as we were on the sandbank without an inch of cover, it was hard to believe that they were not aiming at us. There also seemed to be some mortar fire but none of the bombs landed anywhere near. All we could do was to flatten ourselves on the sand and hope that the boats would not be too long coming back, though we realized that we would probably have to wait at least ten minutes. After about a minute the firing stopped and then, scarcely able to believe our eyes, we saw a boat approaching us. There were two boatmen in it and, more bold than the rest, they had decided to see us all across. Even the firing had not deterred them. As we scrambled aboard, the firing started again, and the Major waded up to his waist to make sure of giving the boat a good shove off. He then found that, owing to the weight of his pack, he could not pull himself over the gunwales. At this point I cannot resist quoting the Major's own classic description of what followed.

"With a great effort, Po Po Tou and Nelson, now safely on board, got me by the seat of my trousers and the underside of my pack and heaved. The boat rolled perilously, shipping water over either gunwale, but I was safely aboard.

"A matting canopy spread over the boat except at the extremeties, where a small poop and forecastle allowed the crew to stand and work their poles and paddles. I found myself kneeling on the poop with my head under the canopy, trembling all over with a mixture of cold and fright. Whenever I tried to change my position to something more tolerable – even to sit – the boat rolled horribly and everyone cursed me in a hoarse stage whisper, in English, Burmese and Karenni. It was not that so much as the influx of water at each attempt that made me desist. It was thus, to the accompaniment of shots, with my head under the canopy, and my behind hideously exposed: with the boatmen heaving away at their paddles, the water chuckling under the boat and swirling among the floor boards – that, shivering with cold and fear, the solemn thought came to me that has been my proudest boast ever since: I am the first British officer ever to have crossed the Irrawaddy on all fours."

By the time we reached the other side it was quite dark. We paid the boatmen for their devotion in silver rupees and they seemed well satisfied. Thornburrow greeted me with the doleful news that our blankets and some Bren gun ammunition were missing. They had been put on a boat with men from another platoon and, when the firing started, they had somehow been mislaid in the mad rush to remove all our kit from the beach to a place of safety. I set all my men searching and went down to the beach to see if I could find anything there. At the edge of the water I saw two disconsolate figures gazing anxiously across the river. Closer inspection revealed C.S.M. Cairns and Peter Dorans.

"What on earth are you doing?" I said.

"Waiting for the Major's boat, sir," Cairns replied glumly.

I don't think I have ever seen two men look more relieved than they did when I told them that the Major was already safely across. They had not seen our boat arrive as the current had forced us to land rather far downstream from where they were standing. While we were talking the Japs on the other bank started firing again, but nobody was hit and after about half a minute they stopped.

As I climbed up the bank again I met the Major. He said that he was afraid he could not wait any longer while we searched for our lost belongings and told me to collect my platoon and rejoin the column which was falling in ready to move off. Half a minute later Brookes the bugler arrived with a message from the Major saying that he would wait while we looked for our kit. As there was nothing to indicate whether the Major sent this message before or after I had met him, I could not tell whether the order to go on searching or the order to get ready to move was the more recent. I sent back a message to say that I had finished searching and was ready to move. In a few minutes the column was under way.

We moved silently and very fast that night as we were afraid that we were being followed. My platoon was at the back and, such was the speed of the column, that in the pitch darkness it was very easy for a man who had stumbled to find, on picking himself up, that he had lost contact with the man in front of him. Twice I had to ride up to the front of the column to ask the Major to stop while we looked for part of my platoon that had got detached in this way. On the third occasion the Major said he really could not wait and the column went on, leaving Dunn, Dennett, Feeney and myself to look for the lost remnant of my platoon. We stumbled about in some paddy fields for some time and at last, Japs or no Japs, I started flashing my torch and blowing my whistle. Thornburrow was with the lost men, as he always had the unenviable job of bringing up the rear of the platoon. He told me later that he was just beginning to give up hope when he saw my torch flashing. We were soon complete again and I am afraid I let fly with my tongue at the man who had caused the break in the column, though I don't suppose he could help it. Luckily the column had gone into bivouac a few miles ahead and we had little difficulty in finding them. We were not feeling very pleased with ourselves. I borrowed what blankets I could for my platoon. Thornburrow and I shared Billy's horse blanket but it was a cold night for some of the men, too cold to get much sleep, so that, although we had crossed the Irrawaddy, our morale was not particularly high. Fortunately we did not realize that we were embarked on what Christopher Sykes called "the terrible second phase of the expedition."*

* If the reader is curious to know how the decision to embark on this second phase was made, he should read the fascinating and, to me, saddening account of this at the beginning of Chapter III in *Orde Wingate* by Christopher Sykes.

# CHAPTER 8

# *Tigyaing to the Hehtin Chaung*

Pegon, the place where we hoped to have our next dropping, is about twenty miles from the Irrawaddy by track but, as the Japs knew when and where we had crossed, we decided not to go straight there. On 11 March we moved a few miles further into the jungle and enjoyed a day's rest, marching a few miles again at nightfall in case our fires had been observed by the aircraft we had heard during the day. There was some delay in front which brought the whole column to a standstill, and while we were waiting to carry on again a Gurkha muleteer in the middle of the column fell asleep. We, at the rear of the column, could not understand what was holding us up and after about fifteen minutes Alex Macdonald sent me up to see what was happening. I found the Gurkha sleeping peacefully at the head of the rear portion of the column, blissfully unaware of the fact that the front portion had moved on some time ago. All our efforts to rejoin them were unsuccessful and we spent the night on our own, joining up with them the following morning.

We marched all that day up a dry river-bed and at the midday halt we contacted the Brigade by wireless to ensure an airdrop at Pegon on the 14th. By this time our wireless batteries were practically exhausted and we had run out of petrol for the motor which we used for recharging them. No petrol had been available in Tigyaing. The signallers just managed to tap out a list of our requirements before the batteries failed.

It was not only the batteries which were run down; we too were beginning to feel the effects of our sparse diet. The rations which were dropped to us were originally intended for para-troops to live on for a period not exceeding five days and, even when one day's ration only had to last one day, it was scarcely enough to sustain us for our kind of work. In practice we considered ourselves lucky if we only had to make one day's ration spin out over a day and a half or two days. After the supply drop at Tonmakeng we were carrying seven days' rations. It was sixteen days before we had another drop. Luckily we obtained supplies at Tigyaing and other places en route but these, when spread round the column, did not amount to much and rice, which, of course, has to be cooked before it can be eaten, is not a good diet to march on.

The problem of rations was a vexed one among the officers. Some of us thought that the only way to ensure the maximum fighting efficiency on short rations was to tell each man exactly how much he was to eat at each meal. I did not favour this policy, partly because of my natural laziness and partly because I felt it was treating the men as if they were children. After an air drop I used to worry the Major until he told us the maximum period for which the rations dropped would have to last; then I would go back to my platoon and tell them how long they must be prepared to spin them out. There was always the risk that one or two of them would lose their self-control and be entirely without rations for the last few days before the next dropping, but in practice this never occurred and I think I was justified in trusting my men to look after their own food.

If it was true that we were all becoming run down, it was also true that we were all becoming highly efficient. It was remarkable how quickly, when we reached bivouac area, mules were unloaded, fed and watered, fires lit, food cooked and eaten and everyone ready for sleep, except the sentries of the Perimeter Platoon. In the morning the routine for moving off was so well known that we were usually quickly on the move.

When we started out on the morning of 13 March we were only a few miles from Pegon, but we ran into another difficult piece of country, a combination of very thick jungle and very steep defiles. If anything, it was worse than the patch we found just before Bonchaung. We halted for our usual three-hour break at midday and the Major summoned his officers. Chewing his last piece of cheese he said plaintively, "I know where I am and I know where I want to go but I can't get there." It was decided that my platoon, minus our mules, should push on independently to Pegon with Denny Sharp and a few Burrifs, to make the necessary preparations for the air drop which was to start at ten the following morning.

It was a trying march; we were all extremely thirsty as we had not come across water for twenty-four hours, so Denny and I decided to make for what looked on the map a sizeable river and then follow it down to Pegon. We moved fast to make sure of reaching Pegon before dark, hacking at the bamboo and clambering up and down rocks all the way. The men stuck it well, though some of them were feeling the strain badly. It was difficult to keep direction and I felt sure that we were going the wrong way, but Denny proved himself a wizard with map and compass. Our frantic efforts to get on made us even more thirsty, so thirsty that our hunger was completely subdued by the overwhelming longing for a drink, but the thought of the water in the river urged us on and, sure enough, thanks to Denny, we struck it just at the point we had been aiming for. It was bone dry.

We trudged wearily along the sandy river-bed, hoping and praying as we turned each bend that we might find just a small pool, but it did not look as though there had been a drop of water there for six months. Night fell and the moon came up and still we dragged ourselves along, by now beginning to forget our thirst in our weariness. At last we saw the roofs of some huts outlined against the night sky and we knew that we had reached our destination. We crept cautiously up to the village, found a good well on the outskirts and soon satisfied our thirst. Better was to follow. The Burrifs went into the village and returned with a report that there were no Japs in the neighbourhood and, best of all, they brought with them some chickens and rice. We moved off about half a mile into the jungle, cooked a meal and slept.

We lit two groups of fires the following morning. Corporal

Litherland and his section were in charge of one group, on a hill-top, which was intended to guide the planes to the area. The other group was on the actual paddy fields where we wanted the supplies dropped. We had everything ready before nine and were just settling down to cook ourselves some breakfast when the Major appeared on his horse, having ridden ahead of the column. Dunn had been preparing an extraordinarily good dish of rice and chicken for me and it was with mingled admiration and regret that I saw him offer it to the Major as soon as he arrived. Looking back, I seem to myself, and probably to the reader, to have been inordinately interested in food. I can only say that I was and we were. In the circumstances I suppose it was hardly surprising.

Punctually at ten o'clock the planes were overhead and we knew that for a few days at least our hunger was over. Five days' rations were dropped but it was necessary to warn the men that it would probably be eight or nine days before the next air drop. Meanwhile we bought all we could from the villagers, including some pigs and a water buffalo which we killed and feasted on that day. The dropping area was not quite so big as the one at Tonmakeng but we soon retrieved the few parachutes which landed in nearby trees. As well as rations, the air drop included petrol for our charging motor and, most welcome of all, mail and newspapers from home. We spent the rest of the day happily reading and eating. The arrival of letters and local newspapers, however old they may be, has a wonderful effect on morale. We were very impressed to notice that some of the Indian newspapers that were dropped had only been published in Calcutta that morning.

The planes did not return that day, though we were expecting clothing and boots to be dropped, as well as blankets for my platoon. In the evening we bivouacked well inside the jungle and there was some excitement during the night when we had to put out a jungle fire which had been started by one of our signal fires. We waited for the badly needed clothes until the middle of the following afternoon and then we were told that the planes were busy dropping food elsewhere and we must wait till the next drop for our clothes. We were just setting out across the open paddy fields when a Jap plane appeared. We were caught right in the open and it was obvious that the pilot had seen us by the way he circled round. Our only comfort was that when he saw us we looked as though we were heading east, whereas our real direction was south.

We did not find water that night and the next day there seemed little prospect of it. The country through which we marched consisted of rocky hills fairly thickly covered with teak trees. What little soil there was on top of the rocks was a curious red colour. The trees were not thick enough to protect us from the heat of the sun and our thirst was becoming acute by midday. We halted by a dry river-bed and, after digging several holes, managed to procure a little muddy water. Occasions like this were a very good test of our water discipline; it demanded much self-control to wait the required period for the sterilizing tablet to dissolve before taking a drink. The Burrifs were extraordinarily skilful in finding the right place to dig for water. It was just one of the many things which we relied on them to do for us.

My platoon had acted as Perimeter Platoon on the previous night so that we were marching at the back of the column. Shortly after setting off after the midday halt, a message came up the front of the platoon to say that Private Byrne had gone back to the place where we had halted to collect some ammunition he had accidentally left there. I sent Feeney back to Sergeant Thornburrow, who always marched in rear of the platoon, with instructions to let me know as soon as Byrne caught us up. He was one of my best men and he should have had no difficulty in following our trail, but somehow I felt uneasy about him. This feeling increased when he did not turn up at the first halt, and in the end I sent back Corporal Berry and his section to look for him. We bivouacked that night by two small pools or large puddles which just sufficed for men and mules. I reported to the Major and told him that Byrne was missing and that I had sent a section to look for him. He was justifiably angry with me for risking a whole section for the sake of one man, although he too had a very high opinion of Byrne. I told him that I felt sure that Corporal Berry would find us, but, as time proceeded, I became more and more gloomy. By the time night was falling I was desperate and I was just setting out to look for Corporal Berry myself when I met him leading his section into the bivouac. My joy at seeing him was tempered by the news that, although they had whistled and searched for several hours, they had failed to contact Byrne. Our charging motor was running all that night and there was a faint chance that he might be guided to us by the sound of it, but when he had not appeared the next morning I gave up hope. He was alone, without map or compass, in a country where there was hardly any water and not a village for miles; I was not the only one who never expected to see him again.

We had another dry and tiring march that day. For some time we had not been using proper tracks but we had marched on a compass bearing, occasionally following small paths which looked as though they might have been made by elephants. That night we stopped on a level plateau without finding water. The Major collected the whole column together and gave us an inspiring talk on what we had accomplished so far and what we hoped to accomplish in the future. Pointing to the east, he told us that through the hills that we could see in that direction ran the famous Burma Road. Another fact he told us, which most of us had not realized, was that our column was operating further east than any other troops from the United Kingdom. This talk did much to raise morale in spite of our thirst. I believe that if we had been allowed to continue operating as a column on our own we could have reached the Namkham Bridge and destroyed it. The Major, who seemed to have unlimited fire in his belly, was very good at inspiring others with something of his own enthusiasm.

The following morning, 18 March, we moved to the neighbourhood of the Nam Mit, a broad, shallow stream. We were all badly in need of a bath as we had not come across a good supply of water since crossing the Irrawaddy. We were beginning to discover lice in our clothes; these uninvited visitors were to stay with some of us for a very long time. The Major decided to spend the rest of the day here and the Burrifs went out in their native clothes to reconnoitre. In the end we stayed in this spot until the evening of the following day, making the most of a very welcome respite.

During this period we were in frequent touch with Brigade Headquarters on the wireless. First a message came through from the Brigadier to say that he had crossed the Irrawaddy with Columns 7 and 8 at Inywa, a point where the Shweli River flows into the Irrawaddy about twenty miles north of Tigyaing. This meant that the whole of Wingate's operational force was now across the Irrawaddy and most of it concentrating in the area known as the Shweli Loop. As the reader can see from the map, this area has the Irrawaddy to the west and the Shweli to the north and east; to the south a motor road ran from Myitson westward to the Irrawaddy. Thus we were surrounded by rivers and roads. The Japanese were to take full advantage of this situation, but for the moment we were preoccupied with feeding and cleaning.

The information that Wingate had crossed the Irrawaddy was followed by orders for us to join forces with 3 Column under Mike Calvert and destroy the Gokteik Viaduct on the railway between Lashio and Maymyo away to the east. Acknowledging these orders, the Major asked for another supply drop on the 20th which would have meant that we only had to make the five days' rations received at Pegon last for six dys. The reply came back regretting that no planes would be available until the 23rd. I was glad I had warned my men that their five days' rations might have to last nine days. The Major acknowledged the receipt of this news and referred the Brigadier to Psalm 22, verse 17: "I may tell all my bones; they look and stare upon me." Wingate, in replying, quoted "It is expedient that one should die for the people." The Major did not pass this on to us, telling us instead that the Brigadier had replied, "Be of good cheer: I will come unto you." This was certainly a more tactful quotation. There was nothing for it but to face the fact that we were going to be very hungry again. We had reports of Japs in the villages and we did not want to draw attention to our presence in the area in view of the fact that such a large part of the Brigade was going to concentrate there, so foraging was out of the question. Doc Aird was seriously worried by the symptoms of some of the men. We were all becoming very thin and a few were showing definite signs of starvation. The Major decided to tell the Brigadier when he arrived that it was essential for us to have a full day's ration every day in future instead of half a day's ration or less.

The Major has related that, when Doc Aird and John Fraser told him that in their opinion the men were in an extremely run-down condition physically, this came as a complete surprise to him. "The very fact of being the Commander," he said, "lends a certain exhilaration to one's acts. It helps one to ignore physical decline." I had a similar shock when one of my men refused to take a message from me to another officer. It had simply never occurred to me that a man might be afraid to walk alone for a few hundred yards through the jungle. I was not afraid to do so; I never stopped to think about it. Feeney, my runner, never seemed to be worried about going through the jungle alone. I asked Sergeant Thornburrow and Dunn for their opinions on the matter. They both told me that many of the men were definitely afraid of being alone in the jungle even for a short time. Thereafter I always sent men on errands in pairs.

I did not have time to bathe on the morning of our arrival at the Nam Mit, but most of my platoon did and Corporal Litherland, who was a barber in civilian life, was busy with his clippers. In the afternoon I started to go down to the river, about half a mile away, and some of my men decided to have another bathe and came with me, offering to show me the way. This was the first time I had let my platoon lead me and an hour later, when we were still searching for the river, I decided that it would also be the last. When we did arrive it was very pleasant and I lay for some time revelling in the sensation, now almost novel, of the water flowing past me. I returned to the bivouac in time to do some reading before it got dark. The

Major lent me the Penguin edition of *Nightingale Wood* by
Stella Gibbons, which was, under those circumstances, far more
congenial reading than *Paradise Lost*. Bill Edge, however,
borrowed my Milton and seemed engrossed in it. I rather
fancied he was reading the description of the banquet in
*Paradise Regained*. We tried to start a literary competition like
the *New Statesman*'s among the officers. It was also suggested
we make lists of suitable film stars for the case of a film on the
Wingate expedition. Someone irreverently suggested Will Hay,
George Formby and Bob Hope for leading roles. I amused
myself by preparing the script for a broadcast by Private Bloggs,
one of our brightest characters, describing his experiences
during the expedition in Lancashire style.

Some of the Burrifs came back and reported a large concentration of Japs at Myitson, a place just east of us on the Shweli
River. We passed this news on to Brigade at once and a few
hours later the answer to our message came in the shape of a
heavy air raid on the place, which must have shaken the Japs as
much as it pleased us. At the same time the order to join up
with 3 Column and make for the Gokteik Viaduct was cancelled
and we were ordered to stay more or less where we were and
cover the movement in our direction of Brigade Headquarters
and its two attendant columns.

The Major was uneasy because we had made a very marked
track from our bivouac to the river in our zeal for cleanliness,
so we moved about a mile west on the evening of 19 March,
stopping near some pools in a dry river bed. Some of John's
Burrifs had not returned from their patrols, so he left a party of
men to contact them at our old bivouac. While they were
waiting this party had the intriguing experience of seeing about
fifty Japs attack the area which the column had just left. Shortly
afterwards two of the missing Burrifs turned up, having run
into the disconsolate Japs on their way home and hurled a
couple of grenades at them before making off into the jungle.

Our air drop on 23 March was to take place in the dry bed of
the Nam Pan, about twelve miles to the north, so we spent the
next few days resting and moving slowly in that direction,

sometimes splitting into smaller parties than a whole column so we left no trace of our direction. I remember concluding a deal with Doc Aird at this time; in exchange for a small slab of chocolate he gave me quite a large quantity of rice that he had saved. In retrospect I believe that he deliberately sought the worst of the bargain. One day we found some rock pools in a dry river bed and I saw some fish rising. Dunn and I were given permission to throw grenades into the pools but the two or three small fish we procured did not seem sufficient justification for having made so much noise.

I had been spoiling for a row with one of my section commanders for some time and the storm finally burst now. In fairness to the man, I should say that he had originally been persuaded by an officer to take a lance-corporal's stripe much against his will and, when it was taken away, he was not in the least sorry. The difficulty was to find anyone to replace him. I tried to ignore the obvious, but it was impossible to deny that Dunn was just the man for the job. The Major agreed and Dunn was give a stripe and made section commander. It meant that I had lost a first-rate batman, but he did so well as section commander that I wished he had been promoted long before. His place as my batman was taken by a pleasant and conscientious Welshman, Private Davies.

We were all saddened by the news that two of the Burrifs who had been sent out to gather information had not returned and the others had heard that they had been caught by the Japs. We could imagine only too well what that meant. Another gloomy portent was that about now the mules began showing signs of weakness. As far as I can remember, we had not had any fodder dropped for them since Tonmakeng, so that, apart from an occasional meal of paddy in a village, they had been living for weeks on nothing but bamboo leaves and, very occasionally, grass. It was not so bad for the horses as we did not ride them often, but the mules were never relieved of their loads on the march. Now several of them suddenly collapsed and it was clear that they had literally carried on until they could go no further. All we could do was to abandon them and their loads. Bill Smyly strongly suspected anthrax and for the next few days mules continued to drop in their tracks. If it was anthrax, we were extremely fortunate not to lose every animal in the column. As it was, we lost about a dozen and then no more.

When we reached our air drop we found that Colonel Alexander and 1 Column were there, having had a supply drop two miles away. They intended to move at first light next morning and they warned us that some Japs had been trailing them. We began to feel that this part of Burma was becoming distinctly over-crowded. That night we slept on the south bank of the Nam Pan, under the thickest covering of foliage I had ever seen. During the night a panther tried unsuccessfully to attack one of the mules, but most of us were sound asleep dreaming of the rations we hoped would be dropped on the morrow.

We had chosen a straight stretch of the river bed for our air drop area but it was not very wide, and it is to the credit of the pilots that most of the parachutes landed where they were wanted and not up trees in the surrounding jungle. My platoon was posted downstream to prevent any Japs approaching from that direction and I could speak to the Major by field telephone. While I was putting my men in position, Major Jeffries appeared with a small party. He used to work independently and his first job in the campaign had been to cross the Chindwin well south of everybody else, dressed as a brigadier, and create a diversion to distract attention from the main crossings. Since then he had had various adventures and he now intended to report to the Brigadier for fresh orders. I was very glad to see him again, especially as he gave me enough rice to feed my hungry platoon headquarters.

We had been told that after this drop we could have double rations for one day to make up for our compulsory fasting, so I had my men ready and eager to collect the platoon's rations. It is easy to imagine our disappointment when the Major rang through to say that the double rations were off as only three days' rations had been dropped in all and he had received a signal to say that the air drop was over. He at once told Brigade Headquarters that we had only received three days' rations. In reply he received orders to march northward with all speed to meet Brigade Headquarters at a rendezvous just outside the village of Baw and a promise that they would have an air drop for us there. Baw was about fifteen miles north of where we were. We were not pleased with the air drop, especially when we found that some of the rations had landed in a pool. We even scowled at some rum that had been dropped. We did not want anything to drink; we wanted something to eat. However, they had delivered a little bully beef for us and some tinned mutton for the Gurkhas, which made a welcome change. We now hoped for a good feed when we joined Brigade Head-quarters at Baw. As far as my platoon were concerned, the most satisfactory item that had been included in the dropping was a bundle of blankets to replace those we had lost at the Irrawaddy crossing.

We left the Nam Pan that evening and marched north until it was dark. Then, to our surprise, we halted and the Major blew the signal for officers to go to column headquarters for orders. We had expected an all-night march, so this summons was rather extraordinary. Going to column headquarters for orders was nearly always a pleasant experience and, however tired and dispirited we might be, we invariably came away refreshed and invigorated mentally if not physically. The Major would sit chatting gaily with Duncan and anyone else who happened to be there, looking up with a smile and a cheery greeting for each officer as he arrived. Eventually he would adjust his monocle and say, "Are we all here? Well now . . ." When he finished he asked for questions and there would often be much joking and laughter over them. Afterwards, he would dismiss us with some parting crack and we would return, grinning, to our platoons. This time we returned with the good news that the Major had decided that we should sleep where we were until 4.00 am.

We were halted on top of a ridge about the middle of the

following morning and I had just made the happy discovery that I was sitting under a tree full of Shan fruit. These look rather like gooseberries and are far more sour at first, but if you keep them in your mouth, they presently turn quite sweet. Suddenly we heard heavy mortar fire from the direction of Baw, and a few minutes later we saw planes circling round that neighbourhood as though trying in vain to drop supplies. Clearly Brigade Headquarters was in trouble and the Major ordered several platoons, including my own, to be ready to leave the column and go with him to the assistance of Brigade as a light striking force. The firing continued for some time but the planes soon disappeared and, although we pressed on as hard as we could, it was obvious that the battle was over before we had gone very far. We were delayed a little by several of the Gurkhas. Not being accustomed to tinned food, some of them had opened their cans of mutton after the dropping and eaten half of the contents. Then they had replaced the rest in the tin and carried it with them until the following morning when they ate it for breakfast. As a result, three of them were in such acute pain that they had to be carried. The other Gurkhas were showing the utmost care for them and there even seemed to be a certain amount of competition among them for the honour of being allowed to carry the sick men.

We were supposed to have reached the rendezvous with Brigade Headquarters near Baw before nightfall but, as the afternoon wore on, it became apparent that we would not be there in time, so the Major went on ahead of us, taking Pam Heald and a party of Burrifs. The arrangement was that he should rejoin us at a certain confluence clearly marked on the map, and that, if he he had not joined us by four o'clock the following morning, we were to make for a further rendezvous well to the north of Baw, near the Shweli River. When the Major left us John Fraser took command and, as we had not found the confluence by the time it was dark, it was decided that we should stop for the night where we were. We knew we were somewhere near the place and there was no point in having the whole column floundering about in the dark. So Duncan went out to look for the confluence and guide the Major to us when he arrived.

I felt very uneasy that night; we were all crowded into a dry stream-bed with steep banks, the men were tired and weak with hunger and I could not help wondering what would happen if the Japs attacked us where we were during the night. I also wondered what was happening to the Major and what had happened to Brigade Headquarters at Baw that day. It certainly did not look as though they would have any rations waiting for us if and when we found them. On top of all this, there was an uncomfortable feeling that we had all walked into a trap. The Japs had let us cross the Irrawaddy but would we ever re-cross it?

It was four o'clock when we started off next morning; the Major had not rejoined us. John and Duncan put on a cheerful face but we all felt pretty gloomy about it. However, our orders were to proceed to the rendezvous north of Baw near the Shweli River and there was really no definite reason for feeling that we would not meet him at this second rendezvous. After covering about a mile, we were just passing a small mere when we were simultaneously hailed by the Major from one direction and by Pam Heald from another. This triple meeting was so miraculous that, as the Major said, it could only be attributed to the Almighty.

After leaving us the previous evening, the Major and Pam had reached the spot where we were supposed to meet Brigade Headquarters but found nobody there. They searched the area thoroughly but in vain, so the Major left Pam and the Burrifs to watch the place in case Brigade arrived during the night, while he himself, accompanied by Jameson, one of the English-speaking Burrifs, set off to rejoin the column at the confluence as arranged. Yet it was very difficult country and, though they searched all night, they could not find the confluence. When it grew light after four o'clock, they knew that we would have started off for the other rendezvous, so they decided to return to Pam, only to find that they were completely lost and could not even find their way back to the place where they had left him. Pam had been given orders to make for the second rendezvous if nobody had joined him by seven o'clock, so when that hour arrived without their having found him, the Major was in despair. He had no map with him and only a very vague idea of the direction of the second rendezvous. He and Jameson had been on their feet, with hardly a break, for twenty-seven hours; they were lost; they had no food. Suddenly they came upon a pool which seemed vaguely familiar and, at that moment the column and Pam appeared simultaneously.

We stopped by the pool while the Major and Jameson had a couple of hours sleep. I took the opportunity afforded by this rest to persuade Alec Macdonald to issue us with some more silver rupees. All the men had started out with twenty-five, but most of these had been spent making purchases in villages by the time we had crossed the Irrawaddy. Meanwhile Duncan had made contact with Brigade on the radio and we were instructed to join them at a spot on a dry river about five miles away where they hoped to have an air drop that afternoon. They could not tell us anything on the air about the previous day's battle but apparently they were still functioning.

It was rough going that day, but, as we marched, we could see the planes dropping supplies in the area we were approaching. When we reached the dry river we found that it had branches leading off in all directions. The column halted while two other officers and myself went out looking for Brigade Headquarters and Brookes blew his bugle at regular intervals. Incidentally, the column call-sign on the bugle was the hunting call, "Tantivy, tantivy, tantivy", or, as Bill Edge used to say, "Old Stibbe, Old Stibbe, Old Stibbe". It was two hours before Brigade was eventually discovered by Denny, less than a mile away, and by the time the column had arrived at the spot everyone had moved off except a small party waiting to receive us. Once again our hopes of a good feed were dashed to the ground. They only had one day's rations and a little bully beef for us but our disappointment was forgotten in our surprise at the news that we were to turn back and make for India.

111

We spent the night there, my platoon acting as Perimeter Platoon, and early next morning, after a short march, we joined Brigade Headquarters and 7 and 8 Columns on the Hehtin Chaung. It was good to be back with them and see so many old friends. We were to stay there for at least twelve hours and we had not been in bivouac long before, much to our delight, George Borrow came to see us. He was looking rather better than he had done last time we saw him; apparently the worst of the jaundice was over. As usual, he was full of interest in everything and everyone. I started talking about the party we were going to have when we returned to India and teased him because he did not seem so sure as I was that we would make it back to India. It was the last time I saw him.

About midday the Major returned from Brigade Head-quarters to pass on the orders that he had received from Wingate. The decision that we should turn back had been made by the authorities in India and Wingate agreed with it. After all, we had proved conclusively that our type of warfare was feasible; we had blown the railway and there were reliable reports that we had created considerable alarm among the Japs, even causing some of their troops to be removed from the Chinese front. Now the authorities wanted us to return to India and, with our invaluable experience, train others in this type of warfare. The return journey was not going to be easy and to move faster all animals and their loads, except for the wireless sets and a few other vital things, were to be left behind. Similarly every man was to carry the bare minimum. News had come in that the Japs were bringing up reinforcements to try and trap us between the Shweli and the Irrawaddy. So we were to move fast in one body to Inywa, the place where Brigade and 7 and 8 Columns had crossed the Irrawaddy a short while back. Wingate thought the last place the Japs would be expecting him to re-cross the Irrawaddy was the place where he had so recently crossed it. Until we were across, there would be no more supply droppings as these would delay us and might attract attention. It seemed unlikely that we would be able to forage in villages,

12. Tending the wounded in the jungle. (*Imperial War Museum*)

13. A tea break in the jungle. (*Imperial War Museum*)

14. A typical communal cell in Rangoon jail.

15. A group of prisoners in Rangoon jail showing the effects of disease and malnutrition.

16.   Rangoon Central Jail: aerial photograph after the Japanese had left in Spring 1945, showing messages for Allied planes on roof.

17.   Major McLeod shows the stump of Corporal Usher's leg which he successfully amputated without anaesthetics.

18. The first day of freedom: a group of released prisoners holding a home-made Union Jack.

19. Allied prisoners of war abandoned by the Japanese at Pegu and rescued by advancing Allied forces are issued with new kit to replace the rags and remnants of their three-year-old clothes.

so it looked as if we had got to make do with what we had for at least another four or five days. Meanwhile steps were being taken to spread rumours that we were heading south. So for as long as possible the Japs would be ignorant of the fact that we were on our way home.

Dunn, or Lance-Corporal Dunn as he was now, had grumbled ever since we crossed the Chindwin because we had not even had a brush with the Japs and, when he heard that we were turning back without firing a shot in anger, he was thoroughly disgusted. However, that evening the Major spoke to the whole column and emphasized that the return journey, even after we were across the Irrawaddy, was going to be no picnic. It was a temptation to feel that all danger was to be avoided and that it would be too bad to be killed on the return journey. We must overcome this feeling. We had to fight our way out and the safety of us all would depend on prompt and resolute action when we met Japs.

There was plenty of meat that day as we started killing off the animals. Mule meat is very tasty and we tried various ways of cooking it. It seemed to keep best when roasted and each man put a good-sized steak in his pack for the march. We abandoned much of our kit on the spot. I opened up the haversack I had filled with medical supplies before leaving India and distributed the contents round the platoon. They included some cod-liver oil capsules which I started taking with one biscuit for a meal. There were also two tins of vitamin tablets. Between us, Thornburrow and I had several packets of biscuits, tins of cheese and bully beef. We divided the biscuits and he carried the cheese and I carried the bully beef. There was an issue of rum that night for the men and I collected my N.C.O.s together and we emptied my water-bottle full of brandy which had not been touched until then. I kept my hip flask for the return journey.

The next morning before it was light the whole force was on its way, our column bringing up the rear of the procession, except for Burrifs who came last to cover our tracks. It is no use pretending that we were in fine fettle. As the Major said, we needed a rest and good food to spur us on again. The Japs, on the other hand, were still fully prepared. All the same it was good to feel that we were on the way home and I, for one, felt very optimistic about our chances.

# CHAPTER 9

# *The Hehtin Chaung to Hintha*

Wingate himself skilfully led the way across country. It was 27 March and we hoped to cross the river at Inywa on the night of the 28th. If we got split up before reaching Inywa, a rendezvous had been fixed a short distance from the village. At each halt a few mules were shot. It was heart-rending business for Bill Smyly who had cared for them so well, and many of the muleteers looked as if they had been weeping. At the second halt, after debating with myself for some time, I decided to throw away my Milton. I had hoped to show it to Edmund Blunden when I returned to Oxford and tell him I had carried it all the time in Burma, but every bit of weight counted and it did not look as if there would be much time for reading.

We stopped at midday in a narrow valley where there were a few tiny pools. I ate my biscuit and cod-liver oil capsule and then went to Column Headquarters for orders. The officers were still there when we heard two or three explosions some little distance to the rear of the column. It sounded like grenades or a small mortar. The Major at once ordered Tommy Blow and myself, with our respective platoons, to go and investigate the matter. I ran back to my platoon and shouted, "Leave the mules, bring your packs and follow me"; in a few minutes we were up the side of the valley.

We searched for nearly an hour but saw and heard nothing, so I decided to rejoin the column. As I had half-expected, when we returned to the valley we found that they had gone. I knew where it was intended that we should bivouac for the night so we set off on a compass bearing in that direction. By this time the men with the Bren-gun were exhausted, so the men in each section took turns in carrying this extra load. I usually rather enjoyed having my platoon on my own but I felt a little bit doubtful about my compass bearing and it was possible that the Brigadier might have changed his mind about bivouacking that night, in which case we would have to make for the rendezvous near Inywa.

We had not gone very far when we came to a wide river bed; I thought it quite likely that the Japs would be watching it, so I bunched the platoon together to rush across it in a body, the text book way of crossing gaps in hedges. I gave the word "Go" and we all dashed forward but halfway across we pulled up in amazement, for there, marching boldly down the river-bed was the Major with the column behind him. It was another miraculous meeting. The Major grinned and held out his hand, and I could not help blurting out, "It's the Almighty again, sir".

Tommy Blow had already returned to the column, having had no better luck than we had. Unfortunately one of his sections had got lost and they never rejoined us, most of them eventually being captured.

The Major told me that, just after he had sent us off, a rather vague message came back to him from Wingate saying everyone was moving on but that 5 Column was to stay behind and ambush anyone who tried to follow them up. It was impossible to lay an effective ambush without being sure just exactly which way the pursuing Japs, if any, would come, so the Major decided that the best thing for us to do was to lay a false trail away in an easterly direction, to distract attention from the main body who were heading roughly north-west. That is why we met the column marching gaily down the river bed and leaving a trail which even the most short-sighted Jap could not overlook. Once again we enjoyed that pleasant feeling we had felt when we came out into the open and marched into Tigyaing.

We followed the river bed through the hills until it led us out on to flat country. Here we lit large fires and brewed some tea. Then, leaving our fires burning and various tempting booby-traps lying about, we moved about half a mile downstream from this dummy bivouac. We knew that we were about a mile from the village of Hintha and the Major decided that the following morning we would continue in the direction of the village and then, while the rest of the column skirted around it, he would go in with the Commando Platoon and deal with any Japs we found there. The jungle on either side of the river bed proved to be very thick and peculiarly prickly so we formed a large square in the Waterloo style and, in this rather cramped formation, we spent the night.

We woke soon after 3 a.m. and prepared to move off as quietly as possible. My temper was somewhat frayed that morning and I vividly remember going up to one of my men who was making an unnecessary amount of noise and hissing, "If you don't shut up, I'll give you such a bang over the earhole." His jaw dropped in amazement; it was the first time I had ever threatened anyone in my platoon with physical violence. It was still dark when we started down the river bed towards the village. My platoon was in front with the Major and the Commando Platoon immediately behind us. We all clutched a grenade in one hand ready for anything. The Major noticed that my Bren-gun mules were up near the front and I hastily sent them further back. After a short distance we found our way blocked by an impassable barrier of thorns and the only way left open to us was the main track into the village. We looked in vain for a way off the track to enable the main part of the column to skirt round Hintha while we went through, but in the darkness the jungle on both sides of us seemed impenetrable. Then, sooner than we expected, we turned a bend in the track and saw the roofs of the first houses in the village before us.

We approached cautiously and noticed that a small track led off to the left just before we reached the houses, and beyond them our track joined another track running at right-angles, thus forming a "T" junction in the middle of the village. A fire was burning on the far side of the third house on the left, lighting the walls and trees with a pleasant glow. I whispered to the Major, "It looks peaceful enough." He nodded and told me to stay where I was while he went towards the fire with two of the Burrifs. He disappeared with them round the corner of the house; a few moments later we heard him shout, "Take that and share it among you!" and immediately there followed a loud explosion. He had seen a group of men sitting round the fire and gone up to them, thinking they were Burmans; fortunately he had recognized that they were Japs half a second before they recognized him, and before they could move he lobbed his grenade neatly into the middle of the fire. At the sound of the explosion we started forward but the Major came skipping back round the corner of the house and called out, "Wait a minute, Philip."

We did not have to wait many seconds before machine-gun fire started from somewhere down the left fork of the "T" junction; the Major told me to take my platoon in with the bayonet. By now we were at the junction and Duncan had come up. My platoon were in threes behind me, facing down the track in the direction of the firing. It was impossible to see much in the dark but there was no time to waste, so I shouted "Bayonets" and told Corporal Litherland and the left-hand section to deal with anything on the left of the track and Corporal Handley and Corporal Berry with the right-hand section to deal with anything on the right. Thus Corporal Dunn was in the centre immediately behind me with his section and I told him to follow me and deal with anything immediately in front. All this took only a moment; the Major shouted "Good luck", I gave the word and we doubled forward.

It is difficult to realize what is happening in the heat of battle and even more difficult to give a coherent account of it afterwards, but I remember seeing something move under a house on our left as we went forward and firing at it with my revolver. Then machine-gun fire seemed to come from several directions in front of us and I hurled my grenade at the nearest gun and we got down while it went off. I was standing up to go forward again when something knocked me down and I felt a pain in my left shoulder-blade. The platoon rushed on past me. What was happening in the darkness ahead I could not tell but there was a confused medley of shots, screams, shouts and explosions. Suddenly a voice beside me said, "Will you take this grenade, sir? The pin's out, but I stopped one before I could throw it." In the excitement I had not noticed one of my N.C.O.s badly wounded on the ground beside me. I managed to take the grenade from him with my right hand and he said, "Thank you, sir," and fainted. There was still some firing and the Major called me to know if I could tell where it was coming from. I told him I thought it was coming from both sides of the track, adding that I had been hit myself. "Hard luck, Philip," he shouted, "you had better get your platoon back now if you can." I raised myself on my elbow and bellowed, "Come back, 7 Platoon" several times as loudly as I could into the darkness; in a few moments they began to reappear.

By now my shirt and trousers were soaked with blood but someone helped me to my feet and I staggered drunkenly towards the Major. The grenade was still clutched in my hand and I solemnly offered it to him saying, "Will you take this, sir? It's just going to go off." He took it from me and threw it towards the Japs. Then he told me to hand the platoon over to Sergeant Thornburrow and I went and lay down at the side of the track by the "T" junction, feeling very fuzzy in the head.

Everything became blurred but I saw Thornburrow putting the platoon into an all-round defensive position on the "T" junction and I remember one of my men, Private Roche, coming up and removing my pack so that he could put a field dressing on my wound; it was in a awkward place and it was difficult to stop the bleeding. I had sufficient presence of mind to remove the last of my rations from my pack in case I lost it. I pushed the biscuits and the bully beef down the front of my shirt.

The firing continued intermittently and the Major sent Jim Harman and the Commando Platoon to try to attack the Japs down the little track we had seen leading off to the left. Alec Macdonald went with them. While this was being done, the Major came over to speak to Corporal Litherland and me but he had hardly begun when a Jap grenade landed beside us. The Major only just had time to throw himself on the ground before it went off; he was on his feet again in a moment and I did not know till long afterwards that he had been hit in the hip by a fragment. Corporal Litherland was wounded in the head and arm but not as badly as a nearby private soldier who had a terrible head wound and started begging me to shoot him to put him out of his agony. Fortunately Doc Aird came up with some morphia. By some miracle, although the grenade had landed scarcely an arm's length from me, I was untouched. By this time I was so covered in blood that the Major was convinced I had been hit again.

Meanwhile the Commandos had put in their attack down the little track and we were all stunned when the word came that Alec Macdonald, who had led them in, had been killed with Private Fuller. Jim Harman, who was with him, had been hit in the head and arm but he and Sergeant Pester went on with their men and cleared the track.

The firing now flared up again in our direction, but my platoon, who had remained calm and steady throughout, only fired when they saw a definite target. It was during the burst of firing that Doc Aird came up with one of his orderlies and dressed my wound. Shots were whistling just over their heads and I offered to move under cover while they did it, but they carried on where they were as calmly as if they had been in a hospital ward. The bullet had gone in through my chest just below my left collar bone, leaving only a very small hole which I had not noticed; the hole at the back where it came out was considerably larger and it was from this that I was losing all the blood.

We were safe at the "T" junction as long as it was dark but it would have been an exposed position by daylight and dawn was breaking. We did not know how many Japs we had killed but it was obvious that their casualties had been far heavier than ours. I was not able to check up on my platoon's casualties but I discovered afterwards that we had lost Corporal Handley, Corporal Berry, Lance-Corporal Dunn and Private Cobb, while Corporal Litherland and one or two others had been wounded. The news came that a way had been found through the jungle at the side of the track, so the Major ordered Brookes to blow the second dispersal call on his bugle. This was the signal for the column to split up into groups which were then to make for the pre-arranged rendezvous.

My platoon remained at the crossroads to cover the withdrawal. Duncan came up to say he had a horse waiting for me down the track. I did not want to leave my platoon, but he insisted. Thornburrow was in charge and the Major was still at the "T" junction when I left. Someone took my pack and said they would put it on a mule and Duncan helped me down the track to where Private Joe Boyle was waiting with a horse. They pushed me on with some difficulty and Duncan told Boyle to lead the horse after one of the dispersal groups that was disappearing down the track. We wished one another luck and he returned to the Major; I never saw him again.

It was not a pleasant ride, although Boyle led the horse as slowly as he could without slipping too far behind the tail of the group we were following. After a while I tried walking, but it was no good, so I mounted my steed again. Then the group in front stopped to let us catch them up and I found it consisted of Bill Williamson and part of the Support Platoon, with some of the Commandos and some Burrifs under Subedar Ba Than. I said that they had better leave me as I was holding them up, but they all refused indignantly.

We started off again and Boyle did his best to make the horse move faster. Then we found that the poor animal had itself been wounded. To add to our troubles it began to pour with rain. When we were about a mile and a half from Hintha I decided it was no good going on; I was weakening all the time from loss of blood, every step my horse took jarred me and I was obviously delaying the others. I told Bill Williamson that he had to leave me behind and at last, very reluctantly, he agreed. I felt quite hopeful that, if only one of the Burrifs would stay behind with me and look after me, I would recover sufficiently to go on after a few days, although I did not relish the prospect of being left to die alone in the jungle. I sat down for a minute and handed over my maps to Bill Williamson, pointing out various important features to him. While I was doing this, I suddenly realized that I was ravenously hungry, so I produced a packet of blood-stained biscuits from my shirt and ate them while I talked to Bill. Then, to my immense relief, Ba Than came up and said that one of his Burrifs has volunteered to stay with me. It seemed almost too good to be true. Meanwhile the men had collected some more field dressings which they most generously gave me. I entrusted Bill Williamson with a verbal message to my parents and asked him to pass it on to George Borrow who, I felt sure, would see that it reached them. (Years later I was to discover that my confidence in George was more than fully justified.) Finally we all wished one another luck and, in a touching gesture, Sergeant Whitehead of the Support Platoon sprang to attention and saluted me. Then they went on down the track and left me, but not, thank God, alone.

I never made contact with the column again and it was not until long afterwards that I heard the full details of their story. The story of their gallant march back to India, the fateful crossing of the Shweli River, the tragic death of Duncan, the incredible hardship they endured and the wonderful help and hospitality given to them by the Kachins is all related in *Beyond the Chindwin* by Bernard Fergusson. When I read the Major's account two years later I realized that I missed the hardest part of the campaign.

The Burrif who volunteered to stay behind with me was Rifleman Maung Tun. I had not previously known his name and, when he told me what it was, it sounded more like "Moto" that anything else, so Moto he became. I learnt from him that his home was in the Bassein district; he was not as tall as most of the Karens and he had cropped hair and a very friendly grin. When Bill Williamson and his party had disappeared round the bend in the track, he led me to a sheltered spot in the jungle and in a short while he had made a bed on the ground with blankets and ground sheets and spread another ground sheet above it on poles to keep off the rain.

I never had to tell Moto anything or ask him for anything. He looked after me that day as carefully and gently and anxiously as a mother looks after a sick child. Although my wound did not hurt me while I lay still, every movement was painful; I also found that when I lay on my left side the blood seemed to collect there, so every time my heart beat there was a squelching sound like a small sponge being squeezed out. Intriguing though this was, I did not lie on that side for long. Every time I had to get up or lie down Moto assisted and supported me; he even helped me to eat and drink. Without my suggesting it, he boiled some salt water and then bathed my wound as though he had worked in a hospital all his life.

Although Moto did not speak much English, we understood one another fairly well and I tried to make him realize how grateful I was. I told him that I thought if we could find food and water I would soon be well enough to move on. The only map we had was a map of the whole of Burma on a silk handkerchief and, with the aid of this, we examined possible routes back to India. He seemed as optimistic about it as I was but he seemed anxious that I should sleep; this seemed a good idea to me to, so I took a couple of morphia pills and for the next few hours I knew nothing.

When I woke up it was evening and already beginning to get dark. There was no sign of Moto anywhere but he had said something about going to look for food so I was not unduly worried. As it grew dark I heard a lot of rustling in the leaves near where I lay and, to my horror, I saw (or perhaps I only imagined I saw) several large spiders crawling towards me. They seemed to be about the size of my hand and I thought they must be attracted by the smell of blood. I managed to keep them away by throwing things at them but each time I frightened them off I heard them rustling towards me again. At last, just before it was dark, I heard a whistle; I answered this eagerly and moments later Moto appeared.

He had put on his "lungi" and returned in the direction of Hintha. One of the villagers had told him that the Japs were still there but he seemed to think they would be going soon. He said that when they had gone Moto could take me into the village and they would be glad to put me up in one of their houses and look after me. Meanwhile, he promised to meet Moto at a certain spot the following morning and give him food and the latest news of the Japs. This sounded very encouraging. We talked things over for a little while, had a few biscuits and some tea, and before long I was asleep again.

The following morning I felt much better. Moto bathed my wound and, about ten o'clock, he set off to meet the villager as arranged. Before going he asked me if I was sure I would be all right, and then, saying he would soon be back, he strode off. I remember watching him go; he was wearing his brightly coloured "lungi" and a khaki shirt, and he had slung his Tommy gun over his shoulder. It was difficult to masquerade as a peaceful Burman civilian with a Tommy gun but no doubt he meant to hide it somehwere if he met anyone. I shouted after him to be careful and he turned his head and grinned.

All that day I waited for him to return, inventing countless reasons for his prolonged absence in an effort to avoid my worst fears. Perhaps the Japs had gone and he was preparing a house for me in the village; perhaps he had failed to find anything at Hintha and was trying another village further afield; or perhaps he had lost his way coming back. He still had not returned when I finally went to sleep that night; the following morning when I awoke I hoped against hope to find that he had returned during the night, but I was still alone. At ten o'clock, when he had been gone twenty-four hours, I decided to wait for him another day and, if he still had not returned, I would have to try to reach Hintha myself. I now had no food left except the tin of corned beef, and the water had almost run out. Fortunately the bathing seemed to have done my wound good and Moto had fixed a dressing on it very securely. If this dressing had slipped I could not have replaced it myself.

The hours dragged by and, as if to torment me further, a bird kept on whistling the recognition signal I had arranged with Moto, so that I was repeatedly sitting up and answering it. Even after I had realized that it was only a bird and not Moto who was whistling, I felt bound to answer every time in case Moto did come; I could not risk the possibility of his coming and being unable to find me because I did not answer his whistle. In the evening I was attacked by swarms of mosquitoes the moment I put any part of my body out from under the blanket. Somehow or other I did not feel despondent; instead I was filled with a desperate recklessness, no longer caring very much what happened. In this mood, I opened the tin of bully beef, ate it and felt much better for it, finished all the water and went to sleep.

The next morning, 31 March, there was still no sign of Moto, but I was loath to give up hope completely and decided to wait for a few more hours. By this time I had a raging thirst; Moto had told me that there was some water quite near so I set out to look for it. My own shirt was still soaked with blood but my slacks were not quite so bad and I pulled them on with considerable difficulty as my wound prevented me from using my left arm. Moto had left behind a blue flannel shirt and it took me about quarter of an hour to struggle into it. In my pocket I still had a grenade but I had somehow lost my revolver at Hintha; my hat had gone too so I put on the one Moto had left. Then, water bottle in one hand and compass in the other, I set out.

I was still very weak and had to keep stopping for a rest. After wandering about in the jungle for about an hour without finding water I was exhausted. I had tried to keep a check on my position with my compass but, to my dismay, when I tried to find my way back to the bivouac, I discovered I was completely lost. I searched for some time but only became more tired, thirsty and, apparently, hopelessly lost; the only recognizable feature was a hill which I knew was not far from Hintha and I decided I must make for it.

Progress was slow and I had to stop for a rest even more frequently, but at length I came upon a track and found a few mules that had been left behind by the column; some were already dead, and some still had their loads on their backs. I decided I was not in a fit state to unload them. I followed the track in the direction of the village and suddenly saw a pool of filthy-looking water; without hesitation I drank my fill of it and replenished my bottle before going on. Once again I found myself approaching the village by the same route as the column had used three days before and once again I knew that the jungle and thorns were so thick that there was no way off the track; I had not intended to approach the village so blatantly but there seemed no alternative. Sooner or later, I felt, I was bound to go into the village for food.

I reached the point before the first houses where the little track branched off to the left where the Commandos has put in their attack; it seemed better to turn down there rather than walk to the "T" junction. I rounded the corner and a few yards ahead of me I saw three or four men sitting in shadow under a tree. For a few seconds we stared at each other. Then they sprang up and, as they ran into the light, I saw that they were Japs. I struggled for a while but it was useless and very painful. They tied my hands and tried to make me kneel and submit to them formally; I refused and, after a time they gave up the idea and, having taken my watch, they led me off through the village. As we passed the "T" junction, I suddenly had an idea that Moto might be somewhere near and managed to shout out, "Moto, Moto, they have caught me" at the top of my voice before they shut my mouth.

Moto could not hear. Later from other prisoners I learned what had happened. Somehow the Japs had discovered where he was to meet the villager and, when he arrived at the spot, they were waiting for him. They also knew that he was looking after a British officer somewhere in the jungle but, when they asked him where I was, he would not speak. They tried to make him speak by beating him and all manner of torture but still he would not tell them; finally they realized that nothing would break his spirit so they shot him.

I cannot put into words what I feel about this man. His utter unselfishness in volunteering to stay behind with me, his devotion in looking after me so well and, finally, his matchless courage in facing torment and death rather than betray me to the enemy – these are things I cannot trust myself to speak of even today. I can never be worthy of the sacrifice he made but, as long as I live, I shall always have the feeling that my life is not my own, and the memory of Maung Tun will inspire me to the end of my days.

# PART III

# Captivity

"The troubles of our proud and angry dust
Are from eternity and shall not fail
Bear them we can, and if we can we must . . ."

A. E. Housman, *Last Poems*.

# CHAPTER 10

## *Hintha to Bhamo*

My captors took me to a camp in the jungle just outside Hintha and started interrogating me at once. I was seated at one side of a rough table and at the other side sat a Jap officer, a Burmese interpreter, whom they called "Mr Mountain", and a Jap sergeant, who spoke good English. I told them my rank, name and number, and that I was wounded, hungry and thirsty, but they seemed anxious to question me further so I pretended to feel faint. They quickly provided two rice balls and some salted fish, and I ate this while they all watched me intensely. Then a doctor came and looked at my wound and dressed it with a red antiseptic called mercurochrome. After that they made me empty my pockets onto the table in front of me. My watch had already been taken and they let me keep my photos, so there was nothing I really minded losing except my phial of morphia pills. I wanted to keep them so that if things became unbearable I could give myself a lethal dose. They left the phial on the table in front of me, and, while I was talking to them I picked it up, gesticulated with it for a moment, and then slipped it into my pocket again.

At first they appeared to be friendly. Why, they asked, had I allowed myself to be captured? I told them that I had been wounded. "Ah," they said, "but a Nippon soldier would kill himself rather than be captured; a Nippon soldier is very brave." I told them that our religion did not allow us to escape trouble by suicide and they considered this for a bit. Then, after the conversation had proceeded on these lines for a few minutes, they started business.

"Where are your friends going to?" they asked.

I pretended not to understand. "What place are the British troops advancing to?"

I said I could not tell them.

"But you must know; you are an officer. You must tell," they said.

I answered that I was only allowed to tell them my rank, name and number, and that I was not going to tell them any more. I mentioned International Law and they laughed and said that the British did not keep International Law as they bombed hospital ships. "International Law is made by men and not by God," they said. They continued asking where our troops were going and I went on refusing to tell them until at last they told me that if I would not give them the information I must die the following morning. Very seriously and as a great favour, they asked me whether I would prefer to be beheaded or shot. After a few moments consideration I said I would prefer to be shot. Then they tied me to a tree, leaving me there to think things over.

I felt surprisingly relaxed, partly because I was pretty certain that they wanted the information so badly that they would not shoot me, but I suspected they would go to any lengths to make me talk. From what they had said, I gathered that they still did not realize that our Brigade had turned round and was on its way to India. They seemed to know more or less where our troops were, but they did not know in which direction they were moving. I, of course, knew that they were heading north or north-west and that in order to cover this withdrawal Wingate had tried to spread rumours that they were moving south. Taking all this into consideration, I made up my mind what I would do if, as I expected, the Japs started to be tough. The decision I made was not a brave one. Perhaps I ought to have decided not to say a word, whatever the cost, but I am not a hero and, after thinking it over, I realized that if I was careful I could avoid too much torture for myself and also do a good turn for the rest of the Brigade. I planned to continue to refuse to talk for a time and then to pretend to give in and tell them, very reluctantly, that the Brigade was moving south.

After about an hour the English-speaking sergeant came back. I believe his name was Tanarka. He was rather fat and pompous and, like many of the Japs, he wore thick glasses. He reminded me of an overfed curate. He was sickeningly friendly; the line he took was that the Japanese army was very kind; in battle they were very brave, but afterwards they were generous to their enemies. He was a Christian, he said, a Roman Catholic, we must be friends and I must stay with him and teach him to speak English better. Did I know William Dunn? They had found William wounded in Hintha and looked after him well, but he had died. He, Tanarka, had seen that he had a decent burial. (I confirmed this from another source later.) There was no need for me to die. I would be well treated if only I would tell them where my friends were going. I need not be afraid. The British would never know that I had given this information. The Nippon army would not give away my name.

This was too much; I stopped him and told him I had no intention of telling him where my friends were going. The smile disappeared from his face, his eyes narrowed behind his glasses and, before I could stop him, he had struck me on the side of the head and knocked me down. I looked up at him reproachfully and said, "That's a nice way to treat a fellow Christian." He did not like this.

"I must do my duty to my country first," he replied awkwardly, and added, "My officer says I have been too kind to you."

Then the smile reappeared and he tried persuasion once more; when I again refused to talk he went off to fetch help.

He was back in a minute with several others, armed with bamboo poles. Here we go, I thought to myself. They threw me to the ground and started beating me all over with the poles. Luckily for me, the poles were rather large and the Japs were rather small so that, apart from cutting my head open, they did little serious damage. I decided it would not be very convincing if I gave in too soon.

Bamboo having failed, they decided to try water; this was more formidable. They laid me on my back and pinned my arms and legs to the ground. Then one of them sat on my stomach and held my nose, while another forced my mouth open and poured an endless stream of water down my throat. The experience is not one that I want to repeat. I stuck it as long as I could and then decided that the time had come to speak. For a horrible moment I thought I had left it too late, but at last there was a pause in the flow of water and I managed to splutter, "Stop, stop; I'll tell you what you want to know." They let me sit up then, and I asked them what it was they wanted me to tell them. They repeated the question, "Where are your friends going to?" Again I showed reluctance to answer, but when they threatened to give me some more water, I gave in very convincingly and told them that the Brigade was going south towards Mandalay. As soon as the words were out of my mouth I appeared to be smitten with remorse and even groaned aloud most realistically. Then I waited to see if they had been taken in and, to my joy, saw that they had. One of them rushed off with the news and Tanarka, all smiles again, came over apologetically and tried to comfort me by saying I had shown a fine spirit and been very brave, but that I was right to tell them and that they would treat me very well. As a reward, I was given some more rice and water, tied to a tree and told to settle down for the night.

Before I fell asleep several Japs came to look at me. Most of them spoke a few words of English. They did not molest me but they treated me in the same way as a small child treats a toy. Their questions and remarks nearly always followed the same lines. Had I a wife? No? Hah! Hah! Indian dancing girls very good? In Calcutta much dancing? Very good. Hah! Hah! English soldier no good; all time dancing and many sweethearts. Nippon soldier very good, very brave, very strong. America no good. Nippon master. Hong Kong, Singapore, Sumatra, Java, Malaya, Rangoon, *Prince of Wales*. Singapore very good. Much whisky. Hah! Hah! White Horse very good. Much cigarette – present from Churchill. Churchill no good. Roosevelt no good. Tojo very good. English soldier, American soldier, fighting no good, dancing very good. Hah! Hah!

This soon began to pall and I was glad when they left me to sleep. During the night one of them brought me a captured British army blanket.

The following morning the Japs struck camp and we marched westwards along the track to Nampaung, a distance of about nine miles. The Japanese commanding officer, a major, was unable to walk as he had grenade splinters in his backside from the battle at Hintha; this meant he was carried in a chair by four Burmese coolies. This meant a considerable halt every twenty minutes, so I did not find the march too hard. I had nothing to carry except my blanket and my water bottle, but my hands remained tied.

The Japs were quite friendly. At meal times I was given my share of rice and a very unpleasant sweet soup; if there was anything left over at the end of the meal they always offered it to me. My enormous appetite seemed to amaze them and, after watching my attempts to eat with chopsticks with considerable mirth, one of them gave me a spoon which I was allowed to keep. They also offered me Pirate cigarettes, which, they said, came from Singapore. I tired of answering their questions about my age, rank and sex life so I started questioning them; they showed no reluctance in answering. I discovered the unit I was with corresponded roughly to a Brigade headquarters in our army and that the major in command controlled all the Japanese troops in the surrounding area. They were collecting information about the movement of our troops from Burmese collaborators who were organized by the obsequious "Mr Mountain" who had helped to interrogate me. They were moving from Hintha to Nampaung in order to be in a more central position; their intention was to remain in that area and intercept our troops as they came south. This piece of information thrilled me as it showed my lies had been well and truly absorbed.

We reached Nampaung in the afternoon and camped outside the village near some water. I was amused by the deferential treatment given to Jap officers. A small bamboo hut was erected for them and the C.O. had a separate hut to himself where he was installed on a camp bed with spotless sheets to the accompaniment of much bowing and scraping as soon as we arrived. As I watched, his orderly approached and offered him a drink from a flask. I looked more closely and saw, to my amazement, that it was my own. Somehow they must have found my pack and the maps in it. After careful thought I realized with considerable relief that there was nothing in the pack with my name on it so I could safely disclaim all knowledge of the maps. The Jap major was obviously enjoying the brandy but he had the decency to send over a small tot for me, and asked about my wound, so I felt rather better about him.

By this time I was beginning to observe the Japs more closely. In appearance they were not very different from what I had expected. There were a few tall ones, but on the whole they were short. Some of them were far more yellow than others; a few had almost white skins. By nature most of them were not physically impressive but it was obvious that they had made themselves extremely fit. They seemed cheerful and hard-working and I saw no reason to doubt that they could endure hardship. I was amazed at the amount of noise they made. On the march, orders were shouted from one end of the column to the other, and in camp the sentries shouted to each other from post to post. In fact they seemed so confident that their Burmese spy system would warn them of the approach of hostile troops that they were revelling in the opportunity to make as much noise as they liked. I also noticed that, although they ate little, they smoked heavily, even on the march.

Patrols were constantly arriving and going out, and messages being received and despatched by Burmans. The wireless set, a smallish contraption, worked with a hand dynamo, seemed to be on the air continuously and, from where I was tied to a tree, I had a good view of everything that was going on. Tanarka was the only Jap who could speak English properly and he was very overworked as all orders to the Burmans had to be transmitted through him to "Mr Mountain". I was an interested spectator when one of the junior officers (Lieutenant Konyshe, I think) issued orders to his N.C.O.s. They arrived with large notebooks and pencils and, after the preliminary bowing, they proceeded to take down practically every word he said, which was more than a little. Then there was more bowing and they all went off to study their notes. I soon discovered that all Jap officers and senior N.C.O.s were extremely proud of their swords. It was difficult not to laugh when one saw a bow-legged little Jap struggling along with a sword nearly as big as himself.

We remained at Nampaung all the next day, 2 April, and, when his other work allowed Sergeant Tanarka came over and questioned me. He wanted me to stay with his unit until the end of the war so that I could teach him English, but I said I preferred to go to a prison camp. He said his Commanding Officer was a very brave man and he gave me details of some of the hardships they had allegedly undergone while fighting on one of the Pacific islands. Many of his questions were infantile and he took down my answers so meticulously I could hardly hide my amusement. He clearly believed everything I told him and it was tempting to see just how much he would believe.

I suppose during the first months of captivity I was interrogated about a dozen times by different Japs. The questions were nearly always the same, though my answers were not so consistent. I told them so many tall stories that I soon lost count of what I had said. Usually an interrogation went something like this:

Q: How many troops are there in India?
A: I don't know.
Q: If you are an officer, you must know. How many are there?
A: I am only a lieutenant.
Q: A lieutenant should know everything. Tell me what you know.
A: Oh well, I suppose there are somewhere between nine and ten million troops in India.

(Pause while this is carefully noted down.)

Q: What regiments are there in India?
A: I can't remember.
Q: Here is a list of the regiments in the British Army. Will
you tick off those that you know are in India?

(Long pause while I tick off about ninety per cent of them,
leaving out an odd one here and there to make it look more
convincing.)

Q: Did you command a platoon?
A: Yes.
Q: How many are there in a platoon?
A: It varies. About 180 usually.
Q: What weapons are there in a platoon?
A: Each man has a machine gun and thirty grenades.
Q: Which way did you come into Burma?
A: I don't know.
Q: You are an officer. You must know. What towns and
villages did you come through?
A: We avoided all towns and marched on a compass
bearing all the way.

And so on; it all seemed too easy but I was amazed when
they produced a typewritten list of the names and addresses of
next of kin of every man in 5 Column. This looked like an
extraordinary piece of intelligence work until I realised that
they had captured the mule that carried our office box. Later I
learnt that this mule had fallen over a steep cliff after the battle
at Hintha and that Corporal Lee, our clerk, in an effort to find
it and the ciphers it was carrying got lost and was subsequently
captured. He died in captivity.

That evening three more prisoners from 5 Column were
brought in; one of them was the same Boyle who had helped
me leave Hintha on a horse. I did not manage to discover much
from them; somehow they had become separated from the
others and some Burmans had handed them over to the Japs.
That night they were tied together in such an uncomfortable

position that they could not sleep but, in spite of my protests, the Japs refused to do anything to make them more comfortable.

I think it was the following morning, 3 April, that there seemed to be much excitement among the Japs and Tanarka came and told us that they had discovered our troops were trying to return to India. I feigned complete surprise and a certain amount of distress. Later they told me they could hear some of my friends talking on the air and that they were saying, "Hello! Hello!" in very faint and weary voices. I tried to seem upset at this although I was tempted to tell them we never used speech on our wireless sets but thought that if I did so it might discourage them from telling me more.

That evening we started back towards Hintha, passing through it in the middle of the night and reaching the banks of the Shweli River in the early morning. Once again the pace was easy as the Commanding Officer still had to be carried in his chair. They gave us our meals regularly but it was always the same, soup and rice. Tanarka came and started practising his English on me; he seemed to know all sorts of quaint words but he often showed ignorance of quite common expressions. I remember, for instance, he used the word "pique" frequently until I pointed out that "bad temper" was the more usual expression.

We crossed the Shweli in a large boat that evening and spent the night in a village on the other side. All the officers dined in state off a real table and chairs in the garden of the headman's house. They had captured some of our rations and seemed to find them a welcome change from rice. Lieutenant Konyshe, who spoke a little English and seemed inclined to be friendly, brought me a piece of cheese after the meal and enquired anxiously after my health. My wound felt much better as it had been dressed every day. We spent the next two days in that area and we were joined by several more prisoners, including Corporal Litherland who had been wounded twice at Hintha.

I now confirmed what Tanarka had told me about Dunn. It was sad news but I felt certain he had never feared death. Before we left Jhansi he had especially asked me to see that whenever there was a fight he would be in it up at the front. He had his wish; at Hintha he was immediately behind me when we moved forward to attack and, when I was wounded, he was right at the front. It is not certain how many Japs he accounted for but I was told that he had fought like a man possessed until he was wounded himself.

Corporal Litherland had been captured several days before I was taken and he said that he saw about forty dead and wounded Japs being carried away; this meant that by comparison our casualties were extremely light.

In the evening of the second day we were crammed on to a lorry and set off for an unknown destination. It was a nightmare ride; we were extremely crowded in the back of the lorry, the road was just a jungle track with slight improvements and the driver drove like a maniac. At every jolt of the vehicle my wound felt as if it had been prodded and for poor Corporal Litherland it was even worse. We went on for hours at the same reckless speed and I was amazed that the lorry held together. One of the Japs told me that their own lorries would not stand up to the wear and tear of Burman roads and that they were using British vehicles taken at Singapore. At last we stopped at a larger place than the villages we had been passing through and we were told this was Bhamo. We were hustled into the guardroom and searched; then they herded us into a small wooden cage at the back of the guardroom. There was just enough space for us to lie down and I, for one, was so exhausted after the ride that I slept through the remaining hours until daylight.

We were now in the hands of a different unit and we saw no more of the Japs who had captured us. Later we all agreed that, as far as we were concerned, our treatment deteriorated the further away we were from the fighting zone. The Japs who had captured us had not treated us too badly, except when they wanted some information, and in later days we looked back on the time we spent with them as one of the less miserable parts of our captivity.

I did not like the look of our new guards. They came and

stared at us through the bars of our cage and indicated, in dumb show, that we were going to be bayonetted. We tried to appear unconcerned but this fate seemed well within the realms of possibility. They gave us nothing to eat and the sensation of being caged in was just becoming unbearable when we were taken out and driven in a lorry through the town. At the far end of the town we came to the jail and a few minutes later we were inside.

# CHAPTER 11

# *Bhamo to Maymyo*

Bhamo jail consisted of a series of solidly constructed wooden buildings surrounded by a high stone wall. Under the British it had probably been quite a good jail, as jails go. There were a few trees in the compound and a Buddhist altar, but otherwise the place was gaunt and solid and bare. The Japanese seemed to be allowing the Burmans to administer local justice themselves and Bhamo jail was still being used for civilian prisoners who were guarded by Burman jailers. The Japanese had taken over part of the jail for prisoners of war and Japanese sentries guarded us.

On our arrival we were searched once again and then put in a large room on the first floor of the building which had a verandah running all around it; instead of walls to separate the room from the verandah there were thick wooden bars. In this room we found about sixty of our men, including about twenty Gurkhas; they were nearly all 5 Column men who had failed to cross the Shweli River.

Conditions in this room were appalling; to begin with we were terribly overcrowded and sanitary arrangements were revoltingly conspicuous by their absence. The Japs would not allow us out of the room for any reason whatsoever and in consequence we had to relieve nature in buckets in a corner of the room. In addition to this stench, there was an incredibly filthy odour from the wounds of some of the men which had not been dressed for many days. We were not allowed to wash. At meal times the jailers pushed rice and vegetable soup into the room in buckets and a mad, savage scramble ensued. Sometimes a few cigarettes were handed in by the Japs or

Burmans and another scramble took place. Our clothes were lousy, the room was dark and there was nothing for the men to do all day but sit on the floor, leaning against the bars, brooding on their misfortune. Most of them had no blankets and they lay on the bare boards at night. Obviously it was up to me, as the only officer, to try to do something about the situation.

First of all I worried the Jap sentries and the Burman jailers about the sanitary conditions, the lack of medical attention and the food; the results were a little better than nothing. The food perhaps improved slightly in quantity but the Burman jailer in charge of it was an unpleasant oily specimen from Rangoon, and I had practically certain proof before we left that he was keeping back for his own purposes a large part of the rations which the Japs were issuing to him and which were supposed to come to us. He always carried the steel shaft of a golf club with him and rather enjoyed poking people with this until one day one of our men set on him; he was more careful from then on. The only improvement in the sanitary arrangements was that we were given something to screen off that corner of the room. Medical attention was given spasmodically by a Jap medical orderly and a Burmese doctor. The doctor would, I think, have come every day if he had been allowed to do so. Fortunately, although the treatment was so irregular, the wounded began to recover; one of the sergeants still had several bullets in his thigh but the wounds began to close up; my own wound was doing quite well.

I made it perfectly clear to the men that in future everything would be distributed fairly and I arranged a system for dishing out the two meals a day which gave everyone his rightful share and avoided the degrading scenes which had occurred hitherto. All the cigarettes received from the Japs and Burmans were handed to me for distribution. I was particularly careful to see the Gurkhas were given their full share of everything. Even with these arrangements there was scarcely enough to go round and at the two daily meals the most we ate was half a mess tin of rice and a few spoonfuls of vegetable soup.

All things considered, the men, both British and Gurkhas,

behaved extremely well. There was one occasion when two of the King's men thought they had not been given their fair share of food and, in the heat of the moment, questioned my right to any authority over them now that we were in enemy hands. I gave them time to cool down and then had a talk to them in my corner of the room. I told them I quite understood their feelings but asked them to put themselves in my position. Would they, in my position, feel it was their duty to try and maintain certain standards and to see that each man, as far as possible, had his fair share of the necessities of life? Or would they just let everything go and allow everyone to sink to the level of animals? They both saw my point and there was no more similar trouble.

The days dragged by. We had about three books in the room; one was the intimate diary of a V.A.D. during the first world war and another was *The Fountain* by Charles Morgan, which I enjoyed until I found the last few chapters were missing. I tried to organize games of various kinds to help to pass the time but the men were really too apathetic to take any real interest.

Some of the local Burman officials came to see us one day and were very sympathetic when I told them of the conditions we were living in, but, although they were clearly pro-British, they were too frightened of the Japs to do much. A Japanese lieutenant used to come and see me often; he was much bigger than the other Japs and had been a champion wrestler; sometimes he would stay for over an hour talking to me in his broken English and sometimes he would bring a few tomatoes, or a cake or cigarettes. He had quite a sense of humour and seemed as amused at some of my comments on the Japanese as I was by his remarks about the English.

Late one night I was taken downstairs into the compound and interrogated by one of the ugliest Japs I had seen. He sat at a table behind two lighted candles and made me stand in front of him while he questioned me. It soon became clear that he belonged to the Japanese propaganda department and that he was trying to make me say that we prisoners felt we had been betrayed by our leaders, that Wingate was a lunatic and Wavell

a criminal fool. I told him as politely as I could that I disagreed
entirely and he then tried to be friendly and told me that he had
come from Rangoon, that he broadcast from there nearly every
night and that John Kerr was in hospital there. After that he
returned to the original subject, but, when I still refused to
denounce my senior officers, he lost his temper and started
jeering at all things British, particularly the British soldier. I did
not trouble to answer him but just stood there and stared at
him till he exhausted himself and sent me away.

One morning after we had been at Bhamo for about a week,
the head jailer came in and gave me a box of about 100 Burmese
cigars which I immediately distributed around the room. I was
then taken downstairs where a tall figure in a khaki shirt and
bright pink trousers strode towards me across the compound.
It was Lieutenant Horton of 8 Column. Ted Horton had been
in the Guards for many years and, some time after Dunkirk, he
had come out to India, been commissioned at Bangalore and
joined Wingate's brigade at Jhansi. He seemed fit enough except
for his feet which were in a very bad state. He had marched so
far that his boots had completely worn out. Before coming to
India Ted had something to do with German prisoners in
England, so he knew how prisoners of war should be treated
and when, on arrival at Bhamo, he heard he was going to be put
in the same room as everyone else, he protested that officers
were supposed to be kept separately. Strangely enough the Japs
had agreed with him so he and I were now put into another
room similar to the big one but much smaller. Here we enjoyed
the luxury of a table, two chairs and two iron bedsteads. The
100 cigarettes which I had so punctiliously distributed amongst
the men were really Ted's and he had paid a large price for them
in a village where he had also bought his pink trousers.

A Burman prisoner called Justice shared our room with us at
night, but during the day he worked in the jail office. Justice
spoke good English and seemed to be a very pleasant young
man. He told us that he had been in the police before the
Japanese occupation and that he was only in jail because of the
jealousy of one of his enemies who had been put in a powerful

position by the Japs. He was very pro-British and we learned much from him about conditions in Burma. He told us that if only we could escape it would be fairly easy to reach the country of the Kachins; however, he did not think there was much chance of our being allowed to escape. Though all the prisoners were now allowed to go down to the well in the compound for a quick wash in the mornings, we noticed that the sentries were on the alert when the men were having their wash and that, when Ted and I went down for our turn at the well, they even loaded their rifles.

We were extremely grateful to Justice as he made life easier for Ted and me in numerous small ways. Through him, for instance, we were able to borrow some books from a Burman official. He also lent us an old pair of scissors and we passed quite a lot of time trimming one another's hair and beards. We enjoyed his company and his cheerful and amusing conversation although we were not very encouraged to hear from him that another Englishman who had occupied our room before we arrived at Bhamo had been taken out to a sandbank by the Irrawaddy by the Japanese and made to dig his own grave before being shot. We had no direct contact with the other prisoners but we gathered from Justice that the conditions under which they were living were improving slightly as time went on.

Ted and I lived in our room for about six weeks and for most of that time we were alone. There are not many people who would not get on one another's nerves if left together for so long under those conditions, with little to do except read, talk, sleep and pick the lice out of our clothes; nevertheless during the whole of that time we never had a row; in fact we forged a lasting friendship there. Although we had only two meals a day we were obviously given considerably more to eat than the men and I did particularly well because Ted often could not face eating his rice. All the same, we were always hungry and we used to watch eagerly for the little procession which approached our room twice a day; first a Jap sentry with a rifle, then a Burman jailer with the keys, then a Burman prisoner to empty our latrine bucket, then two more prisoners with our bowls of rice, followed by a third with our soup and, finally another bringing green tea. We could usually hear them coming because most of the Burman prisoners wore shackles round their legs; sometimes one of the sentries bought us cakes or tomatoes and Justice used to smuggle in sweet potatoes at night when he could.

We had practically no exercise; sometimes we were allowed to walk round the compound for a few minutes after our wash in the morning but never for long. Somehow we kept remarkably fit. Ted used to look after my wound when the Burmese doctor failed to turn up and about six weeks after the battle of Hintha it had completely healed and has never given me any trouble since. The afternoons were the most trying part of the day; the heat was intense as the sun beat down on the tin roof of our room and the high walls around the inside of the jail kept out every breath of wind.

Two or three times while we were at Bhamo the air-raid sirens went but no bomb fell anywhere near. Several times we saw Burmans being flogged. Justice told us that the usual offence was theft. It seemed the jailers did not like flogging so this duty was performed by one of the other prisoners, a vicious-looking specimen who seemed to enjoy it thoroughly. The victim would be brought into the compound and tied to a wooden frame. His bare back was then covered with a cloth soaked in antiseptic. The usual number of strokes was twenty-five. Sometimes the poor wretch would begin screaming before he had ever been struck and I only remember one man who did not utter a sound the whole time. It was not a pretty sight.

We still had regular visits from the tall lieutenant who seemed to have taken a liking to us. Our most unwelcome visitor was a Bengali schoolmaster. He had been employed by the British government before the war and had now sold himself to the Japs as an interpreter and specialist in propaganda. Speaking to us through the bars of our room he used to run down everything British and praise everything Japanese to such an extent that even the sentries told him to shut up. Ted was like a caged lion on these occasions and it was as well for this odious creature that he kept the bars between himself and us.

Looking back on this period of our captivity, I do not remember it as a time of boredom. Ted had an endless fund of reminiscences and he enjoyed telling me about his past as much as I enjoyed listening. He had packed much experience into his time in the Army and, although he was only a few years older than me, his colourful life, especially his time in the Guards, made my sheltered existence seem extremely dull. He had an irrepressible sense of humour and a remarkable gift of mimicry; I can still remember his hilarious account of behind-the-scenes preparations for the Trooping of the Colour. Even behind bars there was rarely a dull moment in Ted's company. If ever the Japs got really worked up, Ted would listen to them with a quizzical expression and his head cocked on one side until they paused for breath; then in an ultra-prim voice he would say "Is that so?"

About 12 May the tall lieutenant told us that those of us who were fit were going to Maymyo. His unit, a battery of mountain artillery, was going there too, so we were to accompany them. We were all assembled in the compound and he made quite a long speech to us, telling us we would march 201 miles to Lashio and from there we would go by train to Maymyo. Anyone who was unfit to march would be left behind and come along later. If anyone fell out on the march he would be shot and if anyone tried to escape, all the prisoners would be shot. We would have the same food as his men. He painted a very pretty picture of Maymyo; there would be a large house for us and we would be paid; there would be bread and fruit and cakes to eat instead of nothing but rice, and we would be allowed to write home. It all sounded too good to be true, and it was, but he seemed to believe what he said and most of us began to hope for better things. He made us march round the compound about fifty times while he picked out those who were obviously unfit; naturally, they hated being left behind but he promised they would follow us later. Most of us had few clothes and some of us had no footwear whatsoever, so we were fitted out with Japanese kit. My own boots were not quite worn out so I stuck to them, but I had lost my hat (or rather Moto's hat) when I was captured. So now I was given a comical Japanese sun helmet. They had no boots large enough for Ted so he had to wear a pair far too small for him with the uppers cut away to let his toes stick out. The whole march was purgatory for him.

The next morning those of us who were fit marched cheerfully out of the jail to join the lieutenant's unit. We were not going to start until the evening and we spent the day in a bombed-out barrack block. One of the officers took Ted and me to his room and gave us a tin of condensed milk during the afternoon but otherwise the day was boring. Nearby there were many mules, most of them captured ones, and the men were told that they would have to lead them on the march. This was a bitter blow as most of them were going to find it difficult enough to push themselves along without the additional drag of a mule. Ted and I were told that we were going to be allowed to ride chargers but our joy was soon dispelled when we discovered that our chargers were barebacked mules. Fortunately the most that any of us had to carry was a blanket, a water bottle and eating utensils; in fact very few had blankets.

Rounding up the mules that evening was not easy and, before it was done, the Japs were in a foul temper. At last the whole unit was ready to move off; the lieutenant, their commanding officer, stood before them and made a long speech, followed by much sword-waving, bowing and saluting. Then a man appeared with a small white box hung around his neck; he stood facing them and they all stood at the salute for some time. We could not understand what it was all about and someone suggested the white box was a camera and that they were having their photographs taken. Later we learned that in the box were the ashes of one of their number who had been killed; these ashes were being taken back to Japan. Apparently this was done whenever possible.

The guns of the lieutenant's battery were horse-drawn and both animals and guns were beautifully kept. All the officers rode horses and I never saw one of them march a step during the whole of the journey. An officer in the Jap army is a being apart from his men and they treat him like a little tin god. The ranks in their army do not really correspond with ours at all. The lieutenant in charge of the unit which accompanied us on the march was really the equivalent of a major in the British army and the major who was in command of the unit which captured me at Hintha was really the equivalent of a brigadier. The Japs could never get over the fact that I was a lieutenant at the age of 21 and would mutter to themselves, "Neejoo eechi? Chooey? Neejoo eechi? Chooey?" – "Twenty-one? a lieutenant?"

We only marched about fourteen miles along a good level road the first night, but it was obvious before we had gone very far that many of the men should have stayed behind. The mules were all fairly well behaved, but even those of us who were fittest were heartily thankful when we turned off the road about two in the morning and found a rest house where we were to stay until the following evening. We were crowded into a very small room, but most of us were soon asleep. We had not realized how weak we had become after living on rice for so long.

Throughout the fourteen days' march rations were brought to us by lorry each day. We were given a pretty generous allowance of rice, vegetables and meat (usually pork), and we had to cook it ourselves in two oil drums provided for the purpose. For the men, exhausted from marching, finding wood for a fire and then cooking two meals a day was an almost intolerable burden, made worse by the fact that the Japs were always vague about time so that we often received orders to prepare to march when a meal was only half-cooked. This caused much exasperation but fortunately the Gurkhas were extremely helpful and expert at cooking the rice. Always at the beginning and end of every march the whole unit was fallen-in in front of the lieutenant to receive their orders from him verbally. When he had finished speaking in Japanese, he would call out to us in English, "Eighteen miles tonight", or whatever the distance was. He was, we had to admit, an impressive officer and quite a kindly man.

The second stage of the march was longer than the first and the road now started climbing through the hills. Looking at some of the men before we started, I thought grimly of the Japs' threat to shoot anyone who fell out. Some of them were still in a state of exhaustion, even after a rest, and many of their feet were in a shocking condition. It was a great relief when the lieutenant allowed the worst cases to ride on the ration lorry; even so, several of the men had to finish the march riding bareback on the mules. Anyone who has experienced the sharp and knobbly backbone of a mule will realize how exhausted these men must have been; I can imagine no more painful means of transport. The road was very similar to the Manipur road, winding up through the hills with always a sheer drop on one side. We climbed all night and halted at a rest house about five miles from the summit. One of the men had developed a nasty abscess and I shall never forget the look of agony on his face as the Jap medical orderly treated it in what seemed an unnecessarily rough and painful manner.

The next stage was about thirty miles long and took us over the summit and down into the valley of the Upper Shweli. The Japs did not stop regularly every hour, but whenever they saw water, they stopped for the mules to have a drink. This meant that we sometimes stopped three or four times in an hour and sometimes not at all for over two hours. Of course the mules did not need watering so often but the Japs got very angry if we did not make them drink at every halt. By the end of this march, even I had ridden a short distance on a mule. I found it was just bearable if I sat on my blanket.

During the third stage we crossed the Upper Shweli by the suspension bridge which 5 Column had once hoped to destroy. It was ideally suited for our purposes and did not seem very heavily guarded. As someone remarked, "It would have been a piece of cake." We halted for nearly twenty-four hours in the market place at Namkham nearby.

Namkham is quite a large place and we noticed the impressive American Baptist Mission Hospital standing on a hill just outside the town. Since the war I have read Dr Gordon Seagrave's book, *Burma Surgeon*, and learnt the brave story of that hospital. It has made me understand why the people of Namkham were so especially friendly towards us. They crowded round us, ignoring the Jap sentries, and showered us with presents. By the time we moved off we had so much brown fudge-like sugar called jagri that we had to give some of it to the Japs. It was while we were here that I was called into a house at the side of the market place and questioned by a Jap N.C.O. He could not speak English and he used a Burman boy, about ten years old, as his interpreter. I must have stayed there for nearly two hours. He was not an official interrogator but just seemed interested in us and wanted to find out as much about the English as he could. His knowledge of the progress of the war was very sketchy. He even showed me on a map how the Germans had overrun large parts of the British Isles.

The remaining stages of the march did not differ much from those that went before. Two stages after Namkham we started climbing again through hills strangely reminiscent of the Sussex downs and our road joined the famous Burma Road. One night, as we were marching into Kutkai, a car drew up beside us and a Jap officer in it asked to speak to me. It was the major who had been in charge of the unit which had captured me. He had now fully recovered from his wounds and seemed pleased to hear that I had too. He apologized for the conditions at Bhamo, gave me some cake and cigarettes, wished me good luck and drove on. I found this piece of courtesy and consideration genuinely pleasing.

In Kutkai, as in Namkham, large crowds of Burmans came to see us. Among our number was a certain Burriff Jemadar who had been attached to Wingate's Brigade Headquarters and who was another splendid example of the devotion and loyalty of the Burma Rifles. On the march he had been extremely ill but he always refused to ride on the ration lorry. It would have been easy for him to escape, especially in places like Namkham and Kutkai but, because he knew what might happen to the rest of us if he did escape, he cheerfully remained with us. Through him we were able to do a little propaganda work among the Burmans, right under the noses of the Jap sentries. The Burmans all had stories of Jap cruelty and of the shortage of supplies and they all asked the same question, "When will the British return?" We were able to tell them that the day of deliverance was coming and that, meanwhile, they must wait patiently and do all they could to hamper the Japs. These Burmans knew nothing about the course of the war and it was touching to find such confidence in the ultimate return of the British among simple people so cut off from the world.

In one village where we were halted some of our more irrepressible men started singing and a smiling crowd of Burmans soon gathered round. When they had finished I caused some amusement by pretending to pass my hat around for contributions, but one Burman took me seriously and put quite a large sum of money into it; it was difficult to persuade him to take it back. The attitude of our guards varied considerably. At times such as this they were quite pleasant, but at the end of a march they were usually very irritable and many of the men were beaten up. Once one of the Japs completely lost his temper and beat all of the men with a bamboo stick.

One of the guards took a particular liking to Ted and sometimes, when everyone had gone to sleep at the end of a march, he would bring us some rice which he had cooked himself. He used to talk to us for a long time when I wanted to sleep but Ted, who had some very good conjuring tricks up his sleeve, used to entertain him for hours. Sometimes this man would sing songs for us which he had picked up from American films; his favourite was "My Blue Heaven". He knew all the film stars and could imitate some of them very creditably.

During the last stages of the march the first storms of the monsoon soaked us to the skin. One night the rain was particularly heavy and it was so dark that it was difficult to keep contact with the man in front. Whenever I hear the tune "Bye-bye Blues", I am reminded of that night for this was the tune Ted Horton hummed as he marched and, although I could not see him as I trudged along behind, the sound of this tune kept me in the right direction.

By the time we reached Lashio I was feeling very fit again, but, even with the help of the lorry, some of the men only just managed to keep up. It was a wearing march and the cattle trucks into which we were herded at Lashio station seemed a welcome luxury. The train journey from Lashio to Maymyo took a whole day. We were all looking forward to better things at Maymyo and there was a general feeling of optimism. The Japanese guards in our truck were also in a cheerful mood; they whiled away the hours of the journey by tormenting a small puppy which they had picked up. Their favourite trick was to apply a lighted cigarette to the most tender parts of its body.

In the early afternoon we crossed the famous Gokteik Viaduct. There were numerous bomb craters around it, some of them only a few yards away from the foundations. Apparently these near misses had shaken the structure considerably, for the train crawled over with extreme caution. We reached Maymyo in the evening, after a long climb. It is beautifully situated in the hills and the climate is excellent so that it is often considered to be the Simla of Burma. As soon as we had arrived our lieutenant handed us over to some Japs who were waiting to receive us and, after a short delay, we were taken by lorry to the beautiful house we had been promised.

# CHAPTER 12

## *Maymyo to Rangoon*

"The beautiful big house" turned out to be the wooden buildings which had been built for the native followers of a British battalion in peacetime. They were simply rows of mosquito-infested rooms, about the size of a horse-box, with a rough wood verandah running along outside. In peacetime they had been strictly out of bounds for British troops.

If we expected better treatment at Maymyo it was not long before we were disappointed. As soon as we arrived a Jap approached Ted and me and, we thought, motioned us to sit down on the ground. We did so, but were at once lifted to our feet again by a couple of swinging blows on the jaw. The object of the camp at Maymyo was to teach us the Japanese words of command, to make us respect the Japs and, above all, to train us in discipline.

Discipline was enforced by varying degrees of corporal punishment, depending partly on the seriousness of the offence but chiefly on the mood of the Japs. Ignorance of a rule or failure to understand an order, even when it was in Japanese, was never considered an excuse. Nearly all the guards carried a club or a wooden sword which they used whenever they saw the slightest reason for doing so. If they were in a good mood, you had your face slapped; if they were feeling a bit liverish, they struck you with a clenched fist; on bad days they would use a rifle butt and kick you on the shins. Whatever they did, the victim was supposed to stand perfectly still at attention; to move only made matters worse. One man actually ran away when he was being beaten up and I saw the Jap catch him, beat him until he could hardly stand up, trip him up and kick him again on the ground. We soon became hardened to this sort of thing but at first it was bad enough seeing it happen to other people. It was not at all easy to get used to being hit without hitting back, nor did we like seeing others being hit and not being able to defend themselves.

The most common offence was forgetting to salute or bow to a sentry. The Japanese looked upon all sentries as direct representatives of the Emperor and they had to be treated as such. Anyone passing a sentry had to bow if bare-headed or salute if wearing headgear. The whole time we were at Maymyo we felt as though we were living on the edge of a volcano and at every step we expected a snarling little tornado to appear and beat us up. Even the most harmless actions might bring wrath down upon us. As often as not a man who was being beaten up would not have the slightest idea of what he had done wrong; the least thing seemed to provoke the Japs. For instance, the day after we arrived various particulars about us were written down by a Jap officer. He asked me what family I had. I said, "Mother and Father". This caused a furious outburst: "Mother and Father! Mother and Father! Americans say Mother and Father. In Japan always Father and Mother." When he had calmed down I told him that in England we always put ladies first.

There were many other prisoners from our Brigade in the camp and among those from the 5 Column were several of the Burrifs. There were also a good many officers from Brigade Headquarters, including Hosegood, the Intelligence Officer. We new arrivals were kept separate from the others and, on the few occasions when we did manage to speak to them, they warned us to be very careful. At night we were locked in our little rooms but they were so crowded that there was hardly space for us all to lie down. Nevertheless, we were always thankful to be shut in at night because it did mean that for a few hours we were free from the prying eyes of the sentries.

At the beginning and end of every day we all had to attend the Japanese prayer parade, which was held in a nearby field. The Japs would all stand facing a kind of altar and there would be a great deal of shouting and praying and bowing in the direction of Japan. We used to call it the "toots" parade because at one stage of the ceremony they all said some responses and every response ended with the word "toots". Of course, we had no idea what it was all about. We were just expected to stand there quietly and bow when the Japs bowed. We did not care for this bowing and I had uneasy memories of a poem about the Private of the Buffs who was faced with a similar situation and died a heroic death rather than conform. Perhaps we should have refused to bow and taken the consequences, but we decided not to treat the matter too seriously. After all, there was no question of our being formally required to renounce our own religion and accept the Japanese one. No doubt some will consider we were weak-minded and cowardly but I am afraid I have not lost much sleep over it.

Each day working parties went out into Maymyo. The usual jobs were digging air-raid shelters or pulling down bombed houses; those who did not go out were employed in the camp, either digging shelters there or weeding. The sick did not have to work, but, unless a man was really sick, he did not report to the Japanese medical officer as the treatment was always so rough and painful. When the working parties returned in the evening there was usually a strenuous drill parade. We had to learn all the Japanese words of command so that we could number in Japanese at roll call, salute correctly, do the goose-step when marching past an officer or sentry and perform various other comical pieces of ceremonial. The only thing to do was to make joke of it all and we did, but woe betide anyone who was caught grinning by the Japs.

We were given three meals a day and the food was well cooked but there was never enough, considering the amount of work we were required to do. Of course the bread and other treats we had been promised never materialized. Every meal consisted of rice and vegetable stew, with sometimes a little meat or fish; all the time we were at Maymyo we never lost the feeling of hunger.

There was only one family of civilian prisoners in the camp

who were either English or Anglo-Burmans; their living quarters were apart from ours but the women had to use the same
primitive latrines as we did. Of course we made things as easy
as we could for them but it was all very embarrassing and
degrading.

We were all interrogated several times on the same lines as
before. The officer who questioned Ted seemed a friendly sort
so Ted ventured to complain to him about the way we were
beaten up. We had been given a particularly harsh beating the
night before on "toots" parade. Without any warning and for
no apparent reason, two Japs came up to Ted and me; we bent
forward slightly thinking they wanted to say something to us;
this was just what they wanted us to do for it gave them the
chance to give us each two real smashes which nearly lifted us
off our feet. Then they went on down the line and did the same
to everyone else. When Ted told the officer this he at first
refused to believe it, saying that a Nippon soldier would never
do such a thing. However, in the end he said he would look
into the matter and that was the last we heard of it.

A few days after we arrived, some more prisoners from our
Brigade were brought in. One of them was in a terrible state
and died after he had been in the camp for only a few minutes.
I was taken with four other men to dig a grave for him in a
cemetery opposite the British church. We had just finished
digging and were preparing to go when we saw a party of our
men arriving with the body in a rough coffin. As the only
officer present I felt that I ought to say some prayers and the
Japs had the decency to allow this; in fact most Japs habitually
showed respect for the dead. I had no Bible or prayer book so I
said a few impromptu prayers for the soul of the dead man and
for his family and for all of us. The men then joined in the
Lord's Prayer and we filled in the grave, saluted and returned
to camp.

The Burmans in Maymyo were still extremely pro-British in
spite of the fact that so many of our bombs, which were
intended for the Japs, had fallen on them. The Japs had
established their G.H.Q. in Maymyo but tried to conceal this

by pretending that G.H.Q. was in Rangoon. They would have been surprised if they had known that the real whereabouts of their G.H.Q. was common knowledge in India. It was quite usual when we went into Maymyo on a working party for a Burman to approach our guard and ask if he could give us a present of mangoes or cakes. Sometimes the guard allowed it and sometimes he did not. Very often, when we were pulling down bombed houses, the neighbours would send us coffee and cake and, once or twice, the guards let us go into a house for refreshments. Of course they came with us but I managed to have a long talk with the lady of the house on one occasion. Her husband was in India and she had tried to join him there in 1942 but missed the last plane for Myitkyina. She was worried about the state of things in India, having heard much propaganda on the subject from the Japs; I was glad to be able to reassure her.

These contacts with the Burmans were really the only bright spots in our life at Maymyo. I think I came nearer to despair at this stage of our captivity than ever before or since. We felt that we were simply the slaves of the Japs; they could treat us as they liked and none of us knew how long it was going to last. An epidemic of dysentery broke out in spite of the rigorous steps taken by the Japs to prevent it. Our morale sunk lower than ever.

Suddenly we were told that those of us who were fit would be moved to Rangoon the following day. Again the Japs painted a rosy picture of the place we were going to and again they promised bread and other luxuries. The officers would have furnished rooms and all ranks would be taken to a cinema show once a week. This time we did not know whether to believe it or not but we felt that anything would be better than staying on at Maymyo. My one regret at going was that we had to leave behind the Burrif Jemadar who had been so courageous and steadfast on the march in spite of illness. Since we had come to Maymyo his condition had deteriorated and he was in great pain. I was able to give him some of my morphia pills but, when we left, he seemed quite happy and resigned to die. I have never been able to discover what happened to this heroic and saintly man.

We started off for the station in high spirits but these did not last for long. The railways in Burma are all metre gauge, which means that the rolling stock is not as large as in England. We travelled in small cattle trucks, twenty-six of us in each. The space in the middle of the trucks by the open doors was occupied by Jap sentries and we had to sit on the floor with our backs to the wall. When we were sitting, there was just room for us, but at night it was impossible to lie down as there was no space for our legs and feet unless we were prepared to have several other pairs of legs and feet on top of our own. There would be loud groans and curses every few minutes when somebody tried to extricate his legs from the bottom of the pile because the pressure had become unbearable. My outsize feet were most unpopular.

The journey took three days and was a continuous ordeal. Long before it ended I had sworn to myself that, if ever I got back, I would never grumble about the railways in India or England again. The roof of our truck was corrugated iron and when the sun got up the heat inside was tremendous. The Japs only allowed us out for a few minutes at halts so we just had to sit in what seemed like mobile ovens while the perspiration streamed from us.

On the first day we went down the well-known zig-zag line between Maymyo and Mandalay, reaching Mandalay soon after a bomb had hit the station. We ate a meal there and then climbed back into the train. After Mandalay the country was, for the most part, flat and monotonous. We passed a large number of wrecked trains, obviously the victims of Allied air attack; the Japanese informed us, each time we passed one of these, that there had been a slight accident. Now and then we were given a meal at halts but we did not do too badly on the whole because some of us had managed to keep some money and this was shared around so that everyone could buy something from the vendors who were still to be found on some of the stations.

At one place where we stopped there were some youths in Japanese uniform. Whether they were Burmese or Siamese we could not tell but, whatever they were, they had joined the Japs and were very full of themselves. They strutted up and down outside our truck, looking at us very disdainfully and brandishing their rifles and bayonets. Ted's lively wit soon rose to the occasion; he leant out of the truck, produced a pencil from his pocket and asked one of them if he might use his bayonet to sharpen it. Even the Japs joined in the laughter.

At last, on the evening of the third day, 6 or 7 June, we reached the bomb-battered station at Rangoon. After some delay, we were fallen in and marched up the broad tree-lined Commissioner Road. We were all so thankful that the journey was over that we were not unduly disheartened when we saw the walls of another jail, similar to Bhamo but bigger, looming ahead of us; sure enough it was not long before we were "inside" once more.

There was a dramatic moment when, after searching us, the sentries opened the gate of one of the jail compounds and herded us in. By this time it was quite dark. As we entered dim figures moved towards us from the other end of the compound. Were they other prisoners or were they Japanese? They paused and we paused; there was a tense silence and then someone shouted, "Come on – it's more of the lads." In a few seconds we were surrounded by an excited crowd of men from our Brigade and, to my astonishment, I found myself shaking hands with David Whitehead. And then, an even greater surprise, out of the darkness as large as life loomed Private Byrne whom we had lost soon after the Pegon dropping. A few minutes later I was led into the building; out of the darkness a well-known voice boomed; "Philip! my dear chap, what on earth are you doing here? You're supposed to be dead." This was followed by a familiar chuckle; there on the floor sat John Kerr; he could not walk and in the gloom I could not see his face but I could tell from his voice that he was still the same old ebullient John.

In a strange way the atmosphere was almost like that of a home-coming. The weariness of our journey was soon forgotten as we talked eagerly to our old friends with whom we were now re-united. When we finally fell asleep on the wooden floors we felt remarkably confident. Whatever the future held for us we knew that we would be facing it in good company.

# CHAPTER 13

## *Six Block*

It is difficult to write fairly of the next two years. Inevitably in some respects they will sound far worse than they actually were. The human mind and body can accustom themselves to almost anything if there is no alternative. Conditions were bad but, once we had adjusted ourselves and lowered our standards accordingly, we became quite used to doing without certain things which we had always looked upon as essential. When we returned to England at the end of the war, we found it difficult to understand why people worried if they could not find a bed for the night or couldn't put milk in their tea; it seemed strange to us to complain so much about the shortages. We knew that it was possible to sleep perfectly well on the floor and, although we preferred tea with milk, we knew it was drinkable without milk. In short, having lived for two years with the absolute minimum of material comfort, we realized what was essential. Even now, although we do not scorn the good things of life, on the material level we shall never be unduly worried provided we have enough to eat, enough to wear and a roof over our heads.

After a time we became hardened and even callous about the everyday sight of suffering and death. Some of us even laid bets as to who would be the next to die. Perhaps this was heartless but it was preferable to the utter misery and total despair which could so easily have overwhelmed us. Everything possible was done to save the lives of the sick but it was worse than useless to grieve over the inevitable.

Some of the accounts which came in from prisoners of war released after the defeat of Japan tell of conditions and cruelty far worse than anything I can report. I do not think they have been exaggerated, as, although I myself never experienced anything as bad as the worst of these atrocities, I have spoken to many who have. I was lucky and it is safer to tell only of things about which I have first-hand knowledge.

The possibility of the Allies being defeated never entered our heads in spite of continuous Japanese propaganda. We had absolute confidence that sooner or later Burma would be re-taken, but along with this unshakeable faith there were three ever-present fears lurking continuously in the background of our minds and occasionally brought to the front by some unusual incident. First was the fear that we might be struck down by disease and die as many of our comrades had died. We had seen that disease and death did not spare even the fittest. Then there was the fear that we might be killed by our own bombs, a fear that was far from groundless. Lastly there was the fear that, when the big attack on Burma came, the Japs would shoot us rather than let us fall into Allied hands. Our names were never transmitted by the Japanese so that nobody knew that we were prisoners; most of us were just posted as missing. We had no contact with the outside world through the Red Cross so that nobody knew of our existence; if the Japs had killed us all, the world would have been none the wiser. Some of us managed to keep these fears in check better than others but I think they hung over us continuously.

Perhaps what helped us most was that we were all together in the same boat, owning nothing but what we stood up in and sharing the same hardships and anxieties. Inevitably as we were living at such close quarters a considerable amount of mutual irritation and ill-feeling was generated between certain individuals but even quarrels and malicious talk made life less monot-ous and took our minds off more sombre matters. Serious quarrels were more than counter-balanced by the many friend-ships which were strengthened by adversity; among the men in particular the spirit of comradeship, the "mucking-in" spirit, was particularly noticeable. Even at the blackest time cheerfulness and humour kept on breaking through and I can honestly say that my time in Rangoon Jail increased my faith in human nature and in the ability of men to rise above suffering and hardship. During the periods of my captivity when I was physically fit I found life at least tolerable; one of the main reasons for this was the staunchness of my friends.

Rangoon must have been a splendid place before the war. Battered and neglected as it was when we saw it, there was still something very impressive about the broad tree-lined roads, the fine government buildings and schools, the long sweep of the water-front, the shady parks with their lakes and, dominating the whole area, the glorious, gleaming Shwedagon pagoda. One felt that if a man had to live in the East, here in Rangoon life must have been most pleasant, and it was not difficult to see why, in spite of themselves, the Japs were envious of an imperialism which could produce such a fine city.

Rangoon Central Jail, to give our new abode its correct title, had not been used as a jail for several years before the war. The main buildings were seven blocks radiating from a central water-tower like the spokes of a wheel. One block contained the solitary confinement cells, and the others, each in its own compound, had five large rooms upstairs and five down. A corridor ran the whole length of the block on each storey and was separated from the rooms by wooden bars; on the opposite side of the room there were five windows with iron bars but no glass. Outside on the ground floor, a verandah of wood and corrugated iron ran the length of the block on one side. The solitary cells were used for new arrivals and for punishment purposes. Of the ordinary blocks, three were occupied by British and American prisoners, two by Indians and one by Chinese. In the compound of each block there was a latrine shed and a long trough of water; a lean-to cookhouse was built against the wall of each compound. At the end of the compound nearest the central water tower there were iron railings so that the sentry could walk round the tower and see what was happening in every compound. Any prisoner who forgot to salute or bow to the sentry on passing this end of the compound was certain to have at least a slapping.

The block into which we were put on our arrival and where we found so many other members of our Brigade was known as Six Block. John Kerr was very surprised to see me looking so fit as I was generally believed to be dead. He had suffered as he was the first officer from the Brigade to be taken prisoner. He had been taken to Myitkyina before Rangoon. Of the men who were wounded and left behind with him he knew for certain that two were dead and was practically certain of the death of the others. His own wound was still very painful but it was healing gradually in spite of the fact that it had never been properly treated and he had never been in hospital. It was impossible to tell how serious the damage inside his leg was and he could not walk on it at all. Nevertheless he was extremely cheerful and as full of vitality as ever.

David Whitehead was looking extraordinarily well although he had collected an amazing number of bullets in odd parts of his body; apparently all his wounds had healed perfectly. David's survival was scarcely less remarkable than the survival of his spectacles. The frames of these were always getting broken; if the Japs were going to beat you up they did not wait while you removed your glasses. I can still see David's stocky figure, his head cocked to one side, his eyes twinkling through lenses held together with innumerable pieces of string, cotton and wire.

"How many bullet holes have you got, David?" we used to ask him.

"Well, lad, last time I counted I think it was twenty-three."

Tommy Roberts had been in the jail but the Japs had moved him on to Singapore with several other officers. Among the prisoners from 5 Column were Brookes, the bugler, and Corporal Jones, the cook. Many of the prisoners from the Brigade had almost reached the Chindwin on the return when they were captured.

At Rangoon I met Stock, the officer with whom I had

differences of opinion at Tonmakeng and earlier. This time we discovered we had much in common and I shall always be thankful that I spent my years of captivity with a man of such amazingly comprehensive knowledge. Strangely enough, although we first met in Burma, we had both been at Oxford at the same time, he at Magdelen under C.S. Lewis and I at Merton under Edmund Blunden. He was captured between the Irrawaddy and the Chindwin about a week after I was captured. To my amusement he told me that one of the first questions to be put to him by his captors was, "Do you know an officer called Stibbe?" When he hesitated, they added by way of description, "He has a very large nose." This made him laugh so much that he could no longer pretend not to know me.

Many prisoners had died on the way to Rangoon, among them Doc Aird. Nobody was more generally regretted; he had been extremely popular with all ranks and everyone was delighted when, in spite of ill-health, he had insisted on coming into Burma with us. I heard from the men who were with him when he died that, with typical devotion, he continued to look after the other sick prisoners as long as he was able to move.

Many other members of our Brigade arrived during the course of the next few months. Everyone who had not come via Maymyo spent some time in the solitary cells before being sent to Six Block. In the end there were over two hundred of Wingate's men in the jail; of these more than half did not survive their captivity.

The officers lived in two rooms upstairs and the men gradually filled up all the rooms as they arrived. There was no furniture in the block at all, except that in the downstairs rooms, where there were stone floors, men slept or tried to sleep on vermin-infested wooden beds; upstairs we slept on a wooden floor. The whole block, like all the other blocks in the jail, was filthy with insects and, in spite of our efforts to get rid of them, we only just managed to keep them in check. In addition there were large numbers of rats and mice. When we arrived we each had one blanket but these began to wear out after a few months. The Japanese issued a few blankets but they were not nearly enough to go around so they gave us old rice sacks instead. It was not long before a man with the remains of his blanket and two rice sacks was considered to be living in luxury; before we had finished some of the men had no more bedding than the remains of one sack. Only the officers were given mosquito nets. Fortunately there was little malaria in Rangoon but mosquitoes were a perpetual torment to the men at night.

The clothing situation was little better. When we arrived we were all pretty ragged and most of us had nothing but the shirt and trousers that we stood up in. Soon the legs were cut off our trousers to provide patching material for the shorts that remained. The Japs produced a very limited supply of needles and cotton and one or two men, under Private Berkovitch, acted as tailors. Occasionally there was a small issue of Jap clothing but it was quite inadequate and we came to consider ourselves lucky when the Japs gave us some dirty old rags to use as patching material. Clothes were unnecessary during the day and we all went about in very brief loin cloths but it was very difficult to find enough cloth even for one of these. We had to wear our clothes for roll-call, and at night to protect our bodies from mosquitoes as far as possible. As for footwear, only a few lucky ones still had wearable boots; the majority went barefoot or clattered about in home-made wooden sandals.

The only water supply was the trough in the compound. We could dip our mess-tins into this and splash water over ourselves but soap was issued so rarely that it was only possible to use it about once a week. Frequently the water supply broke down, sometimes for over a week at a time, especially after air raids. When this happened, all water had to be drawn from a well in the jail and, as the Japs would scarcely let us draw enough for cooking purposes, we just had to go dirty.

When we arrived in Six Block the senior officer was a New Zealand Flight-Lieutenant. To him fell the onerous task of looking after the interests of the prisoners and at the same time satisfying the demands of the Japs as far as possible. He was in a most unenviable position. The Japs would give him some unreasonable order and they expected him to see that it was carried out; if he tried to do so the prisoners complained bitterly and if he did not do so the Japs became even more unreasonable. Naturally he came in for plenty of criticism but few of us would willingly have taken his place.

Only one of the Japanese in the jail spoke English really well and all official orders were transmitted through him. He was like one of Strube's little men, nervous, puny and bespectacled. At heart I do not think that he was unkind and it was obvious that he did not like having to transmit some of the orders from his seniors. On the other hand, he was fanatically patriotic and I have seen him work himself up into such a frenzy that tears streamed down his face; he trembled from head to foot with rage if he thought any disrespect was being shown to Japan or to the Japanese army.

Roll-call, or "tenko" as the Japs called it, took place in the morning and evening and was quite a ceremonial affair. All the words of command were given in Japanese and we used the Japanese numerals when we numbered. We fell in by rooms and, as soon as the Jap guard commander came through the gate of the compound, we were all called to attention by our senior officer and gave him an "eyes right" which he solemnly acknowledged. Then each squad was called to attention in turn and numbered ("Ichi, Nee, San, She, Go, Roko etc."). Then there was another "eyes right", a mass bow or "keri", and we fell out. Quite often tenko was enlivened by an odd beating up here and there, usually with fists but at least on one occasion with a wooden sandal; indeed hardly a day passed without one of us being beaten up on some pretext or other, at times not very seriously and at other times savagely with blows from a rifle butt and kicks on the shins thrown in. It all depended on the temper of the Jap concerned and we all had our turn at intervals.

After morning "tenko" there was breakfast, and then the work parties went out to work either in Rangoon or somewhere in the jail. In the early days the officers did not have to work but an officer went with each of the men's work parties and gave the words of command for goose-stepping past the sentries by the water tower and again as we marched out of the jail through the guard room. Some of the parties came back for the midday meal and others cooked their own food where they worked. Evening 'tenko" took place after supper, just before dusk, and by 10.30 we all had to be in our rooms and stop talking. Once a week, on Thursdays, no work parties went out. Thus the days passed, not pleasantly but at least busily.

The chief topic of conversation in Rangoon was food; sex was very much an "also ran". Here, even more than during the campaign, we realized how much morale depends upon food. Never have so many taken so much interest in so little!

Our staple diet was rice and vegetables. We became very familiar with the properties of rice. We found, for instance, that you can stuff yourself with rice to bursting point and yet feel hungry again in half an hour; not that we often had the opportunity to do this. We discovered that rice is far more filling when it is wet and soggy and we got to know the various grades of rice, from the high grade white rice to the low grade red rice, swept off a warehouse floor. One would have thought that, whatever else we lacked, we would never go short of rice in Burma, but frequently we were not given enough for every man to feel that he had had sufficient.

The most common vegetables were marrows, sweet potatoes, beans, pumpkins, brinjals and cucumbers. Sometimes we had new potatoes, tomatoes and onions. There were occasional issues of cooking oil and curry powder and also of dhal, a kind of lentil, and gram, which is a very hard kind of pea, usually given to horses or mules; these issues became less and less frequent as time went on. The supply of meat was very irregular; during good periods we sometimes had it three times a week and during bad periods not more than once a fortnight. Occasionally it was pork, but usually it was beef and there was never very much. We always counted the number of pieces of meat in our stew and a man who got four small pieces was considered to have done extraordinarily well. We received our sugar or jagri ration pretty regularly but it did not amount to more than a teaspoon per man per day. There are two schools of thought about the sugar; one held that each man should be issued with his ration and the other thought that the cooks should keep it and put it in with the food. I belonged to the latter school as it was such a small amount that I could not be bothered with the trouble of collecting it and keeping the ants away from it. It seems a trivial matter now but feeling ran very high on such subjects.

A regular and most unpopular feature on the menu was gruel. This was made out of rice bran (the ground-up husks of rice) and was most repulsive. Those of us who could stomach it felt obliged to eat it as it was our only source of Vitamin B and thus some safeguard against beri-beri. Our only drink was Burmese green tea without milk or sugar.

The cooking was done by some of our own men and, for a time, until I had to go sick, I was messing officer. Unfortunately I took over the job at the beginning of the monsoon and I could not have chosen a worse moment. All the cooking was done over wood fires and we were issued with a ludicrously small supply of firewood. Several times, in desperation, we had to use rafters and odd pieces of wood from the building; Corporal Jones and several others were badly beaten up and sent to the cells for a while when the Japs discovered this. The wood shortage was acute before the monsoon, but when the rains really began the situation became impossible.

All the firewood in the jail was stacked in the open and men from each block were called out in turn to draw the ration for their block. The men from Six Block were always called out last and we always had to take the wet wood from the top of the pile which had been thrown on one side by the men from the other blocks so that they could take the dry wood from underneath. It was impossible to keep the wood alight without constant fanning and this only made it burn more quickly and give off less heat. The result was that we used our meagre supply of wood in half the normal time and the meals were never properly cooked. The Japs refused to do anything about it, although we frequently explained the situation to them, and

they always turned nasty if the meals were served late. Sometimes, in order to try and save wood, we missed a meal, and
often the meals were nothing more than a piece of raw cucumber
and some half-cooked rice. This was not nearly sufficient for
the men to work on but there was remarkably little grumbling.
The men could see the cooks were doing their best; some of
them worked from dawn to dusk in a smoke-laden atmosphere,
fanning the fires while the sweat poured off them and tears
streamed down their faces from their smarting eyes. Firewood
was indeed a perpetual nightmare and it was more than infuri-
ating not to be able to cook what little food we had.

In addition to the rations issued by the Japanese, we were
able to buy a few extras. The men were paid coolie rates for the
work they did on work parties; this was little better than not
being paid at all. The officers were supposed to receive the same
pay as their equivalent rank in the Japanese army. Before we
received our pay a considerable sum was deducted for a
mythical item called messing. A further sum was carefully paid
into Japanese War Savings on our behalf and we all gave half of
what we actually received to a fund for buying extras to improve
the food for everybody. This left a lieutenant with twenty-four
rupees to spend on himself. With this we could buy cigars, eggs,
nut toffee, jagri, meat, soup, bananas, pineapples, mangoes,
tomatoes, onions and various other extras when they were
available which was unpredictable. To begin with the prices
were extortionate and, as the Japanese currency became more
and more worthless, inflation set in; before the end of our
captivity one egg cost five rupees (about 40 pence). Nevertheless, the arrival of our weekly order of purchases was an event
and gave us something to look forward to. The Japs used to
issue a few cigarettes occasionally but the smokers among us
nearly all made their own, crumbling up the Burmese cigars we
were able to buy and sticking the paper together with rice. Even
so, the men nearly always seemed short of something to smoke.

With the monsoon came disease and death. Dysentery, ulcers
and beri-beri all took their toll. Conditions were ideal for a

dysentery epidemic and it is really surprising that we did not suffer more heavily from it. The latrine sheds with their leaky tin buckets must have been a perfect breeding ground for germs. We kept the dysentery cases in a separate room from the others but there were so many flies to carry the infection that it made little difference. At times the flies at Rangoon were so numerous that you could kill four or five on the ground with one blow of a fly swat. The place literally crawled and hummed; I realized for the first time why the devil was called Beelzebub. When a man had dysentery really badly, he soon became too weak to move and had to relieve himself where he lay. The medical orderlies did their best to wash the foul bedding every day but it was impossible when the water supply broke down. I will not attempt to describe the filth and stench in which we lived in spite of every effort to keep the place as clean as possible.

I had seen several men die of dysentery when I developed it myself. We had no doctor and the Jap medical orderly who came occasionally could only give us charcoal and what we called "creosote pills"; these seemed to be quite effective. Our own medical orderlies seemed to think that I should not eat anything solid, so for eight days I lived almost entirely on fluid, but I only became thinner and worse. On the eighth night the officer next to me, who also had dysentery, died in his sleep and my own pains became worse than ever, and I began to wonder how long I would last. The next morning, for the first time, the Japs allowed Colonel Mackenzie, the Medical Officer from Three Block, to come across for a few minutes to Six Block. He told me that I had starved enough and put me on a light diet. From that day I began to recover.

Many of us suffered from tropical ulcers. We called them jungle sores because they were similar to those we had suffered from at Patharia, only far worse. The least little scratch seemed to go septic at Rangoon and quickly develop into a large ulcer; the flesh simply rotted away and in its place came quantities of evil-smelling matter. A small graze on my leg soon turned into a sore more than two inches in diameter and took seven months to heal. This was small compared to some; several men had sores which were as big as dinner plates and their flesh rotted away right down to the bone. The task of clearing the pus out of these sores and washing the dressings, which had to be done over and over again because of the shortage, was enough to turn even a cast iron stomach; but the medical orderlies stuck at it hour after hour. They had very few antiseptics; sometimes they were given a little acriflavin and some eusol but for the most part they had to use copper sulphate or blue stone as we called it. The sores were painful enough by themselves, but with blue stone or a salt pack on them the pain was excruciating. Several men died of these jungle sores.

The disease which claimed the most victims was beri-beri, which is caused through lack of Vitamin B. Our only real source of supply for this vitamin was the repulsive rice bran gruel; there is no Vitamin B in the polished rice and, of course, bread was unheard of. Often even this bran proved insufficient and it was pathetic to see some of the fittest men suddenly develop beri-beri, knowing that nothing could be done for them. A few did manage to keep it in check by eating huge quantities of bran but in most cases nothing seemed to stop it. At one time the Japanese gave us some Vitamin B tablets but there were not enough and the supply soon ran out. The disease seemed to attack men in two ways; some of them developed chronic diarrhoea and grew thinner and thinner until they died. Towards the end they were literally skin and bone and the pictures which have been published of some of the emaciated victims of Buchenwald and Belsen are no worse than the sights which daily met our eyes in Rangoon. Others swelled up to an enormous size, starting at the feet and working upwards until their faces were nearly twice the normal width. This swelling was caused by quantities of fluid under the skin and it was ghastly to see men becoming more and more inflated with water until they could hardly breathe and, finally, their hearts stopped beating. We knew that anybody might develop the disease at any time. I cannot forget the look of fear and horror in the face of one particularly fine and intelligent young soldier when he recognized the unmistakable signs of beri-beri in himself, but before he died he, like all the other victims of the disease, became mercifully resigned and apathetic. Some became delirious before the end and we would be woken at night by their crazy shouting. One man suddenly sat up in the middle of the night and, in macabre and grotesque imitation of Gracie Fields, started singing at the top of his voice, "Walter, Walter, lead me to the altar". A few minutes later he was dead.

At last, towards the end of the year, the Japanese released Major Raymond Ramsay from the solitary block. He had been the senior Medical Officer in our Brigade and his arrival filled us all with optimism. He exuded an atmosphere of confidence and efficiency and the debt we survivors owe to him is inestimable. His arrival in Six Block was a turning point but he was, in fact, faced with a heart-breaking job, for he had the knowledge to tackle the situation but was deprived of the means as he was given hardly any drugs to work with. Nevertheless, with tremendous faith and perseverance, he gradually reduced the death rate, until only one or two men were dying each month whereas, at one time before his arrival, we had at least one death every day and as many as four on one occasion. He even found an effective way of dealing with jungle sores.

Soon after Major Ramsay's arrival in Six Block, the Japanese sent in two American airmen who had been shot down near Rangoon. They were terribly burnt and had been kept in solitary confinement for some time without having their burns dressed, so that when they arrived in Six Block they were a mass of maggots. One of them had practically nothing left where his face had been. It took more than an hour and a half to dress each man's burns and the stench was so foul that the medical orderlies assisting had to work in relays, but Major Ramsay, with superb determination, worked on them without stopping. The agony of it cannot be described; hardened as we were, their screaming turned us sick; they could not help themselves and, in their hell of pain, they cursed everyone and everything, even the doctor who was trying to help them. They had the last of my morphia pills but it was not enough. All the Major's efforts were in vain and they died after a few days.

I have not told and cannot tell the full tale of pain and death; none can say what agonies were daily borne in silence and unobserved. Sixty percent of the prisoners from Wingate's Brigade died. Of those already mentioned in this book, Corporal Litherland, Corporal Lee, and one of the Bennett twins died in Rangoon. I should also make special mention of Corporal Hardy, who was captured because he insisted on remaining behind with a friend who was wounded. Both he and his friend died. Nearly always they died peacefully, usually in their sleep. In almost every case towards the end they seemed to lose the will to live and to become quite content to go; once this happened we knew that nothing more could be done.

The Japanese allowed us to bury our dead in Rangoon Cemetery and towards the end they even provided rough coffins and a Union Jack, whereas, in the early days, the bodies were simply sewn up in rice sacks. All the occupants of the block would fall in to give a final salute to their dead comrade as his body was slow-marched out of the compound. The officers took it in turn to take the simple funeral service and we erected home-made wooden crosses. A plan, showing the position for each grave, was kept but I am afraid it soon became impossible to distinguish where any individual lay buried. It is good to know that a fine memorial has been erected over the last resting place of these men, for they died in the service of their King and Country just as much as if they had fallen in battle. To Major Ramsay and all his medical orderlies the highest praise is due. It would be invidious to single out any particular one for mention for each one cheerfully undertook a job which would make the stoutest heart quail and which, besides being distasteful in the extreme, often proved a vain expenditure of effort.

One incident in our first few months at Rangoon was particularly tragic. The Japanese Medical Officer at Maymyo had been using some of our men as human guinea pigs, injecting germs into them to see the results. One party of prisoners arrived from Maymyo in a terrible state. They told us that they had been injected with malaria germs; nearly all of them died soon after arrival. One of them went delirious and the following day he was missing at morning roll-call. We managed to conceal his absence from the Japs, but, when a thorough search of the compound failed to reveal any trace of him, we thought it was obviously better to tell the Japs that he had gone rather than let them discover it for themselves. Somehow in his delirium, the man had got out of the compound and out of the jail. Nobody ever found out how he did it. For a white man to try to escape from Rangoon was sheer madness. The Burmans in that area were mostly so frightened of the Japs that, even if they did not betray him, they would certainly not assist him; besides the nearest Allied territory was thousands of miles away.

As soon as the Japs were told that the man was missing they took drastic action. Our senior officer, the New Zealand Flight Lieutenant, was sick, but the acting senior officer and various men whom the Japs quite wrongly suspected of assisting the escape were clapped into solitary confinement. The rest of us were locked in our rooms and spent the time wondering what was going to happen. On the evening of the second day the cooks were allowed to cook a meal for us; the following morning we were paraded in the compound in front of the Japanese Commandant. The escaped man was brought in; the poor fellow had obviously no idea what was happening. The Commandant announced that he had been brought back to the jail by Burmans and that he would receive the severest punishment. He was then led out and none of us ever saw him again. As for the rest of us, the Commandant said that he would be lenient and that we could carry on as usual provided that we promised not to try to escape. We were all required to sign a document to this effect and, after some discussion among ourselves, we did so. We felt that, after all, a promise extracted by force and by one's enemies is not binding and the chance of a good opportunity of escape presenting itself seemed very remote. After a few days, those who had been sent to solitary confinement came back, considerably shaken by their ordeal. The Japanese guard commander who had failed to notice that there was a man missing at morning roll-call was severely punished and he, in his turn, retaliated on the British officer who had been in charge at the roll call. The officer came back from the cells with terrible bruises on his face where he had been beaten up. He was never the same after this incident and, many months afterwards, he died of heart trouble. During the days when we had been locked up, the sick received no attention and this probably hastened the end in many cases.

As the monsoon began to slacken off Allied air raids on Rangoon began again. The jail was quite conspicuous from the air and I believe it was known to house Allied prisoners of war but, as it was situated near the docks and the railway station, not to mention various Japanese headquarters, it was only to be expected that bombs would land in or near it. Before we had arrived it had already been hit several times and once the Japanese guard had been wiped out in their guard room.

The first air raid I ever experienced came in the middle of the day: I was laid up with my jungle sore in the Block Sick Bay which was one of the upstairs rooms. We heard the planes coming and crawled to a window to watch; they were flying low and quite close by. Suddenly there was a sound like several express trains approaching at full speed during a thunderstorm. It was quite the most terrifying sound I had ever heard. We flattened ourselves on the floor while the building seemed to shake itself like a dog. Those bombs were some distance away but we started at once to build air raid shelters in the compound in the form of trenches with sheets of corrugated iron across the top.

I don't mind admitting that I was frightened, very frightened, by those air raids; somehow, to be killed by our own bombs seemed such a stupid end to everything. John Kerr and I shared a trench and never strayed far from it when the warning had gone. We had been joined by some American prisoners who were shot down over Burma and they were full of stories of a wonderful new bomb sight which could drop bombs on a pin head; however, we noticed, with some amusement, that their confidence in it did not prevent them from making quickly for their trenches whenever they heard the siren. One afternoon we heard the planes coming and took to the trenches as usual. The bolder spirits used to wait until the sound of the bombs falling warned them to duck down. On this occasion they reported that a formation was flying just above us, with one plane lagging behind. Then they took shelter abruptly as the thunderous roar of the falling bombs began. This time it was louder than before and we crouched trembling in the bottom of our trenches. There was a massive explosion and the earth shook so that we expected the sides of the trench to fall in. A few moments later we emerged into a cloud of dust to find that a stick of bombs had fallen across the jail, landing in the compounds of Two and Three Blocks. Some British and Americans were killed in Three Block but the Indians in Two Block suffered the most casualties.

After this we were all pretty nervous about air raids. We had comforted ourselves with the thought that a bomb falling on the jail was just a piece of bad luck and not likely to happen again, but the following night there was another raid and Three Block compound was hit again. I think Allied bombing depressed us more than anything the Japs ever did. Our nervousness was mingled with exasperation. A total of well over a dozen bombs fell in the jail while it was being used as a prisoner of war camp and about thirty prisoners were killed.

It was difficult to decide whether we disliked day or night raids the most. By day we could see what was happening and we hoped that the planes could see where they were dropping their loads, but as they came in formation by day and all dropped their bombs at the same moment, there was always the risk that we might receive the bombs of any planes slightly out of formation. On the other hand, at night they used to fly over the target one at a time to drop their bombs and, although it was dark, we did feel that there was a little more precision about this. All the same, the hours and hours of crouching in our trenches, bitten by mosquitoes, counting the planes as they made their runs, deafened by the very noisy and inaccurate anti-aircraft fire and watching the searchlights, which the Japs handled rather well, were, to put it mildly, rather trying. Nevertheless, when the target was well away from the jail, we enjoyed air raids, especially when we could hear Jap ammunition dumps blowing up for hours after the raid was over. Once Ted Horton, with a party of men, had to go and dig up an unexploded bomb; fortunately this only happened once.

If we were frightened of air raids, most of the Japanese were terrified of them and if a plane flew over while a party was outside the jail, the guards would quite often run for cover and, in a panic, forget all about the prisoners they were supposed to be guarding. Once during a night raid, they caught some Americans smoking in their trench and gave them a very severe beating up. The day after an air raid they were usually in a particularly foul temper.

My jungle sore kept me on the sick list from August, 1943 to January, 1944 and during that period the officers were given a piece of ground in the jail to cultivate. We grew pumpkins and tomatoes and a few onions, but our most successful effort was a vegetable which was known and eaten as spinach. Actually I think it was a kind of weed but it grew most prolifically and spinach and spinach-water became a regular stop-gap on the menu. The men's work parties did various odd jobs in Rangoon, chiefly digging deep air raid shelters and dummy anti-aircraft positions; they also did some gardening. The work was hard and very often the Japs in charge were extremely unpleasant. Sometimes in the early months parties had to go and unload ships in the docks; for a long time the men used to come in with odd things concealed about their person such as soap and cloth and books. We all became adept at stealing anything we could lay our hands on and we amassed quite a large number of books in this way. Eventually the Japs took to searching everyone who re-entered the jail after a day's work.

Books were a boon, especially for the sick. John Kerr had been given a copy of H. G. Wells' *Outline of History* by a friendly Jap at Myitkyina; this was a wonderful standby both for reading and for discussion purposes. We had many books from the library of a man called Donald Moxton; I have often wondered what kind of man Mr Moxton was. I am sure he would not have begrudged us the use of his books; even the dullest of them were very useful for making cigarettes. Among the more worthwhile books brought in by work parties and eagerly devoured were *Wuthering Heights*, Daphne du Maurier's *Rebecca* and *Jamaica Inn*, J. B. Priestley's *English Journey* and *Midnight on the Desert*, Lytton Strachey's *Eminent Victorians* and some H. V. Morton, Warwick Deeping and Rosamund Lehmann, to mention only a few. I find now that I can often remember books I read in Rangoon far better than books I have read more recently.

Officially we were not allowed to sing in jail unless we had gained permission to have a concert on our weekly day off, but most of the Japs did not interfere unless the singing in the Block became too loud in the evenings. We had quite a number of concerts; our star turns were Corporal Clegg, who composed and performed songs in the George Formby style, Campbell and Yates who sang very pleasantly together and a big rollicking Welshman called Morgan, who bubbled over with good humour and put on some priceless comic sketches. Tom Stock gave a series of extremely interesting lectures on a wide variety of subjects and these were always well attended. He was also the Professor Joad at three Brains Trusts which I organized, taking good care that I was always the question-master. We also had some inter-room spelling and general knowledge competitions.

There was little time or space for games other than card games and chess but we had several home-made packs of cards and chess sets in the block. At one time the officers played deck tennis in their room. The most lasting craze was for horseshoe quoits. We had some keenly contested quoits competitions and some of our amateur bookmakers ran very successful books; others did not do so well. It all kept us amused.

As the months went by quite a large number of American airmen joined us in Six Block; they had all been shot down in raids over Burma and, before coming to Six Block, they went through a gruelling period of solitary confinement. The Japanese seemed to have a particularly strong dislike for American airmen; some of them were at first sent to a smaller jail in

Rangoon which was known to us as the military police jail. Here the treatment was extremely cruel; from all accounts it was a miniature hell on earth. The full story of what went on within its walls will never be told nor shall we ever know how many died there.

For some months I lived in the same room as the Americans so that I got to know them very well. Like us, they were a mixed crowd and it would be foolish to pretend that I liked them all; on the whole I got on well with them and I was happy to count one or two of them among my best friends. Not everyone shared my views on this subject but, as has frequently been pointed out, much of the bad feeling between Britons and Americans is caused by their refusal to treat one another as foreigners. Because we speak more or less the same language, we are irritated when we find our ideas and behaviour are not the same. Someone once pointed out that if the Americans spoke Russian we would think they were extraordinarily charming. There were also a number of Australians in the jail and, although I had heard mixed reports of the Australians, I can honestly say that those in Rangoon were, without exception, extraordinarily fine types. I particularly remember one Flight Sergeant, a giant of a man with a face like Abraham Lincoln, who could perform amazing feats of strength when necessary and yet could dress a jungle sore as patiently and gently as a trained nurse.

In December 1943, Major Loring was sent over from Three Block to take command of the prisoners in Six Block. He brought with him Captain Henstock as his adjutant, and two cooks. The prisoners in Three Block had been in Rangoon since the British withdrawal in 1942 so that they were far more experienced in dealing with the Japs and in making the best of everything than we were. Major Loring was a man of great energy and determination with a lively sense of humour; he had a wonderful knack of cajoling things out of the Japs. Ably assisted by Tiny Henstock, he soon improved conditions in Six

Block. Major Ramsay's arrival had been one turning point and this was another.

For Christmas the Japs gave us a holiday and extra rations, and the cooks excelled themselves and gave us a really good feed. In the morning we had a carol service, conducted by Lieutenant Brian Horncastle, and then a sports meeting. In the evening there was a concert with alternate turns by British and Americans. The Americans had assured us for some months that their General Stilwell, or "Uncle Joe" as they called him, had announced his intention of spending Christmas in Rangoon, so that when one of them appeared in the middle of the concert dressed as "Uncle Joe" with a "Sorry I'm late, you fellows", he received an uproarious welcome. We finished with community singing and finally "The Star Spangled Banner" and "God Save the King". We always finished our concerts with the National Anthem. Thousands of miles from our own people and surrounded by our enemies, we sang it with more fervour and emotion than ever before.

Brian Horncastle, who had conducted the Christmas carol service, died early in 1944. He was a sincere Christian and utterly good-natured. When he died all ranks felt that they had lost a friend to whom they could always turn for help. When he had gone the outward signs of religion disappeared from Six Block, except among the Roman Catholics. The attendance at the weekly services on our rest day gradually dwindled until they petered out. I do not think this was necessarily a sign of loss of faith or that anyone ever felt he had been abandoned by God; it merely showed that under those circumstances the men found that they gained more help and inspiration from their personal prayers and private devotions. Those at any rate were my own feelings.

It was about Christmas that we began to hear persistent rumours of the collapse of Germany. Where they started nobody knew, but they were brought in from outside by work parties. It was difficult not to believe them as they were so detailed, even giving full and convincing particulars of the terms imposed by the Allies. Our false hopes were not finally dispelled until the arrival of some fresh prisoners who were able to deny the rumours with some authority.

Apart from rumours and scraps of news eagerly gleaned from new arrivals, our only source of information was a Japanese propaganda paper, printed in English and called *Greater Asia*. We were issued with weekly copies of this for some time, until the news became so bad from the Jap point of view that it ceased to appear; it was a bombastic rag but we found it quite amusing and, reading between the lines, we gained some idea of what was happening. One feature in it we relished particularly; this was a long serial poem in praise of the Japanese by a Mr Banerjee. No Poet Laureate has ever been guilty of such obsequious doggerel.

Soon after his arrival in Six Block, Major Ramsay had told John Kerr that he was going to walk without crutches within a few months. This seemed extremely optimistic as John's ankle joint was stiff and almost unmoveable and the nerves of part of his foot were completely dead. However, under the Major's instructions, he persevered with exercises and I gave him daily massage. There came a day in Spring 1944 when John managed to limp unaided for a short distance. This was a moment of real triumph and he yelled with a joy we all shared. From then on he made rapid progress so that later in the year he could move about inside the compound quite easily.

With the aid of a musical American, John and I planned and started rehearsing a bigger and better concert. The rehearsing had to be done in the evenings after the men had done a hard day's work but everyone taking part was most enthusiastic. Then, to our annoyance, at the beginning of May when we had nearly finished rehearsing, the Japanese decided that they wanted to have all the American and Commonwealth prisoners in Six Block; this meant transferring a large number of men from Three Block and John and I were among those who had to go to Three Block to make room for them in Six Block. Ted Horton, Tom Stock and quite a few others were to come with us, but it meant leaving many friends behind and this made it a sad occasion. However, we could not argue with the Japs, so on 12 May, 1944, we said goodbye and, carrying our extremely scanty belongings, we walked across to Three Block to start a new chapter in our life at Rangoon.

# CHAPTER 14

# *Three Block*

The inmates of Three Block had nearly all been taken prisoner during the withdrawal from Burma in 1942 so that by comparison we were new boys. From them we learned of the cruelties of the early days in Rangoon, the solitary confinement, the starvation, the refusal by all ranks to broadcast for the Japanese and the subsequent mass beatings and humiliations. Many of them, more than a third of their number, had died, but now conditions had improved somewhat and those who remained had become accustomed to prison life and were fairly fit by comparison with the occupants of Six Block. There were men from many different regiments, a large proportion of them regular troops with many years' service in the East to their credit. As far as possible those from the same regiment lived in the same room. There were soldiers from The Duke of Wellington's Regiment, The King's Own Yorkshire Light Infantry, The Inniskillings, The Cameronians, The Gloucesters, The West Yorks and The Lancashire Fusiliers.

The senior officer was Brigadier Hobson, who had been a liaison officer with the Chinese Army. He was a fine looking man and he never ceased to strive for improved conditions, although this involved him in many a trying ordeal with the Japs. Colonel Power of the Dogra Regiment was second-in-command; his tact and kindliness smoothed out many difficulties in our somewhat turbulent community. The Medical Officer, Colonel Mackenzie, I have already mentioned. He was a rugged Scot with great courage and strongly held opinions. Both colonels were quite old but they stood up to the buffetings of life with exemplary fortitude.

## Three Block

During my time in Three Block I made many new friends, and there were few evenings when I did not spend the time between roll-call and lights out talking to someone or other. Perhaps under these circumstances we had a better chance of discovering our friends than we shall ever have again. Among officers and men there was no lack of amusing and interesting characters, but the list of their names, so full of meaning to me, might be monotonous for others.

The cookhouse in Three Block was run by two large Yorkshiremen, Sergeants Hansell and Martin; their bluff humour appealed to me particularly and I passed many lively evenings in their company. Corporal Godwin, a Leicester man, and his friend, Sergeant Dobbs, were employed by the Japs to keep the ration store tidy. Godwin was not tall but he was immensely thickset and as hard as nails. Sometimes he would steal whole sacks of gram or dhal from under the nose of the Japs and the whole compound was constantly benefiting from his skilful "fiddling". Hansell and Martin were adept at this game too.

All cases of serious illness were sent to Six Block. So inevitably the atmosphere in Three Block was more cheerful; we were not constantly being brought face to face with death nor the sight of living skeletons. My own health remained pretty good except for a bad spell of stomach trouble which lasted for five weeks at the end of the 1944 monsoon. When it was over I was incredibly thin but Colonel Mackenzie put me on a special course of exercises under the supervision of Private Jones of the Gloucesters, a physical training expert, and I soon built myself up again.

About July there was an outbreak of cholera in the jail; the Japs were very frightened about it and rigid measures were taken to stamp it out, including inoculation. Somebody in the Block had a copy of Kipling's poem "Cholera Camp"; reading this did nothing to lessen our anxiety, but, thanks mainly to Major Ramsay and a number of volunteers from Six Block who risked their lives looking after the victims of the disease, the epidemic was checked after about a dozen deaths.

The officers in Three Block had a nursery garden where they

worked and grew vegetables in the same way as the Six Block officers. During the monsoon there seemed to be a shortage of labour and we were put on harder work such as demolishing buildings, carting bricks, moving girders and, at times, sacks of rice. We normally wore our clothes, such as they were, outside the jail but on one memorable occasion the population of Rangoon was edified by the sight of British officers dressed only in the briefest of loin-cloths, pushing cartloads of manure through the streets. We amused ourselves by imagining what the reaction of the members of the Poona Club would have been if they could have seen us! For a few months at the end of 1944 the officers were taken off all work. The only explanation we could think of was that the war was going so badly for the Japanese that the Jap Commandant was anxious lest he should be made to work when it was his turn to be taken prisoner. However, this respite did not last for long and we were soon back on gardening, with occasional other jobs when there was a labour shortage. We took turns in accompanying the men's working parties and going through the ceremonial drill required when marching in and out of the jail.

For the most part the officers did not have to work nearly as hard as the men; most of the men's parties were concentrated on the enormous task of digging an underground air-raid shelter for the Japanese headquarters in Rangoon in the grounds of the Nyoma School. The digging went on for months, and then many more months were spent piling a huge mound of earth on top of the shelter. On this job the men were treated like slaves; even coolies would not have been made to work so relentlessly. The hours were long and it is convincing proof of the basic toughness of the British that they were able to stand up to this work so well in that climate and on that diet. Beatings were frequent; one particularly brutal Jap was christened the "bulldozer".

By the time the job was finished, the air raids on Rangoon were becoming heavy and many of the coolies left the city. So our men were sent to take their place unloading sacks of rice from barges on the river. If anything, this work was even more exacting. As the manpower situation deteriorated, the Japanese demands on us became more and more exorbitant, until even our unfit men were working at the docks from dawn until dusk, eating their breakfast before daylight and their evening meal after sunset. No lights were allowed by the Japanese during the hours of darkness so that the chaos at these meals was indescribable. After much agitation by the Brigadier, working hours were made a little more reasonable, but the men were still appallingly overworked and they now only had a day off about once a month, instead of once a week. This meant they never had any time to wash their clothes as they were out of the jail throughout the hours of daylight. Warrant Officer Richardson of the RAF had picked up the Japanese language with uncanny skill and he did splendid work at the docks, wheedling, soothing and cajoling the Japs into a more reasonable frame of mind. Conditions on work parties would have been far worse if he had not been there.

Life went on against a background of cruelty and suffering. In Six Block men continued to die, though with diminishing frequency. Medical supplies continued to be pathetically inadequate, but, for the purposes of propaganda, the Japs photographed Major Ramsay, clad in white, treating a healthy looking prisoner on a comfortable bed with a prominent array of medicine bottles in the background; this was a piece of cruel cynicism very hard to forgive. Fresh prisoners, mostly airmen, came in and were put in the solitary block. We never heard the full story of their sufferings and privations but we were quite accustomed to the sounds of blows and screams from the direction of the cells and we heard that more than one man had died as a direct result of Japanese beatings. The food for the solitary block was cooked in our cookhouse by our cooks and we tried to send them of our best, but we knew that the Japanese barely gave them sufficient to keep them alive. When the cells became full, many of their occupants were moved into Eight Block; we had no contact with them at all, but we could see that they were in a very poor way.

To a large extent the attitude of the Japanese depended on the

Commandant; we had several during our time. The first ones were more or less swine, but the last one was, by comparison, almost a gentleman. I think his name was Captain Tazumet. He appeared to have several British medal ribbons so we thought that he had probably fought with us in the First War. On several occasions, such as the cholera epidemic, he behaved very decently and, as far as I know, on no occasion during his term of office did we have any evidence that he was directly responsible for any act of cruelty. When one of the American officers ventured to approach him on the subject of the terrible conditions in the solitary block, he said he regretted them but that he was acting on orders from above.

We gave most of the Japs nicknames and they were not very complimentary ones as a rule. Pluto, Monkey Face, Tarzan, Limpy, The Ape and the Moulmein Terror were all familiar figures. There were some who usually behaved quite reasonably but there were a few who had never been known to beat up anyone; some of them took a savage delight in it and seemed to look upon it as a kind of sport. It is only fair to point out that slapping was a recognized and regular punishment in the Japanese army.

There was a lighter side to life. John Wilde, an officer in the Lancashire Fusiliers, was a veritable genius at producing concerts and a song he wrote in jail called "When my soldier days are over" certainly deserved to become a hit. Our only musical instrument was a mouth organ but, under the leadership of Sergeant Smith of the Gloucesters, a very melodious band was formed, the members making the noises of the various instruments in the same way as the Comedy Harmonists. Altogether there was an imposing array of talent in Three Block and John Wilde was able to put on several concerts in revue style which were far better than anything I have seen produced by ENSA.

John Kerr and I appeared twice in these concerts as Colonels Bygadsby and Burrough-Pegg, complete with monocles and Oxford accents. Our turn consisted of dialogue, anecdotes and songs in the manner of the Western Brothers with much scandal and scurrilous comment on topical events thrown in. The refrains of the songs were on the usual lines; "Try to ignore it, you chaps!", "It's all such a terrible bore!", and "Always give a 'keri' to the Nips, fellows!" For some reason, in the jail, we almost always referred to the Japs as the Nips and a "keri" was the Japanese word for a bow or salute. We spent many happy hours preparing and rehearsing our script and it certainly seemed to go over well with almost everyone; most of it was unfit to print but I can remember that one of our songs ended with the words:

> "We think this rising sun affair has gone a bit too far
> But Lord Mountbatten's fixing an eclipse,
> So always give a 'keri' to the Nips, fellows
> Always give a 'keri' to the Nips."

A certain Private Williams could imitate the Japs to perfection and in the middle of one concert, dressed as a Jap sentry, he stormed into the room, shouted at the Brigadier and delivered a tremendous tirade in pseudo-Japanese; the Brigadier bowed and treated him with the utmost deference but he was not the only one who was completely taken in. In Three Block we had room to play football in the compound and we had some very energetic and enjoyable games, despite a good deal of vagueness concerning the rules. Tom Stock, the source of practically all knowledge in the jail, gave some of his more fascinating lectures at intervals; as I slept next to him I used to glean much from our conversations and felt that, from an educational point of view, my years of captivity were not a complete waste of time. A great deal of bridge was played by certain sections of the community and the game of Holy Dido was also very popular.

Sometimes articles brought in by the work parties were raffled and I was lucky enough to win a Japanese tooth-brush and a tube of tooth-paste which lasted me for many months; until then I had been using charcoal to clean my teeth.

Of course food remained a perpetual source of interest. Ted

Horton became messing officer after we had been in Three Block a few months and each room sent a representative to make suggestions and complaints about the food at the periodical mess meetings which he held. The rations issued by the Japs fluctuated considerably and so did the wood supply, but the cooks became extremely skilful at making cakes and pastries out of the rice flour which we ground ourselves and, considering the meagreness of the rations and the terrible lack of variety, we really fed amazingly well. The sentries apparently thought that our cooks were cleverer than their own as they freqeuntly came and sampled our meals. Food was sent up to the rooms in buckets and the task of dishing it out fairly was indeed a heavy responsibility. On days when there was meat in the stew every piece had to be counted.

Rumours about the progress of the war continued to come in with the work parties and we were also able to signal the solitary block for news from fresh prisoners; this was really our only reliable source. Some of the Americans could only give us the latest news about film stars and dance-band leaders but, on the whole, we managed to gain quite a good idea of how the war was going. In 1944 several prisoners from the Second Wingate Expedition were brought in and we were delighted to hear news of some of our friends. Wingate himself was now a Major General and Major Fergusson had led a brigade into Burma on his second trip. The news that gliders had been used and the details of the improved rations and the vast equipment and air support for this second expedition cheered us tremendously but we were soon very downcast at the news of the death of Wingate himself. The Japs lost no time in telling us all about it and they also told us some wonderful tales of their advance on Imphal. Some of them even informed us that they were shelling Calcutta from the Manipur Road but this was no more fantastic than their claims that London and Washington had been flattened by Japanese bombers. News was inevitably several months old. For instance, I think it was August, 1944, that we received our first definite information about the long-awaited D-day. Sometimes we found pamphlets dropped on

Rangoon by our planes, in spite of all Jap efforts to prevent this.

Much of our news came through the Chinese who were able to translate stolen Japanese newspapers. The senior officer in the Chinese block was General Chee, a charming man who spoke perfect English. He had resisted persistent attempts by the pro-Jap elements in China to gain his support and his confidence in our ultimate release never wavered. The Chinese in the jail were pleasant enough, though inclined to be unruly. There was, however, a bad element among them and, to our horror, one of them attacked General Chee one night, stabbing him in the stomach. Peritonitis set in and Colonel Mackenzie risked his own life performing an emergency operation on the General without the proper instruments or antiseptics. The gallant effort was in vain and General Chee died on the eve of the events for which he had waited so long with unswerving faith. Our suspicion that the murderer was the tool of the Japs was strengthened by the fact that he was henceforward used as a servant boy by one of the Japanese NCOs. Colonel Mackenzie had previously performed at least one successful amputation in the jail, in spite of lack of proper drugs and instruments.

Some of the Indian prisoners were persuaded by promises of better conditions to join Chandra Bose's Indian National Army, which made an abortive attempt to invade India with the Japanese. We saw a great deal of this Indian National Army in Rangoon and it was a considerable force. I find it difficult not to believe that many of the prisoners who joined had every intention of going over to the British at the first opportunity. The majority of Indian prisoners refused to have anything to do with the INA and remained consistently loyal. One Gurkha Subedar was ordered by the Japs to write an essay on what he thought of the British; he simply wrote in block capitals: "The British always have been and always will be the finest race in the world." For this he was put into solitary confinement.

All the men in Three Block with any mechanical ability were made to work in Japanese workshops some distance outside

Rangoon. They all lived in the same room in the block and formed what was known as the mechanics' platoon. Graham Hosegood was the officer in charge of them, but he fell ill at the end of 1944 and had to return to Six Block. He had always been most solicitous for the welfare of the men and he was widely mourned when he died early in 1945; his patience and cheerful friendliness had made him universally popular. When Graham went over to Six Block I was put in charge of the mechanics' platoon or "The Scruffs" as they called themselves after I had lectured them about their personal appearance and reproved them for being so "scruffy". Sergeant Smeraldo became my platoon sergeant and we made ourselves most unpopular for a week or so by carrying on a smartening-up campaign in the platoon. However, after a certain amount of initial unpleasantness, "The Scruffs" seemed to settle down to their new regime quite well. One of them provided Ted Horton and myself with a cut-throat razor by grinding down an old car spring which he had picked up in the Japanese workshops. Ted and I used it every other day and, although he would never trust me to shave him, he used to shave me quite regularly.

As time wore on Allied air raids in Rangoon became heavier and we began to see Super Fortresses quite frequently. One day at the end of November I was put in charge of the work party digging the huge air raid shelter for the Japs at Myoma School. While we were eating our midday meal the sirens went and we soon heard the roar of the bombers approaching; for some reason, on this occasion, none of us felt inclined to take cover; we just sat in the open and continued to eat. The planes appeared directly over our heads and still we did not move. Suddenly the familiar sound of falling bombs began. It was too late to take cover, so we just flung ourselves on the ground while the bombs crashed down on the station, a good quarter of a mile away. They must have been heavy bombs for the force of the explosion made the ground heave beneath us and we were considerably shaken when we got to our feet. We then saw a terrible sight; a giant Fortress was spinning slowly to earth with smoke and flames pouring from it but the crew were indicated by several white blobs in the sky. The plane crashed with a sickening rending sound quite near to us, amid the cheers of the Japs who exuberantly claimed that their anti-aircraft guns had shot it down. The crew who soon joined us in the jail, told us that one of their bombs had exploded under the plane when they pressed the release button.

This was the last air raid we experienced when bombs were dropped anywhere near the jail and, from then on, although the raids were heavier, they seemed to be concentrated on the Japanese dumps and workshops on the outside of Rangoon and on Mingaladon airfield. We had a very good view of the massed daylight raids; sometimes nearly a hundred and fifty Fortresses came over, but our exhilaration at the sight of so much destruction was often marred by the knowledge that the mechanics platoon were working in workshops in the middle of the target area. They had several miraculous escapes and the Brigadier complained to the Japs about their being forced to work in a danger zone; the Japs retorted that the whole of Rangoon was dangerous. Luckily the Japs were eventually forced to evacuate these workshops so that the mechanics no longer had to work there.

Christmas, 1944, could not have been merrier under the circumstances. The Japs were really generous by their standards in giving us extra rations and the cooks toiled like slaves and worked wonders. We asked if we might send a few extras to the men in the cells but the Japs would not allow it, saying that the airmen in solitary confinement were being treated as criminals because they were guilty of indiscriminate bombing. We all had too much to eat that day. In the morning there was a Carol service and a basket-ball tournament and the Japanese allowed our friends from Six Block to visit us. In the afternoon there was an excellent concert, and the sing-song in the evening could not have gone with more of a swing if we had all had a few pints of beer.

At the beginning of January, 1945, we were told that a batch of mail had arrived for us. The excitement was tremendous. This was our first contact with our homes and some of the men had not heard from their families for nearly three years. The Japs kept us waiting for over three weeks while they censored the mail and many of the men received nothing. My parents had sent eight postcards with twenty-five words on each, through the Red Cross at Tokyo in the hope that I was a prisoner, although they had had no official news of me except that I was wounded and missing. It was wonderful to know that all was well at home but at the same time terrible to feel that they had no news of us. At last, on 28 February, we were all allowed to write one postcard of twenty-five words; needless to say those postcards have still not arrived.

In March, 1945, some of the men discovered a large supply of soap in the Jap stores and nearly fifty bars found their way into Three Block. I had one bar and so did several other officers but we kept it well away from the prying eyes of the Jap sentries. The rooms were quite often subjected to searches by the Japs and already they had discovered quite a number of men with stolen property; the consequences had not been pleasant. The punishment of making a man stand hatless at attention in the sun for several hours was very popular with the Japs at this period. One day an officer left a piece of this stolen soap in a place where it was at once spotted by a Jap sentry on his daily tour round the block. Then the trouble started for, on investigating, they found over a hundred bars of soap missing from their stores. Actually some of the Japs had been stealing it themselves, but, in order to conceal this, were determined to prove that we had done it.

The block was searched from top to bottom time after time and several more bars were found in the possession of officers. There were beatings and threats of mass punishment; Godwin and another man, who confessed to having stolen some soap in order to prevent the whole block being involved, had a very bad time. Twice we were kept standing on parade for three hours or more and nearly a week we were kept on tenterhooks, particularly those of us who were in possession of some of the beastly stuff. Many people buried their soap but it was difficult to do so without the sentries seeing. I hid mine in various places about the compound but it seemed to shriek aloud wherever I put it; finally I shredded it up and scattered it in the garden and, when it was gone, I felt as if I had destroyed the last clues to a murder. Eventually the whole affair died down and we decided not to risk another reign of terror. Tragically Godwin never fully recovered from the effects of the beatings he had at this time and there is little doubt that this was the cause of his early death some years after the end of the war.

It is difficult to convey any idea of the atmosphere in which we lived. Normally it was far from gloomy; we were all completely accustomed to the life; the craving for sugar and fats had long disappeared and our stomachs were fully acclimatised to our monotonous diet. The primitive sanitary arrangements, the constant bowing to the Japs, the rats and mice and smaller vermin which crawled over us in the night, the complete lack of privacy, the prevalence of scabies and the sight of men covered from head to foot with ringworm – all these and many other things which would have revolted us normally were now a routine part of our lives and passed unnoticed. When there was a Jap in the compound everyone was on the alert and ready for anything, but at other times we lived in an atmosphere of cheerfulness and often hilarity. The sound of laughter and badinage was almost continuous and the Japs themselves provided endless material for ribald comments, while little things like a history of the huge waxed moustache of the Cameronians' Piper Birse were a constant source of amusement. Life was a strange mixture of despair and laughter.

By this time we knew the Japs quite well and had pretty definite opinions about them. In view of what has happened during the last forty-five years, my considered opinion of the Japanese, written just after the end of the war, may be of some interest:

First of all I would say that, like every race, the Japanese contain good and bad elements, so that sweeping condemnation or praise is quite unjustifiable. I feel bound to place on record that, in spite of all the cruelties I have witnessed, I see no reason why the Japanese should not eventually become a truly civilized race, once their fanaticism is rooted out and they are subjected to the right influence. No doubt the process will take several generations, but I have seen Japanese behave decently at times and, apart from their fanaticism, they appear to have as good a chance of becoming civilised as any other race.

It is far easier to understand why the Japanese have committed atrocities than it is to understand why the Germans have done so. The Japanese have only been in contact with the rest of the world for a very short period and, during that time, they have been practically untouched by Christian influences. Under the thin veneer of the outward signs of civilization lie all the lusts, cruelties and superstitions of a backward medieval race in Europe. They are like children masquerading in grown-up clothes and, like children, they are desperately afraid of not being treated as adults. I feel sure that this latent inferiority complex, this feeling that they are not really the equals of the Western democracies, lies behind most, if not all of the outrages they have inflicted upon the world.

I am not putting forward these opinions because I advocate a lenient policy towards the Japanese; on the contrary, I think it is essential that we should treat them as firmly as we can without being vindictive. We must realize that most of them are incurable fanatics. I do not know how many of them still believe in hara-kiri, but I do know that many of them expected the war to last long after they were dead and they spoke glibly of a hundred years of warfare. To a nation with this mentality, their present defeat will seem nothing more than a temporary set-back. It is also important to remember that they can easily build up the myth that their armies were not defeated and that they were beaten only by the atom bomb.

The ordinary Japanese has the mind of an adolescent; his cruelty to animals, his attitude towards sexual matters, his ability to swallow the wildest propaganda, his childish irritability and petty attitude to life all indicate this. He is easily led and consequently it has been possible to establish a discipline in the army compared with which the Hitler Youth were a wavering and disorderly rabble. That it is quite customary for them to stand stiffly to attention while they are beaten for even a trivial offence is just one illustration of this iron discipline. Therefore, let us not be willing to believe in any apparent change of heart in this generation of Japs; they are easily led but most of them have been led too far to turn back. I believe we can only try to keep the present generation under control and prevent them from passing on their ideas to a future generation. If we can do this, and it will not be easy, Japan may yet make a real contribution to the progress of mankind.

Reading this account of my time as a prisoner of war forty-five years later, I am dismayed by the casual and matter-of-fact tone of parts of my narrative which seems at times to amount to callousness. Perhaps the truth is that those of us who survived managed to do so by developing a protective insensitivity. If so, this was not a deliberate process but, in our efforts to avoid feeling sorry for ourselves, we probably became less aware of the troubles of others. In the early days of our captivity at Bhamo, Ted Horton and I certainly had a grim warning of the opposite attitude to life. We were joined for a time by a young officer who had been attached to Brigade Headquarters before he was taken prisoner. Physically there was nothing seriously wrong with him when he joined us but his morale had broken down; all he could do was brood on his own misfortunes and those of his comrades. Ted and I tried hard to rouse him from his despair; when sympathy failed, we tried cajolery and then downright rudeness but nothing could stir him from his misery. In the end he died because he had lost the will to live.

One lasting boon which we have gained from our experiences is the ability not to worry about things which are beyond our control. We have learnt that there is nothing to be gained from anxiety and that, in any situation, one can only do one's best and then leave the outcome to Providence. This attitude to life, which can be exasperating to others, also involves, as far as possible, taking one day at a time and not dwelling unduly on the past.

## PART IV

# Deliverance

"Oh how comely it is and how reviving
To the spirits of just men long opprest
When God into the hand of their deliverer
Puts invincible might . . ."

John Milton *Samson Agonistes.*

# CHAPTER 15

# *The March*

Every year as Christmas approached we had said, "We are sure to be out by Christmas," and when Christmas passed we said, "Something is sure to happen before the monsoon"; then we had resigned ourselves to the misery and perpetual damp of the rainy season and built our hopes on Christmas again. At the beginning of 1945 we really seemed to have some good grounds for hoping that we should be spared a third or, in the case of the older prisoners, a fourth monsoon in Rangoon. The heavy air raids and fighter sweeps were a visible sign that something was happening; even *Greater Asia* could not entirely conceal the fact that the Japs were not having it all their own way and the rumours which poured in seemed too good to be true. It was difficult to believe all the talk of Mandalay, Meiktila, Toungoo, Magwe and Prome, but in April the work parties began to report a large exodus of troops and Japanese civilians from Rangoon. Friendly Burmans passing us in the street and even members of the Indian National Army would murmur, "It won't be long now". But the question in all our minds was, "Will they arrive before the monsoon?"

As the population lost faith in the Jap currency, prices rocketed to fantastic heights and, while the Japs brought large stocks of food and firewood into the jail for safe storage, the shortage of supplies in Rangoon itself became even more acute. To add to the distress the water system had been put out of action by Allied bombs and everywhere the Burmans were frantically digging wells. The Japs tried in vain to turn them against the British by pointing out the obvious fact that it was because of our bombs they had no water.

In the middle of April the atmosphere became very tense and the Burmans started rioting and looting in the town. We heard the sound of firing in the streets outside, and numerous columns of smoke, which seemed to indicate sabotage, could be seen all over Rangoon. The Japs in the jail, however, showed no sign that anything unusual was afoot.

Finally, about midday on 25 April, we were told that all fit British and American prisoners would be leaving for an unknown destination that afternoon. We were to march and we would have to carry anything we wanted to take with us. At this late hour the Japs opened up their stores and produced large stocks of clothing and boots which they issued on a lavish scale; at the same time the cooks were allowed to draw as much food as they could cook.

It was a day of tension and foreboding. Those of us who were leaving felt that all our hopes of an early release were shattered and we gloomily faced the prospect of further years of waiting in a prison camp elsewhere. Those who were being left behind knew that they would possibly be shot by the Japs before the British arrived or else killed by allied bombs or shells. There was an air raid in the middle of the day but we were all so absorbed in our hectic preparations that we hardly noticed it.

John Kerr had to be left behind; although he was by now remarkably mobile it was clear that he could not cope with a long march. I scribbled a hurried note to my parents for him to give them in the event of his being released. I think we both felt pretty grim about being parted. Our friendship was such that, although we were complete strangers when we met in India, there was by now little that we did not know about each other's family and past life. When eventually I met members of John's family I felt that I had known them for years.

In the late afternoon it started to rain but it had almost stopped when we set off up the Prome Road. Many of the inmates of 8 Block came with us; only the worst were left behind and those who came were a pathetic sight; terribly pale and emaciated, most of them not yet recovered from their ghastly months in the solitary block. The Japs even made some of the men come on the march who had been in the cells until that morning. I can only describe the march as I and others in comparatively good health found it; for these sick men the ordeal was infinitely worse.

We must have looked a motley array as we marched off. The cooks were pushing handcarts packed high with rice and other stores, and the rest of us were carrying our belongings in bundles wrapped in rice sacks. We were wearing a strange variety of Japanese clothing and rags; some of us had Japanese boots on our feet and others, like myself, were wearing home-made sandals; many were marching barefoot. I trudged along immediately behind Brigadier Hobson and we carried our bundles of belongings suspended from a bamboo pole which we supported between us, frequently shifting the pole from one sore shoulder to the other. Most, if not all the Japs from the jail seemed to have come with us and they marched beside us while we moved in columns of threes. Even the Commandant was marching and before long he told the Brigadier to put his bundle on one of the hand carts. Thereafter, my friend, Greg Kirwan, a South African RAF officer, took the other end of my bamboo pole. I could not have had a better man to share the hardships of the march with me; he was always calm and cheerful. At halts we used to nibble jagri together and his flow of whimsy was an endless delight.

All through that night and the succeeding night we were passed by lorries and cars of all descriptions loaded with Japanese and Indian National Army troops heading away from Rangoon. There was not much traffic in the opposite direction. It took us several hours to leave Rangoon; even in its battered state it was still possible to tell what a fine city it had been. We passed many fires and behind us there were frequent explosions as though the Japanese were destroying all their dumps. Suddenly we heard the sound of planes diving above us. Greg said quietly to me, "They're Japs," but the others apparently thought differently; Greg and I were left shaking with laughter in the middle of the road while everyone else, Japs included, dashed for the ditch or leapt over the hedge. Even the Commandant laughed when he realized the mistake.

Colonel Mackenzie had refused to be left behind in spite of his age, and before long the cooks were pushing him, and several others who showed signs of collapse, on their already overloaded carts. We were all exhausted and footsore when we stopped in the early hours of the morning and went to sleep under some trees about a hundred yards from the road.

We spent the whole of the day of the 26th resting under the trees, apart from an occasional roll-call. The Japs arranged an elaborate system of air sentries and everyone was ordered to remain perfectly still under cover if aircraft were heard. We were anxious not to stay where we were any longer than was necessary, for we knew we were in the middle of an area which was being periodically subjected to concentrated bombing as it was quite near to Mingaladon Aerodrome, but the Japs explained that it was not safe to move along the road by day owing to the Allied fighter patrols. Our two meagre meals had to be cooked a good half mile away where there was a supply of water; the task of carrying the food was no light one.

The Commandant issued detailed instructions to the Brigadier about what we were to do if aircraft appeared while we were on the march; he ended by saying that if we did as his men told us we would be quite safe. "My soldiers are here to protect you," he said; "if necessary they will give their lives for you." I am afraid we were not particularly grateful for this offer.

Several times on the march that night we had to take cover at the side of the road when the planes were heard. The Japanese appeared to be suffering from nervous strain and became very irritable. We noticed that some of them found the march very hard going. The Commandant tramped along, chewing the corner of a towel which he frequently used for mopping his face. For the most part we marched in silence, pondering on the gloomy prospects for the future. We still did not know where we were going; the most likely guess seemed to be that we were going north to cross the Sittang Bridge, which is the most southerly route to Moulmein and Thailand. This was confirmed in the middle of the night when we reached the junction where the Prome Road goes to the left and the Pegu Road to the right. We took the Pegu road.

By this time my sandals had rubbed large sores on my feet and I decided to try marching barefoot. The road surface was fairly smooth and I got along quite well but there was a good deal of glass lying about and some people had their feet badly cut; it was not easy to avoid it even by moonlight. Frequently we came to a place where a series of deep holes had been made in the road to take explosive charges for demolition purposes and every bridge we passed was prepared in this way. The cooks had considerable difficulty in steering their carts through the mazes of potholes, overladen as they were with the sick as well as stores.

The march that night seemed endless. The road ran on for miles in a dead straight line across a featureless plain of paddy fields. At last, in the distance, we would see some trees, which usually indicated a village, and, we hoped, a suitable place to rest but, after miles of marching, we went straight through the village and on to the flat plain beyond. The same thing would happen at the next village and the next. At irregular intervals we had short halts and I always fell asleep the moment we stopped, only to be awakened a few minutes later to stumble on again. Word came up to the Brigadier that one of the officers had been taken ill and fallen out. We could not make out why he did not ask to be put on a cart as the others had done; perhaps he thought the poor cooks had already enough to push. We never saw him again and nothing has been heard of him since. Probably the Japs killed him on the spot. At last in the early morning we rested for about an hour but when we had to start again we were stiffer and sorer and wearier than ever. We struggled on a few miles further and stopped for the day about nine o'clock in a small hutted camp under some trees by the roadside.

It was impossible to sleep much that day. The Commandant insisted that we should improve the natural cover from the air and later in the day a large formation of gleaming Fortresses flew directly over us with their deep sinister roar. We crouched, fearful and helpless, waiting for the thunder of their bombs as we still imagined that we were in the target area but they turned and headed towards Rangoon. During the day I cut my hand badly on some glass but the Jap medical orderly showed great concern and bandaged it up very carefully. There was a constant shouting of orders and warnings of aircraft overhead; the officers had to take it in turns to act as air sentries. We had two more scanty meals which did little to remove the feeling of depression which had hung over us since we left Rangoon; nevertheless, most of us tried to put on a cheerful exterior and I remember Private Byrne was grinning as usual. During the day I had a word with Sergeants Hansell and Martin; although they had the responsibility of cooking our meals and the exhausting task of pushing the carts on the march their morale was still characteristically high.

That night, as we were crouching in bushes at the side of the road, listening to aircraft overhead, we heard a peculiar series of heavy explosions from the direction of Rangoon; as we marched on we could hear them going off in groups of twelve at regular intervals of an hour or so. Some of us thought it sounded as though Rangoon was being shelled from the sea and we thought anxiously of our friends left behind in the jail; others thought the road behind us was being bombed and others that it was simply the Japs blowing up stores and installations in Rangoon. I believe this last guess was the correct one, though at the time I favoured the naval bombardment theory. Behind us, and in front, we could see large glows in the sky, apparently caused by fires. Obviously events were now moving fast but it looked as if they were too late to save us.

Later in the night we had just overtaken a convoy of bullock carts when one of our planes came over flying low; we dived for cover, but the pilot had obviously seen something; he circled over us for what seemed a very long time while we crouched waiting for the sound of his machine guns. Instead there came a ringing explosion. When the plane had gone at last, we found that it had dropped a small bomb among the bullock carts behind us.

Ahead of us, towards Pegu, we could see a glow in the sky and throughout the night we heard rumbles from all directions. The moon, which had helped us avoid the rough parts of the road, had set by this time and the road ran between dark plantations on either side. The rest of the night was a prolonged torment to our sore feet and aching bodies. The upper parts of my feet had been rubbed raw by my sandals, so that I could not put them on again, and now my bare soles which had given little trouble while the road was smooth, began to fail me. On and on we went, hardly bearing to put our feet down at each pace on some fresh agony. Ahead of us the voice of the Brigadier boomed back, "Holes on the left", or "Bad patch just here", or "Glass on the right there", but most of us had long ago given up trying to avoid the hazards; we concentrated, as if in an awful endless dream, on trying to put as little weight on our feet as possible. If it was so agonizing for us, it is hard to imagine what it can have been like for the poor men from 8 Block and the solitary cells. Greg and I took it in turns to take the front end of the pole. At the front end you never knew what you were going to put your feet down on next and at the back end you could tell when you were coming to a bad patch every time you heard a sharp intake of breath from the man in front of you, but there was nothing you could do to avoid it. On and on, with a few minutes' precious sleep snatched at halts, and then at last dawn found us in a daze of weariness and pain, a few miles short of Pegu.

The Japanese were in an awkward predicament; the place where we were supposed to lie up for the day was some miles ahead on the outskirts of Pegu but, owing to delays on the march, we had failed to reach it before daylight, and to move along the road except at night was suicide. There were some deserted houses in the woods a few yards away from the road and as it grew light we were hustled off the road into the area around them. We had hardly reached the sparse cover of the trees when our planes came over, doing their daylight patrol up and down the road. Nobody moved as they flew overhead. The hand carts were still standing on the road and it was quite obvious they drew attention to the area we were in. During the whole of that day there never seemed to be a period of more than fifteen minutes when our planes were not overhead; they seemed to be watching our area constantly for any suspicious movements. Frequently they fired their guns as they swooped down over us; at times it seemed that they were firing at something on the road and at times they were firing at the woods in which we lay but, in spite of some narrow escapes, nobody was hit.

It is impossible to convey the nervous strain and the mental torture of that long day. To be machine-gunned by our own planes seemed to be the crowning horror. Each time they screamed down over us, nerves were stretched to breaking point. The empty houses were, like most houses in Burma, raised off the ground on posts; we crowded underneath them, though it was very doubtful whether they gave us any real protection from machine-gun bullets, to say nothing of cannon fire. Many of us spent most of the day lying on a sunken track which ran nearby through the woods. It felt safer here, though when the planes were overhead it seemed hideously exposed. To sleep was out of the question; there was no water and to light a fire to cook a meal would have been to draw even more attention to our whereabouts. The Japs began to behave very strangely. We prisoners were spread out under the houses and trees over quite a large area but there were only one or two Jap sentries on duty and they hardly took any notice of us at all. The rest of the Japs disappeared into a house a little apart from the others. During the afternoon the possibilities of escaping were being widely discussed. It was difficult to decide what the chances were. Obviously it would be simple for men to slip away individually or in small groups if the Japs did not increase their vigilance and by the evening a number had already done this on their own initiative without the Japs noticing. One of them returned after a few hours, reporting that the attitude of some Burmans that he had met was so unfriendly that he had thought better of it. It was impossible to tell how far away from the nearest British troops advancing down from the north we were, and we did not know whether or not the explosions that we had heard during the night from the direction of Rangoon indicated a landing there from the sea.

Ted Horton, Sergeant Hansell and Sergeant Martin seemed eager to escape while the going was good. I was undecided. It was a decision which each man had to make for himself and I would never have forgiven myself if, by persuading them to stay, I had involved them in several years more imprisonment. Finally I made up my mind to stay with the Brigadier for the present. I feared what the consequences might be for him and for us all when the Japs discovered how many had escaped during the day; to add to the number would only make matters worse. I also felt that later the chances might be more favourable.

Colonel Power and the other senior officers went into conference with the Brigadier and the possibility of a mass escape was examined. Clearly, if we all acted together according to a pre-arranged plan, it would not be difficult to overpower the guards who only numbered about fifty to our four hundred odd. Then, if we all remained together as a large body, we had little to fear from the Burmese villagers, even if they were to prove hostile. We were still moving roughly northward in the general direction of our own troops and the Brigadier decided that, as a better opportunity would probably present itself later, it would clearly be foolish to escape prematurely and run the risk of being rounded up again by the Japs. Anyway it was already evening and there would not be time to make plans and circulate them before we set off again, so the Brigadier issued an appeal to the men through their officers, urging them to stick together until such time as a mass escape could be organized with a fair chance of success.

Sergeant Dobbs and Corporal Godwin, whom the Japs had taken ahead of us in a lorry to see about rations, came back with the news that while they were on the outskirts of Pegu during the previous night, the place had been subjected to continuous heavy bombing for several hours; we trusted that there was not going to be a repeat performance while we were passing through Pegu that night.

At dusk we fell in on the road for roll-call. About thirty of us were missing and we wondered what was going to happen; to our astonishment the Japs did not even seem surprised and we carried on as if nothing had happened. Before we set off I noticed, with considerable relief, that Ted Horton and Sergeants Hansell and Martin were still with us.

The Japs seemed to have abandoned most of their kit and the hand carts were left behind. So I now shared my pole with the Brigadier, and Gregg marched on his own. We were all extremely thirsty as we found no water during the day. Tom Stock, who still had some in his water bottle, shared it with the Brigadier and me. When people question whether there is such a thing as pure unselfishness, I quote this action of Tom Stock's as an example.

The sick could no longer ride on the carts. So they had to be helped along by their friends and the Japs grew impatient because we did not move faster, but we took little notice of them; the Brigadier even snapped back angrily at one of them who tried to urge him on. As we approached Pegu, we fully expected the bombing of the previous night to be renewed, but, for the first time for over twelve hours, not a plane could be heard. The place was in ruins and only the framework or the more solidly constructed buildings were still standing. As we crossed over the bridge over the Pegu River we saw the Japs preparing it for demolition and, about an hour later, we heard it go up behind us. We were all thankful to be safely clear of the place.

On the outskirts of the town we halted and a Jap officer in a staff car pulled up and spoke to the Commandant for several minutes; then we started off again, leaving the road and following a rough path which ran beside a railway line in the shadow of the embankment. In the moonlight the country seemed very featureless, an occasional group of trees in the distance indicating that there was a village. Some of the men had fought over this area in 1942 and they told us that the railway led to the Sittang Bridge. At places the path petered out completely and at other times we had to walk along the line for some distance; for the most part we kept to the shadow of the embankment. The moonlight seemed unusually bright and at intervals we had to lie flat against the slope while planes flew overhead.

How far we went that night I do not know, but it seemed the longest march I had ever done. We passed a few pools of water but the Japs would not let us quench our raging thirst, though, to our amazement, one or two of them handed round their water bottles. Our feet, which had been painful enough on the road, caused us endless agony on the rough ground so that our hunger and thirst and fatigue seemed minor inconveniences. In spite of the Japs, the column began to straggle; several men said they could go no further but their friends dragged them along somehow. One officer from 8 Block collapsed and was never seen again.

Everything began to seem utterly fantastic and the crazy dreams which floated through my mind during snatches of sleep at halts seemed no more unreal than my waking impressions. My only clear recollections of the night centre round the Brigadier; his spirit was magnificent and, although he was as weary and footsore as any of us, he seemed to have found some fresh source of energy. As I followed behind him, he was continually turning round with an encouraging word and trying to find a less painful way of carrying our pole. At halts, when the rest of us simply dropped where we stood, he would hobble round enquiring how we were and trying to persuade the Japs to let us stop and have a drink. Colonel Power, despite his age, was standing the strain of the march remarkably well but Colonel Mackenzie was in a pitiful state; he is said to have asked the Japs to shoot him on the spot but Sergeant Hansell and Sergeant Martin came to the rescue and carried him between them. None of the cooks had slept much since we left Rangoon and, while we rested during the day, they had been busy cooking but these two cheerfully undertook to carry the Colonel now that he could no longer ride on a cart. Somehow at the end of the march they still had him supported between them.

At last, in the early hours of the morning, the Brigadier approached the Commandant and told him point blank that, unless we had the prospect of a rest and a drink and something to eat, we could not go much further. To our surprise the Commandant accepted this statement quite calmly and sent one of his men ahead to look for a suitable spot where we could lie up for the day. About an hour and a half later we stopped in a shady village on the left hand side of the line. Dawn was just breaking and none of us guessed what the coming day had in store for us.

# CHAPTER 16

# *29 April, 1945*

The village where we halted had a long and unpronounceable Burmese name which I have tried in vain to remember. It was pleasantly situated in a large grove of trees and appeared to be deserted, though another village a few hundred yards away was still inhabited, as we discovered later. The moment the Japanese allowed us to fall out, we chose suitable places, well under cover of the trees, where we could try to sleep. We were so busy doing this that we did not notice that our guards had disappeared. Suddenly someone shouted to us to pay attention while the Brigadier made an announcement. We were all standing within earshot and we turned towards where he was standing in an open space in the middle of the village, hoping that he would tell us we were going to be allowed to rest all day or give us some similar information; I do not think any of us dreamt what was coming.

There was a sudden unearthly silence and, speaking in a strained but clear voice so that everyone could hear, the Brigadier said, "At last I can tell you something that you have been waiting to hear for years; we are all free men." There was an audible gasp of astonishment and a few seconds passed while this amazing news sank in; then there was a shout of joy as the full realization of what it meant came over us. We all went completely crazy, patting one another on the back, shaking hands, laughing and weeping simultaneously.

The Japs had gone. The Commandant had sent for the Brigadier when we arrived in the village and informed him that he was going to release us. He advised us to stay where we were until our troops advancing from the north arrived and he gave the Brigadier a note in Japanese saying that we had been officially liberated, so that we could show this note if we encountered any Japanese troops withdrawing. Whether he did this on his own initiative or on instructions from above we never discovered, but there was a strong rumour that his second-in-command and other subordinates wanted to shoot us rather than let us go alive. When he had finished talking, the Commandant shook hands with the Brigadier and went off to join his men who had already moved away some distance. In the light of subsequent events, it seems unlikely that they escaped from Burma alive.

We were free. The strain under which we had lived for so long was suddenly lifted and the feeling of relief was almost unbearable. Now for the first time for years we could look forward confidently to the future we had almost despaired of at times, to our homes and families, to a civilized life instead of a bare existence. For years all this had seemed a dream so utterly desirable that we hardly dared to imagine that it could ever come true and, now that it had happened, we were almost too dazed to realize it.

When we had calmed down a little, the Brigadier appealed for the co-operation of all ranks until we had made contact with our own troops. Everyone was to remain under the cover of the trees except those detailed for special tasks. The most immediate need was to make contact with our aircraft and signal our presence to them. Squadron-Leader Duckenfield and other RAF personnel quickly laid out a ground strip in the nearby paddy field, using all the available white clothing. The message they put out indicated who we were and asked planes to drop a wireless transmitter. A Union Jack, manufactured in record time from suitably coloured clothing, was also laid out.

It was not long before the inhabitants of a nearby village approached us. They seemed very friendly and offered us some rifles and a machine gun which they had kept hidden for years. They also produced some rice and vegetables with which the cooks began to prepare a meal. According to them, there were hundreds of Jap stragglers in the neighbourhood and many of the Burmans were hunting them down. This was soon confirmed when rifle fire started only a few hundred yards away; apparently there were some Japs quite near and the Burmans were attacking them but we could not quite make out what was happening and after a while the noise died down.

To the east we could see a range of hills and, after a short time, a tremendous artillery barrage started from the north-east, the nearest shells landing about a mile and a half away. This was followed by what sounded like a tank battle and aerial bombardment combined and then there was more shelling. It was obvious that the advance of our troops was being preceded by a huge screen of fire power. We only hoped that it would not be turned in our direction.

Several planes came over at a high altitude but did not seem to see the sign that we had laid out; we were quite confident that they would see it eventually and we did not mind waiting a little longer now. Four hundred of us had been lifted from utter wretchedness to incredible happiness on that Sunday morning in an unknown village about seventy miles north of Rangoon. We sat waiting for over an hour, talking excitedly and watching the distant battles; then it was decided to set fire to a straw stack and to try flashing mirrors in the sun in order to attract the attention of our aircraft.

I suddenly realized how dirty I was and went over to the village well to have a wash. There was plenty of water and several others were doing the same. I was just enjoying the sensation of feeling comparatively clean when some planes came over lower than before. Squadron-Leader Duckenfield and some of his men stood by the ground strip waving a piece of cloth at the circling planes which now came in much lower. There was immense excitement; at last, we thought, they had seen our message and we looked up hopefully as they wheeled over us. Then there was a searing burst of machine-gun and cannon fire and a small bomb exploded in the middle of the village. Before we could take cover the planes behind were coming in and, as I ran naked through the trees, another bomb exploded about five yards from me; a stout tree-trunk shielded me from the fragments and I ran on. Ahead I saw a dry pond about five feet deep. Several men were already huddled in the bottom of it but I leapt down just as the next plane swept over. We clung together desperately trying to hide ourselves as the planes came over again and again. Twice bullets hit a tree above our heads, sending showers of splinters down on us. At last they seem to have exhausted their ammunition and we crawled out dazed and trembling, scarcely expecting to find anyone else still alive in the shattered village, but, miraculously, apart from a villager, there had only been one casualty; it was the Brigadier.

Nobody could blame our airmen for what they had done. They saw a village full of people and they naturally assumed that they were Japs. How were they to know that four hundred British and Americans had suddenly appeared out of the blue in the middle of no-man's-land? The Brigadier had established his headquarters in one of the empty houses and, when the first planes swooped down, there was no time for him to take cover; a burst of bullets penetrated the roof of the house and killed him outright. It was bitterly cruel that anyone should be killed during his first hours of freedom and by our own planes, but it seemed a piece of inscrutable irony that the only one to die was the man who had striven so long and so valiantly that as many as possible might see this day. The tragedy of it hung over us all for weeks.

Now we were desperately eager to leave the village before the planes returned and, almost before they had gone, many men had made for the open fields or the shelter of some woods about half a mile away. It was impossible to organize anything and for a time it was each man for himself. Just outside the village was the railway station where there were some fairly deep trenches. Some of us waited in these for a while and discussed among ourselves the best course of action. Planes appeared again while we were talking but they did not come very near. It seemed a grave mistake for us all to scatter without any instructions but most people had already gone and we none of us wanted to remain in the village. We decided to lie up in the neighbourhood until nightfall and then collect again at the station for further consultation. I hurried back into the village to collect my clothes, not wasting any time about it, and then I joined Warrant Officer Richardson and we went out into the middle of the paddy fields. We now felt that we wanted to get away from all trees and buildings and anything in the least conspicuous from the air; we lay down in the open, hoping that we were invisible but the sun beat down on us, we were attacked by thousands of ants and we still felt extremely visible, so we were not sorry when someone brought a message that we were wanted back at the station. Some parties of Japs had been reported in the area and we decided to organize look-out posts to give warning of their approach. I took four men and my old friend Colour-Sergeant Beatty of the King's; we stationed ourselves in a small brick building beside the railway line, taking it in turns to look out over the fields to the north-west. We could see odd figures moving in the far distance along a road but no Japs appeared.

The afternoon dragged on. Planes flew over at a distance and some Burmans appeared and we asked them to bring us food. We had had nothing to eat except jagri for nearly forty-eight hours, but until then we had not noticed our hunger. Several people had seen parachutes landing in the far distance but there was no sign of any troops coming our way and the morning's battle seemed to have died down. A Burman reported that all villages along the line were being bombed and we could hear the sound of bombing in the distance. As it began to get dark, a message came to say that the headman of a village about three-quarters of a mile away on the other side of the line had offered us all hospitality for the night. Colonel Power, who was now the senior officer, decided to accept.

By nightfall a large number of us had collected in this friendly village, though many were still missing and had not been seen since the strafing. There was no sign of Ted Horton or Sergeant Martin, but Sergeant Hansell was there and, with Tom Stock and one or two others, we were conducted by a friendly Burman to his house. It was spotlessly clean and he asked us to make ourselves comfortable while he went off to get a meal. In a nearby house I found Sergeant Dobbs and a party of men but we seemed to be in a different part of the village from everyone else and we decided that it would be wise to keep a sentry on duty all night. We also ascertained the position of the nearest air raid trench. Our Burman host soon came back with the meal, a most delicious curry and rice, and when we had eaten our fill one of the villagers produced a rifle and said he would stand on guard. I was feeling too weary to worry much about anything, but Stock, who seemed inexhaustible, carefully arranged a system of sentries for the night and armed them with a club. It was a strange situation. We were free, yet at any moment we might be attacked by Japanese or bombed and shelled by our own people; in spite of this we could hardly keep awake.

Apart from the sentry, we were just falling asleep when Major Lutz, one of the American officers from 6 Block, appeared. He was a stocky little man and I am afraid I had sometimes found his super-efficiency and self-assurance rather irritating in the jail; now there was good reason to be profoundly thankful for these qualities and I trust that his remarkable courage and initiative have received the recognition they deserve. After the strafing that morning, he had disguised himself as a Burman and, with the help of a guide, had made his way to the nearest British troops. When he had told his story he learned that, after attacking the village that morning, our planes had reported there was something strange about the place and the proposed bombardment of the place had been cancelled until the matter was investigated. Major Lutz was able to provide all the information that was required and he was then sent back with instructions to have as many of us as possible ready to be picked up at a certain place by a patrol that night.

Our weariness vanished as he told us this news and we were on our feet in no time while he gave us careful instructions as to where to go and what to do. He then went on to tell the others. We knew that there were Japs about, so, taking our leave of our Burman host and apologising for the shortness of

our stay, we made our way through the darkness to the railway
line and crept silently along it towards the village we had left so
hurriedly that morning. I was leading the way when I suddenly
ran into a frightened man coming from the opposite direction;
he had been hiding somewhere since the strafing and, on
returning to the village in the dark, had bumped into someone
who, from his language, appeared to be a Jap. I calmed him
down as best I could and told him to follow us. As we
approached the village we were challenged and gave the password as we had been instructed by Major Lutz. We were then
ordered to approach and found Ted Horton and quite a large
party, including Sergeant Martin, waiting for us.

We waited some time while all the men with whom it was
possible to make contact were assembled and then we set off
northwards across country led by Major Lutz and a Burman
guide. After we had passed through another village we started
to climb a gentle slope. Suddenly a tense voice rang out through
the darkness ahead; Lutz replied and we knew that at last we
had made contact with our own people. Figures appeared from
the darkness and a smiling Indian officer of the Frontier Force
grasped each one of us by the hand as we came forward, saying
"Thank you, thank you". Why *he* was thanking *us* we could
not imagine but most of us were too overwhelmed to reply.

In a kind of dream we moved on. There was a cheery Scottish
officer in charge of the patrol and he told us to lie down if there
was any firing and leave everything to his men. He asked us a
few questions and gave us the latest war news. Germany was as
good as finished, Burma was almost liberated and Rangoon was
expected to fall within a week. Over and over again he repeated
how thrilled they were to rescue us, and we replied truthfully
that they could not be half as thrilled as we were.

We walked on, escorted by efficient looking Indian soldiers,
all grinning with delight. Soon we came to some lorries which
were waiting for us. They helped us on board and, after a
bumpy half mile, we reached a good road. Sitting there in a
British truck, speeding away from the Japs towards our own

lines, we knew that at last our troubles were over. We were really free; we had to keep reminding ourselves of this incredible fact.

Half an hour later we were shaking hands with the officers and men of a battalion of the West Yorkshire Regiment. They gave us a tremendous welcome and led us off to have our first civilized meal, washed down with tea, real tea with sugar and milk. We just could not express our feelings or thank them enough. Finally we gathered round the fire, drinking rum and talking, they being as eager to hear our story as we to hear theirs. Sitting there in the firelight I could not help noticing how fit they all looked compared with us, how confident and enthusiastic they seemed and how touchingly pleased they were to see us. It was early morning when our hosts led us to our blankets and we went to sleep in a mood of utter thankfulness, completely carefree for the first time in years.

# CHAPTER 17

# *The Journey Home*

We had never seen anything like the 14th Army which was driving the Japs before it as it advanced down Burma. The tremendous array of equipment and vehicles, the enormous air support and supply system, the fitness of the men and the superb organization all astonished us, but what impressed most was the wonderful spirit about it all. Every man seemed eager to finish the job and was absolutely confident of success. In order to advance faster the troops had volunteered to go on half rations so that petrol could be dropped to them instead of food. The men in the West Yorkshire Regiment must have gone very short to feed us as they did. It was also good to see so many of Wingate's ideas being put into practice on a really large scale.

Nothing seemed to worry the 14th Army. A typical instance of this occurred when we were awakened the morning after our release by the sound of firing nearby. Bullets whistled over our heads and we lay waiting and wondering what was happening. For a while nobody seemed to take any notice. Eventually a Major strolled over to where we lay and said quite casually, "I am awfully sorry you've been disturbed like this; some Japs appear to have got into the Perimeter. I'm just going to wake a few of my fellows to deal with them." This happened quickly and we all went to sleep again.

Things happened so quickly during the next few days that we felt increasingly that we were living in a dream. We were issued with clothes and kit, interviewed by the Press, photographed, addressed by Senior Officers, and medically examined all in the space of a few hours. Everywhere we went we were cheered on our way by British, American, Indian and African troops. We were puzzled by the letters SEAC which we saw everywhere, standing for South East Asia Command; we decided that they stood for Supreme Example of Allied Co-operation! The other prisoners were gradually recovered and brought in and planes arrived to fly us out. I took my leave of Burma on a dusty airstrip one morning when twenty-four of us fell in under Major Loring and, for the benefit of a crowd of onlookers, went through the ceremony of roll-call in Japanese for the last time. A few minutes later our Dakota was heading for India. Over Prome, which was still held by the enemy, the Japs took a parting shot at us with anti-aircraft guns, and there was a brief halt for a meal at Akyab. That evening we touched down safely in India. It was 1 May, 1945, three years to the day since I had left home.

We shall never forget the kindness and hospitality shown to us during our few weeks in India. Everywhere it was the same. I cannot recall all the parties I enjoyed in Officers' and Sergeants' Messes, in hotels and clubs and restaurants. Everywhere I went I found someone I knew. I met many old friends from the Royal Sussex, including my faithful Atkin, and at Poona I had a wonderful reunion with Sergeant Thornburrow who had been awarded a well-earned Military Medal; we celebrated well into the night with Sergeant (now Company Sergeant Major) Rothwell who had won the BEM. At Karachi there was another great welcome from RSM Cairns MM, and Sergeant (now CSM) Marchbank. There were celebrations right across India and the final seal was set on my happiness when I received a letter bringing good news of my parents and brothers at home.

Before I left India I found out what had happened to nearly all my friends. It was a grievous shock to learn that George Borrow had been killed in the same plane as Wingate; he had been awarded the Military Cross for his courage on the first expedition and he had gone into Burma again as Wingate's ADC. Major Fergusson had been awarded the DSO and returned to Burma leading a Brigade of his own, as had Major

Calvert. Among those who went in again were John Fraser, Bill Edge, Jim Harman and Bill Smyly. Sergeant Pester and Corporal Peter Dorans had both been awarded the DCM and were still very much alive. I was delighted too to hear good news of Pam Heald, Bill Williamson, Gerry Roberts, Feeney, my runner, Dennett, my groom, and that Ba Than and Nelson had escaped from imprisonment but Robert, Po Po Tou, Jameson and many others were still missing. In all about sixty five per cent of Wingate's Brigade had reached India safely after our expedition.

It was also good to know that those who were left behind in Rangoon jail had returned safely and later I heard the full story from John Kerr. After our departure, the jail was guarded by a squad of very raw Jap recruits. During the night of 29 April, Wing Commander Hudson, an Australian Air Force Officer in 8 Block, discovered that these Japs had departed, leaving a farewell note for the prisoners which expressed the hope that they might all meet again on the battlefield. For the next few days Hudson, with John Kerr as his adjutant, more or less ruled Rangoon from the jail, playing a superb game of bluff. They issued orders to the Indian National Army Units who then asked to be taken prisoner, and to the Burma Defence Army who had turned pro-British. On 2 May a Wing-Commander Saunders crash-landed his plane at Mingaladon airfield and made his way to the jail. He was able to tell the prisoners that Rangoon was going to be bombed by twenty-nine squadrons prior to a landing from the sea. This was grim news and there seemed no way of informing the Allied Forces that the Japs had abandoned Rangoon. Wing Commander Saunders set off down the river in a small boat to try and make contact with the Naval Headquarters ship directing the landing at the mouth of the Rangoon River. Those left in the jail waited anxiously, fearful that he would not reach his destination in time to stop the air bombardment; the following day planes came flying over very low and, when they had dropped supplies instead of bombs the prisoners knew that Wing-Commander Saunders had done his job well. Some SEAC newspaper correspondents were the first to arrive at the jail, closely followed by the Navy, and it was not long before all the prisoners were on their way by boat to Calcutta.

From my platoon Private Byrne and Private Nicholls survived their imprisonment and, among other members of 5 Column mentioned in this book who were released were David Whitehead, Sergeant Skillander, Corporal Jones, the cook, Corporal McGhie, Brookes, the bugler and Private Joe Boyle.

On the evening of 7 July we left Karachi in a Transport Command Dakota and, after touching down during the night at Bahrain and Baghdad, we reached Lydda the following morning. We spent two idyllic days bathing in the Mediterranean at Tel Aviv and then continued our journey via El Adem in the Western Desert, Malta and Sardinia. The sun was rising as we crossed the French coast near Marseilles on Sunday, 10 July and we flew over France all morning. When we reached the Channel, the weather became so bad that we saw nothing of England until we came down to land. Suddenly our plane burst out of the clouds and there below us were the green fields of Somerset. For a few minutes we circled the aerodrome at Merryfield; then we touched down gently and in a moment our feet were on English soil once more. There was no need for any speeches; it was enough to know that we were home again.

# EPILOGUE

## *(Written in 1945)*

Now it is all over and I return to my old life. Whether I am wiser than I was when I joined the Army as a young undergraduate I cannot tell, but certainly I am happier. It is true that the first ecstasy of release is over, and the unspeakable joy of homecoming, but there has been no anticlimax. Along with a deep feeling of thankfulness there is a conviction that it has all been supremely worthwhile. Before we set out Wingate prayed that, having done all, we might "see the fruits of our labours and be satisfied". We little dreamed how fully that prayer was to be answered.

Yet Wingate had seen beyond the end of the war. Even as we went into battle he had said: "Our aim is to make possible a government of this world in which all men can live at peace and with equal opportunities." That aim has been achieved and that possibility is here now for us to make into a reality if we will. Wingate has said nothing of a dream world of ease and prosperity, because he saw peace as a time when men can and must make sacrifices. Because we have seen the fruits of our labours and been truly satisfied we should not hesitate to face the tasks of the future with confidence. If we are content to rest now we shall lose what we have gained, for without sacrifice there can be no peace.

Perhaps I was foolish to try to write this book so soon after the events described, and at a time when, not having put pen to paper for more than two years, the crudity of my style or lack of it was bound to be painfully obvious. I have left unsaid so much that could and should be said. How inadequate have been my attempts to tell of Wingate and Fergusson and my efforts to

227

convey something of the courage, gaiety and endurance of my companions. How many tributes have been left unpaid, and how many men to whom I owe a heavy debt of gratitude have not been mentioned in this story, but, named or unnamed, the memory of their comradeship abides. My own halting words cannot express what I feel half so well as these lines written by Edmund Blunden.

> Now my mind
> Faint and few records their showings,
> Brave, strong, kind –
> I'd unlock you all their doings
> But the keys are lost and twisted.
>
> This still grows,
> Through my land or dull or dazzling
> Their stream flows;
> But to think of them's a fountain,
> Tears of joy and music's rally.

Message left by the Japanese when
they abandoned Rangoon Jail

Rangoon
29th April. 1945.

To the whole captured persons of Rangoon jail.

According to the Nippon military order, we hereby give you liberty and admit to leave this place at your own will.

Regarding food and other materials kept in this compound, we give you permission to consume them, as far as your necessity is concerned. We hope that we shall have an opportunity to meet you again at battlefield of somewhere. We shall continue our war effort eternally in order to get the emancipation of all Asiatic Races.

Nipon Eto

∴ the chief officer of Rangoon Branch Jail.

# SONNET FOR MY MOTHER

## *written in Rangoon jail*
## *1 May 1944*

Two years have passed, two long and joyless years
Since last I saw you smile or heard you speak;
And yet the thought of those unwilling tears
Which ran unheeded down your oft-kissed cheek
Still rips my heart. No earthly words can tell
The depths of love and sorrow which our souls
Plumbed in those precious moments of farewell;
But grief can never linger in my mind
For long when you are there, as happiness
Always comes with thoughts of you. I find
Serenity as if from your caress,
And often among the daily doubts and fears
Of life, or when temptation seems too strong
Your unseen influence prevents or cheers.

APPENDIX

# Order of Battle, No. 5 Column
# Wingate Expedition 1943

**Column Headquarters**
Column Commander: Major B. E. FERGUSSON, The Black Watch
Column Adjutant: Lieut D. C. MENZIES, The Black Watch
Administrative Officer: Captain A. I. MACDONALD, The King's
  Regiment
Medical Officer: Captain W. S. AIRD, R.A.M.C.
Air Liaison Officer: Flight-Lieut D. J. T. SHARP, R.A.F.
Cipher Officer: Lieut W. EDGE, The South Wales Borderers
Animal Transport Officer: 2nd Lieut W. SMYLY, 3/2 Gurkha Rifles
Column Sergeant Major: C S M J. CAIRNS, The King's Own Scottish
  Borderers

**Detachment of the Burma Rifles**
Commander: Captain J. C. FRASER, The Burma Rifles
          (also 2nd-in-Command of Column)
Second-in-Command: Lieut P. A. M. HEALD, The Burma Rifles
Officers: SUBEDAR BA THAN, The Burma Rifles
         JEMADAR AUNG PE, The Burma Rifles

**Support Platoon**
Commander: Captain T. C. ROBERTS, The King's Regiment
Second-in-Command: Lieut W. WILLIAMSON, The King's
  Regiment

**Commando Platoon**
Commander: Lieut J.B. HARMAN, The Gloucestershire Regiment
Second-in-Command: Lieut D. WHITEHEAD, Royal Engineers

**Rifle Platoons**
No 7 Platoon Commander: Lieut P. G. STIBBE, The Royal Sussex
  Regiment

No 8 Platoon Commander: Lieut J. M. KERR, The Welch Regiment
No 9 Platoon Commander: Lieut G. ROBERTS, The Welch Regiment
Reinforcement Officer: Lieut T. BLOW, 14th Punjabi Regiment
(No. 8 Platoon Commander)